Beyond Oppression

Beyond Oppression

Feminist Theory and Political Strategy

M. E. Hawkesworth

CONTINUUM • NEW YORK

1990

The Continuum Publishing Company
370 Lexington Avenue
New York, NY 10017

Printed in the United States of America

Library of Congress Cataloging-in-Publication Data

Hawkesworth, M. E., 1952–
    Beyond oppression : feminist theory and political strategy / M.E.
Hawkesworth.
        p.   cm.
    Includes bibliographical references.
    ISBN 0-8264-0456-1
    1. Feminism—United States. 2. Sex discrimination against women—
–United States. 3. Women—Legal status, laws, etc.—United States.
I. Title.
HQ1426.H314   1990
305.42'0973—dc20   89-39094
                                                                          CIP

For Lucy Freibert

Contents

Acknowledgments

This book grows out of my conviction that feminism and social justice are inextricably linked, a conviction that arose from my readings of the classic texts of political philosophy and that has been strengthened by my participation in feminist politics. The arguments advanced here have benefited greatly from the helpful suggestions of a number of my colleagues. Special thanks are due to Kathleen Shortridge, Mary Shanley, and Ruby Reimer for comments on my analysis of contemporary feminist conceptions of the good polity. I am grateful to William Connolly, Murray Edelman, Cecil Eubanks, John Gunnell, and John Nelson for insightful criticisms of my discussion of feminist rhetoric. Diane Fowlkes, Margrit Eichler, Frank Cunningham, Mary Wyer, and Nancy Theriot have helped me to avoid a variety of mistakes in analyzing feminist theories of knowledge. Christine DiStefano, Rita Mae Kelly, Joan Tronto, and John Cumbler offered constructive suggestions for the development of my arguments concerning constitutional mechanisms that might contribute to a world worthy of feminist allegiance. I am especially indebted to Judith Grant who read most of the chapters in draft form and whose insightful critiques stimulated my thinking on a wide range of issues. I owe an enormous debt to Landis Jones who afforded me course relief in order to complete the manuscript. Finally, I would like to thank Philip Alperson, whose intellectual support, computer assistance, and willing assumption of household responsibilities made the completion of this project possible.

9

Research for this book was conducted under the auspices of grants from the Commission on Academic Excellence and the College of Arts and Sciences of the University of Louisville. Their support is gratefully acknowledged.

Introduction

Feminism is a political movement inspired by a belief in the fundamental equality of men and women and committed to the eradication of gender-based injustice.[1] Feminist theory explicates the conception of gender equality towards which feminists strive. It analyzes concepts central to the social construction of masculinity and femininity and examines the manner in which these gender constructions circumscribe an individual's life prospects in determinate social formations. Feminist theory investigates the dimensions of inequality that have characterized women's existence in diverse societies. It explores the causes for the subordination of half the species and the factors contributing to the perpetuation of gender inequities. Feminist theory also envisions a sexually egalitarian polity and offers prescriptions for social transformation, identifying strategies for the realization of social, economic, and political equality for men and women. Although the issues addressed by feminist theorists are fairly well defined, feminist theory is not univocal. On the contrary, drawing upon various tenets of liberalism, Marxism, socialism, psychoanalysis, critical theory, hermeneutics, and deconstruction, feminist theorists advance rich and varied conceptions of a sexually egalitarian political order.

Feminism and feminist theory are much maligned and misunderstood. Despite its concern with issues of justice and equality—issues integral to the legitimacy of contemporary political systems—feminism is frequently depicted as a movement of interest only to women, or indeed as a private interest group devoted to advancing the interests of a narrow subset of women. Despite its focus on questions of human nature and political order—questions central to political philosophy since its inception—feminist theory is characterized by its critics as a marginal endeavor that offers little of interest to social and political theory. Despite detailed demonstrations by feminist scholars from a wide range of disciplines that key disciplinary methods and concepts derive their force from distorted gender stereotypes which undermine their theoretical adequacy and explanatory power, feminist critiques have failed to make major incursions into traditional academic disciplines. Despite the generation of systematic evidence documenting an array of social practices advantaging men and disadvantaging women, feminist prescriptions for redressing specific inequities have failed to win popular assent. Indeed, despite feminism's promise to engender more humane and equitable social relations, the "failure of feminism"[2] has been proclaimed prior to the realization of major feminist objectives.

That feminism encounters criticism and opposition is not surprising, for feminists face formidable obstacles associated with any movement that challenges established traditions and entrenched power. But the pervasive caricature of feminist objectives, the successful severance of feminist issues from related questions of freedom, equality, and justice, and the removal of feminist concerns from the contemporary political agenda are matters of grave concern. If feminism is to achieve its benign objectives, then efforts must be made to comprehend the factors that contribute to its premature dismissal. Theoretical, rhetorical, and political objections must be identified and engaged. This book contributes to that effort by defending the feminist project against its detractors, by demonstrating the validity of feminist theory as an intellectual endeavor, and by illuminating the contributions feminism can make to the achievement of a just political order.

Among the most profound obstacles to feminism is a set of beliefs that construes feminist objectives as impossible, undesirable, and unnecessary. The conviction that women's role is "natural," hence desirable and unalterable, provides a firm foundation for the rejection of feminist arguments concerning the social construction of gender relations. In order to shake that conviction, it is important to trace the social origins of a variety of conceptions of gender. The identification of differences between the sexes that are relevant for social and political organization has been a recurring motif in philosophical and religious analysis. Linking particular notions of gender difference to specific thinkers—a task that is taken up in Chapter One—may go some way towards dispelling the belief in the "givenness" of gender.

To demonstrate that specific conceptions of gender originate in the works of specific thinkers may eliminate simplistic commitments to naturalistic notions of gender, but it does not in and of itself address the issue of the best theoretical account of gender. Among the various conceptions of gender advanced in the Western tradition, which is most illuminating? Which goes farthest in capturing the truth about the nature of men and women? In assessing competing theoretical accounts of a phenomenon, philosophers consider a number of related factors including internal consistency and coherence, depth of explanatory power, richness of insights, problems illuminated for further research, significant omissions, and implications for modes of being in the world. Chapter One also suggests that, in terms of these criteria, feminist accounts of gender offer a marked improvement upon traditional accounts. Feminist theorists have revealed substantial defects in traditional philosophical and religious claims about women. Moreover, in problematizing gender, feminist theory illuminates new areas for philosophical investigation and identifies new issues in need of political solutions.

A second type of belief that poses a fundamental obstacle to feminism suggests that feminism has outlived its usefulness. Depicting feminism as a political movement that mobilized women in the nineteenth and twentieth centuries to fight against laws and practices that severely constrained their life prospects, proponents of this belief suggest that feminism is no longer needed. On this view, feminist success in eliminating discriminatory legislation, establishing affirmative action programs, and achieving meaningful equality of opportunity has created the conditions for a postfeminist world in which further feminist effort is unnecessary. Those who believe that contemporary feminism is irrelevant to a world in which the historic bases of sex discrimination have been eliminated and which functions according to principles of merit and free choice seldom examine the range of social practices featured in feminist analysis. Chapter Two considers a range of contemporary social practices that continue to privilege men. The persistence of practices imposing palpable harms upon women suggests not only that feminism is as important now as it has ever been, but also that claims of sexual equality will continue to remain illusory until feminist remedies are implemented.

If some of the impediments to the realization of the feminist project can be traced to uncritical acceptance of traditional beliefs and to a conflation of the rhetoric of sexual equality with the status of women in the contemporary world, other obstacles originate within feminist discourse itself. Feminist theory is intimately tied to a transformative project. Feminists work to illuminate the systematic and pervasive nature of women's oppression in order to create a world in which meaningful equality reigns. Indeed, feminists frequently suggest that meaningful equality requires a complete restructuring of power relations, a restructuring that encompasses both public institutions and private relations. But how is this restructuring to take place? What political strategies will suffice to achieve a sexually egalitarian polity?

To accept that feminism is essential to the eradication of the unjust constraints circumscribing women's lives does not imply that all feminist approaches are equal in their ability to explain women's oppression, to forge an alliance for the elimination of sexual inequality, or to envision a sexually egalitarian polity. There is much in feminist discourse that operates within a negative dialectic, vacillating between claims of victimization and perfectionist expectations, and positing a level of masculine evil and womanly beneficence that fuels caricatures and dismissals. If feminism is to win the allegiance of a political majority, it is important to explore the specific problematics that have constrained feminist discourse, curtailed its analytic rigor, and circumscribed its persuasive power. Chapters Three through Six examine the coherence and the fruitfulness of alternative feminist approaches to questions concerning the nature of women, gender equality, truth and political order. Through a sustained critique of explicit claims and tacit assumptions concerning knowledge, politics, women's oppression, models of politicization, and strategies for social transformation, these chapters distinguish that which is valuable in feminist discourse from that which is ill-conceived and self-defeating.

No political movement can maintain momentum without pragmatic objectives that embody respected principles, afford a rallying point for mass mobilization, and provide a frame of reference against which progress can be measured. Since the defeat of the Equal Rights Amendment in the United States, American feminists have lacked a focal point for their organizing efforts. Theoretical disagreements about the causes of women's oppression and strategies for political transformation have generated multiple proposals for political action, but none has won support from a large coalition of feminists. The final section of this book—Chapter Seven—attempts to remedy this deficiency by identifying a pragmatic political strategy for moving beyond gender oppression. It advances a theoretical solution to the problem of gender inequality that would empower women to resist male hegemony. In developing a constitutional proposal for the achievement of sexual equality and defending this proposal against possible objections, I hope to make a case that can win the support of a wide range of feminists and capture the allegiance of a popular majority willing to work toward the realization of gender justice.

Part One

Provocations of Feminist Theory

Chapter One

The Reification of Difference

From the standpoint of nature, men and women are closer to each other than either is to anything else. . . . The idea that men and women are two mutually exclusive categories must arise out of something other than a non-existent "natural" opposition.[1]

Homo sapiens is a sexually dimorphic species. As such, sexually mature men and women have different physical characteristics and different reproductive capacities. Underlying these physical differences, men and women have an array of species characteristics in common. How these numerous commonalities come to be eclipsed by cultural constructions of gender difference is a central question for feminist inquiry. The conversion of biological sex (male and female chromosomes, hormones, and reproductive organs) into social constructions of gender (clusters of traits associated with masculinity and femininity) is important because it influences the distribution of burdens and benefits in society, the assignment of occupational and social roles, and the development of individual identity and aspiration.

The reification of difference is a social process that draws upon the resources of tradition, language, literature, philosophy, science, and religion to accredit notions of inherent oppositions in male and female nature, character, and potential. Central to the process of reification is the transformation of contentious claims about gender into autonomous "facts."

17

Within and through this process, gender differences are discussed in the language of discovery rather than invention. All traces of human authorship of disputable ideas disappear as conceptions of masculinity and femininity are characterized as "given in nature," "ordained by heaven," or "biologically determined." Accredited as "natural" and "normal," the traits deemed essentially male or female are treated as immutable rather than as culturally produced and alterable. Once entrenched, reifications of difference so thoroughly obfuscate what men and women have in common that they are routinely appealed to as justification for a range of social practices that treat men and women differently.

This chapter will trace the reification of difference in some of the classic texts of Western philosophy and religion.[2] The point is not to suggest that these are the sole sources of conceptions of gender difference nor that they are uniquely responsible for the reifications of gender in contemporary societies. Rather, the intention is to illuminate the mechanics of gender construction, the process by which certain characteristics are attributed to women, accorded social significance, and taken as grounds for differential treatment. Familiarity with the mechanics of gender construction in these classic texts may heighten awareness of parallel processes in contemporary cultures that typically escape detection.

In considering some of the classic works of Western philosophy as paradigmatic of the reification of difference, this chapter will focus on the transitions from discussions of human nature to claims concerning gender essentialism. It will explore the narrow range within which the social construction of gender has operated, conceiving difference in terms of gradations (equating more with male and less with female), dichotomous oppositions, and variations selected from an indefinite series of possibilities. In addition, it will examine the use of these constructions of gender as legitimations of male dominance. The final sections will consider the problem the reification of difference poses for feminists both in their attempts to challenge defective conceptions of human nature and in their efforts to situate themselves in relation to Western philosophical tradition.

Gender in the Classic Canon

Conceptions of human nature attempt to identify the *differentia specifica*—that which all members of the human species share and that which separates them from all other species. Within the Western canon, a number of characteristics including reason, speech, and free will have been identified as distinguishing features of human existence. But whether men and women share equally the defining characteristics of the species has been a subject of remarkable controversy and equivocation among some of the world's greatest thinkers.

As the "father" of Western philosophy, Plato can lay claim not only to the development of the first systematic philosophical anthropology but also to the initial philosophical elaboration of an inherent gender hierarchy. Plato suggested that humans possess a tripartite soul. Within the soul, reason, spirit, and appetites vie for ascendency. The part of the soul that achieves mastery in this struggle dictates the nature of a person's character and interests and thereby shapes the individual's ambitions, choices, and actions. According to Plato, the highest form of life is possible only for those individuals who achieve a just order in the soul, one in which reason rules temper and passions.

In Plato's view, both men and women can develop just order in the soul. For this reason, all offices and occupations in a good society ought to be open to both sexes. Yet despite this seemingly egalitarian stance regarding competition for positions of status and power, there are other passages in Plato's works that suggest the outcome of such equal opportunity is not likely to be equal numbers of men and women either in public office or at various rungs of the occupational hierarchy.[3]

In The Republic, Plato asserts that, when considered as a group, men are superior to women in all areas of endeavor. "The one sex is, so to speak, far and away beaten in every field by the other."[4] Similarly, in the Timaeus, Plato notes that "Human nature being two-fold, the better sort was that which should thereafter be called 'man.' "[5] Exactly how much better men are than women can be glimpsed in Plato's claim that "Evil and cowardly men are reborn as women, that being the first step downwards to rebirth as animals."[6] Although he insists that women are educable and can be trained to assume far more diverse social responsibilities than was typical for women in his society, Plato also indicates that the task of educating women will be more difficult and less efficacious than educating men. He argues that men are more gifted students than women: they learn more quickly; they are faster at putting their thoughts into action; and they are more skilled in applying their knowledge to problem situations and in making new discoveries by creative extrapolation from existing knowledge. Women also suffer from a number of moral defects according to Plato: "Women's weakness and timidity makes them sly and devious."[7] Precisely because "women's potential for virtue is less than a man's," Plato suggests in the Laws that women "need to be controlled, less they get up to mischief."[8]

If women are slower to learn and if they lack a degree of excellence men typically possess, then men and women are not likely to fare equally well in any competition. Nor should they. For those committed to human excellence would quite rightly select the more talented competitor for positions of social importance. Thus Plato advances ambiguous views on women. On the one hand, he admits that any particular woman could outperform any particular man in any specific task. A policy of equal opportunity under rules of strict competition is judicious, then, because it ensures that an individual's life prospects are determined on the basis of merit and that society thereby reaps the benefit of the maximal use of talent. On the other hand, however, Plato develops a conception of gender difference that fosters expectations of women's diminished performance. By suggesting that men and women differ not in kind but in degree and that the structure of this difference is one in which men have more and women have less of most talents, Plato lays the groundwork for the legitimation of male dominance.

When men hold the major social, political and economic roles in society, it is easy to assume that it is because they have succeeded in a competitive struggle and have claimed their rightful reward. But what of instances where no competition has taken place, where men were accorded privileged positions on the presumption that they would outperform women? Plato's construal of gender differences in terms of typical male superiority and typical female inferiority may structure expectations so thoroughly that some may believe that there is no need for a test. Convictions concerning women's inferiority may override concern for specific tests of individual merit and thereby legitimize male power even in the absence of real competition among men and women. The doctrine of equal opportunity in conjunction with the assumption of male superiority may supplant actual competition on the grounds that the contest is superfluous, the outcome a foregone conclusion.[9]

Aristotle's treatment of gender introduces language that moves beyond differences in degree to suggest a fundamental opposition. In the *Metaphysics*, he notes that "Female and male are contrary and their difference is a contrariety."[10] In explicating this notion, he suggests that men and women are members of the same species; but they are opposites in that the female is a privation of the male. To support this view, Aristotle advances arguments concerning the gendered nature of the soul, sexual differentiation in reproductive function, and sex-specific virtues.

The conception of the soul advanced by Aristotle is a complex of nutritive, sensitive, and rational elements. In Aristotle's view, gender has a profound effect since women differ from men in each dimension of the soul. Women have diminished nutritive requirements and therefore need less nourishment than men. Women are deficient in desire; as evidence Aristotle cites women's "passive" role in copulation. Moreover, women are defective in rationality: the deliberative faculty that enables individuals to regulate their actions is inoperative in women. It exists but it lacks "authority."

With respect to reproduction, Aristotle suggests that women play a relatively minor role, providing the soil that nourishes the seed, the nutrients, and the matter from which life is generated. Men contribute the greater part in reproduction by giving life its form, essence, or soul. If women are the material cause of life, men do far more by providing both formal and efficient cause.[11] "The female always provides the material, the male that which fashions it, for this is the power that we say they each possess, and this is what is meant by calling them male and female."[12] In recognition of their lesser role in the generation of life, indeed of their inability to contribute form to reproduction, Aristotle dubs women, "impotent males."[13]

In addition to marked deficiencies in all elements of the soul and fairly insignificant contributions to the reproductive process, Aristotle argues that women's virtues differ from those of men. In the *Politics*, he insists: "Clearly, then, moral virtue belongs to all of them; but the temperance of a man and of a woman, or the courage and justice of a man and of a woman, are not, as Socrates maintained, the same; the courage of a man is shown in commanding, of a woman in obeying. And this holds of all other virtues."[14] As illustrations of other sex-specific virtues, Aristotle notes that a woman's "glory" lies in silence, in preserving not acquiring, in having true opinion not wisdom, and in friendships of inequality not equality.[15]

In constructing his theory of gender difference, Aristotle relies upon evidence that is imperceptible. In positing the soul as the key locus of women's inferiority, he structures a claim that is impervious to refutation by evidence drawn from the senses, for the soul exists in a realm that is neither visible nor tangible. Moreover, in advancing claims about reproduction, Aristotle controverts the physical evidence and attributes superiority to the male role, again on the basis of an invisible essence. Yet despite his creation of a site beyond the senses as the locus of significant gender difference, Aristotle insists that the opposition between men and women is "preordained by the will of heaven."[16] And despite the active, vibrant presence of real women in his culture, Aristotle conceives women primarily in terms of absence, and privation, in terms of the invisible essence that they lack.

Aristotle argues that sexual difference had important implications for the organization of social life. As "defective males," women could not be expected to assume the same social and political responsibilities as those free of defect. According to Aristotle's construal, nature has lessons that humans must heed in developing a sound social order. Those whose deliberative faculties have full authority must be granted the power to act freely according to their best judgment; those unfit for such tasks should be placed under their command and trained in the art of compliance: "Although there may be exceptions to the order of nature, the male is by nature fitter for command than the female, just as the elder and full grown is superior to the younger and immature."[17] Thus, Aristotle also advances a legitimation of male dominance, cast in terms of a clear assertion of male superiority, but a superiority rooted in the imperceptible realm of the soul.

If Plato and Aristotle develop conceptions of women as men *manqué* in terms of either diminished capacity or privation, Christian doctrine construes women's difference in terms of a range of vices. What is critical to the understanding of gender difference is not so much what women lack but what they possess in abundance. For in this view, women are excessively inclined towards weaknesses of the will, temptations of the flesh, and a general propensity towards evil. The biblical story of Eve, who is assigned blame for the introduction of evil into the world, figures prominently in the attribution of wickedness to women. According to Tertullian, every woman bears the shame of Eve; none can escape the ignominy of the first sin: "You are the devil's gateway . . . you are the first deserter of the divine law; you are she who persuaded him whom the devil was not valiant enough to attack. You destroyed so easily God's image, man. On account of your desert—that is, death—even the Son of God had to die."[18] Tertullian suggests that women should openly acknowledge their guilt by their dress, demeanor, and behavior. They should manifest their inherent difference by donning a veil, assuming the posture of those in mourning, and engaging in unending acts of penitence.

The story of Eve's creation from Adam's rib has also been used by Christian theologians to explain women's difference. St. Paul suggests that Adam was made in God's image, but Eve was made only in the image of man.[19] Augustine transforms this notion into a complex account of women's heightened corporeality. According to Augustine, as the original of the species Adam incorporated both spirituality derived from his likeness to God and corporeality. Because Eve was created from Adam's rib expressly for the role of helpmeet in the physical task of reproduction, she symbolizes the corporeal side of human nature in a way Adam does not. Where Adam symbolizes spirituality, rationality, and the possibility of transcendence of the body, Eve symbolizes material existence.[20] Augustine does not deny that Eve, as a creature of God, also has a compound nature comprising body and soul. But he suggests that the corporeal is more truly her nature and as such is responsible for her stronger propensity to sin.[21]

By symbolically grafting the spirit-body dualism onto a conception of male-female difference, Augustine generates a neo-Platonic argument for the "natural" subordination of women, for "flesh must be subject to spirit in the right ordering of nature."[22] Interpreting the relations of Adam and Eve as prototype for all relations between men and women, Augustine develops a conception of women as inherently inferior on the basis of their debasing carnality. Augustine's conception constructs women not only as fallen and carnal but as uniquely dangerous to men: for women have the power to distract men from the higher concerns of rationality and spirituality, and to mire them in carnal pursuits.[23] The lesson of Eve is again instrumental: the temptations women pose cause endless pain and suffering. Thus men must use all the resources in their power to avoid temptation. Avoiding sin, disciplining desire, and controlling women are interrelated aspects of men's duty to conform to their higher natures.

St. Thomas Aquinas draws upon both Aristotelian and Augustinian precedents in his discussion of women. Adopting Aristotle's notion of women as "defective" or "misbegotten" males, Aquinas explains women's existence in terms of an accident to the male sperm that precludes the reproduction of a perfect likeness of its origin, that is, another male.[24] Defining the *telos* of women in terms of their reproductive function, Aquinas suggests that women's immanence renders them incapable of the spiritual, intellectual, and moral accomplishments of men. For all nonprocreative activities then, Aquinas suggests that men should seek the assistance of men: "It was necessary for woman to be made, as the Scripture says, as a helper to man; not indeed as a helpmate in other works, as some say, since man can be more efficiently helped by another man in other works, but as a helper in the work of generation."[25] In addition, in order to supplement Augustine's argument that men reflect the image of God in a manner different from and superior to the image found in women, Aquinas introduces an analogy of the differences in degree between superior and inferior angels to support his case.[26] Thus, Aquinas links claims concerning a hierarchy established by heaven with claims about the "natural" rule of reason over body and the logical superiority of the perfect over the imperfect to form a seamless web that ensnares women in perpetual subordination and restricts them to tasks related to reproduction.

The reification of difference in Christian doctrine draws heavily upon biblical myths, accorded incontrovertible authority as the divinely revealed word of God. Inherent gender differences in the imperceptible soul are supplemented by references to the order of creation (Adam first) and the material of creation (dust and God's breath for Adam, Adam's rib for Eve) to support claims concerning men's just precedence. Women's capacity to give birth is interpreted as their sole function. Tied symbolically to the body, women's corporeality is subtly converted to carnality. Men's sensual desires are taken as proof that women are inveterate seductresses, and in quick succession claims concerning excessive lust, greed, sloth, guile, and virtually every other vice are put forth as descriptions of women's essential character. The dangers posed by women's weak character and carnal nature necessarily require men to assume both secular and religious control of women. For the havoc wreaked by women's propensity to sin is no less ominous in the city of Man than in the city of God. To the legitimation of male power in terms of avoidance of chaos and protection against danger, Christian doctrine adds the paternalist claim that male rule is necessary for women's own sake. Women's eternal salvation turns upon due submission to their male superiors.[27] Men must assume the responsibilities of leadership for the sake of women's immortal souls.

With the advent of modern political thought, an almost Orwellian "doublespeak" becomes the norm in discussions of gender: women are recurrently depicted as equal and inferior. John Locke provides an interesting illustration with his insistence that all human beings are equal, rational, governed by principles of reciprocity and fairness, and, as such, capable of self-rule.[28] The equality of men and women, typified in the shared responsibilities of parenting, serves as a cornerstone in Locke's refutation of patriarchal power as the absolute ground of political authority. For Locke insists that the fact that mothers share power with fathers in the care and education of children proves that the father's power cannot be absolute.[29] Locke also introduces crucial aspects of the relations between husbands and wives to demonstrate that, although the relation is one based on consent, conjugal association is not a form of political association. Indeed, the "subjection that every wife owes her husband" and the "power that every husband has to order the things of private concernment in his family as proprietor of the goods and land there, and to have his will take place in all things of their common concernment before that of his wife"[30] are cited as clear evidence that the limited, hierarchical relations of conjugal society are distinctly different from the political power to make laws (with the penalty of death and all lessor penalties) for the preservation of property, the defense of the nation and the common good.[31]

Locke suggests that the primary function of conjugal society is the care and education of children until they reach the age of reason and are able to govern themselves. Consonant with his view that consent is the only means by which rational agents can commit themselves to additional obligations, Locke classifies conjugal society as a voluntary compact. Thus, in consenting to marriage, it would appear that men and women provide a paradigmatic example of the way that rational, self-governing individuals order their relations. Yet, in claiming that women consent to marriage, Locke calls into question women's rationality, the foundation of human equality.

Locke establishes a fundamental criterion for rational action: in acting voluntarily, no rational being can intend to worsen his/her condition. Consent to marriage calls women's rationality into question, precisely because consent to conjugal society is consent to a permanent relation of subordination. Locke describes decision making in marriage in the following terms: "But the husband and the wife, though they have but one common concern, yet having different understandings, will unavoidably sometimes have different wills too. It therefore being necessary that the last determination (i.e. the rule) should be placed somewhere, it naturally falls to the man's share as the abler and the stronger."[32] Thus, in consenting to marriage, women consent to subordinating themselves to their husbands' will. In Lockean terms, a fully rational being would never agree to such a contract. The logical conclusion is that women cannot be fully rational.

Locke suggests that the validity of this logical inference is further demonstrated by biblical exigesis. Genesis records God's dictum in addressing Eve: "And thy desire shall be to thy husband, and he shall rule over thee."[33] In addition to God's providential order that women be subject to their husbands, Locke notes that "generally the laws of mankind and customs of nations have ordered it so, and there is, I grant, a foundation in Nature for it."[34] Within Locke's texts, then, the rationality of women and the power of mothers are asserted when convenient to a refutation of claims concerning the patriarchal legitimation of monarchical power, even as they are challenged by the very nature of the marriage contract. All humans are not really equal in a Lockean world. Those who through some defect do not develop full rationality must always be directed by the will of another.[35] Despite initial claims concerning the absence of any "natural" subordination, Locke offers an account of gender differences that vindicates male rule in the guise of husbands' natural right in the apolitical realm of conjugal association.

Rousseau also advances an account of the original human condition in which humans are equal, independent, innocent, and perfectible.[36] Cataloguing the devastating corruption of the human race as a consequence of ill-conceived modes of social organization, Rousseau devises both an ideal political order and a detailed educational regimen intended to restore human virtue. Yet, within the ideal democratic society of the General Will where liberty and equality are attained through universal participation in decision making about collective concerns, women have no place among the citizenry. Their sole role lies in the generation and nurturance of moral males who can assume the responsibilities of public life. Moreover, in designing an educational program to produce self-reliant, virtuous, and public-spirited men, Rousseau insists that a markedly different curriculum is required for women: "They must be trained to bear the yoke from the first, so that they may not feel it, to master their own caprices and to submit themselves to the will of others."[37]

Rousseau's educational prescriptions are instructive because they ingeniously display the means by which gender differences can be created and inculcated in a species in which individuals have unlimited potential and malleable characters. In *Emile*, Rousseau abandons the arguments that he developed in the *Discourse on the Origin of Inequality* to prove that the "natural" equality of men and women lay in their abilities to subsist independently. He harnesses the rhetoric of natural law to insist that men and women ought to be different: "In answering the different ends for which nature has designed them . . . a perfect man and a complete woman should no more resemble each other in mind than in feature, nor is their perfection reducible to any common standard."[38] In addition, he suggests that the difference that nature ordains must be understood to be hierarchically organized:

> In the union of the sexes, both pursue one common object, but not in the same manner. From their diversity in this particular, arises the first determinate difference between the moral relations of each. The one should be active and strong, the other passive and weak: it is necessary that one should have both the power and will, and the other should make little resistance. This principle being established, it follows that woman is expressly formed to please the man.[39]

Intent upon designing educational institutions to conform to the mandate he has discerned in nature, Rousseau suggests that a sex-specific curriculum must be created to teach women their duty in relation to men:

> The education of women should be always relative to the men. To please, to be useful to us, to make us love and esteem them, to educate us when young, and take care of us when grown up, to advise, to console us, to render our

lives easy and agreeable; these are the duties of women at all times, and what they should be taught in their infancy.[40]

Perhaps what is most remarkable about Rousseau's recommendations for the training of women are the precise mechanics he identifies for the production of docile, good natured, self-sacrificing creatures:

> Girls ought to be active and diligent; nor is that all, . . . they must be subjected all their lives to the most constant and severe restraint, which is that of decorum: it is therefore necessary to accustom them early to such confinement, that it may not afterwards cost them too dear; and to the suppression of their caprices, that they may the more readily submit to the will of others. If, indeed, they are fond of being always at work, they should be sometimes compelled to lay it aside. . . . Deny them not the indulgence of their innocent mirth, their sports and pastimes; but ever prevent their sating themselves with one to run to another; permit them not for a moment to perceive themselves entirely freed from restraint. Use them to be interrupted in the midst of their play, and sent to work, without murmuring. Habit alone is sufficient to inure them to this, because it is only affirming the operations of nature.[41]

Surveillance, discipline to ensure conformity, continual interruptions and distractions, frivolous commands, and rigid control are the key to women's successful socialization. When indulged systematically, they will produce a woman of excellent character. Despite the fact that Rousseau graphically details the kinds of techniques that are required to produce a docile woman, he claims that these artificially induced traits are altogether "natural" and in conformity with heaven's design. "Heaven did not make women attractive and persuasive that they might degenerate into bitterness, or meek that they should desire mastery; their soft voice was not meant for hard words, nor their delicate features for the frowns of anger. When they lose their temper, often enough they have just complaint; but when they scold, they always put themselves in the wrong."[42]

Having invented essential sex differences, developed socialization mechanisms to produce them, and employed the rhetorics of naturalism and divine ordination to justify them, Rousseau also advances an additional, paternalist legitimation for gender-specific training of children. Appealing to the notion of women's best interests, Rousseau suggests that these stultifying educational practices are essential to a woman's chances for happiness:

> The first and most important qualification in a woman is good-nature or sweetness of temper. Formed to obey a being so imperfect as man, often full of

vices, and always full of faults, she ought to learn betimes to suffer injustice, and to bear the insults of a husband without complaint. It is not for his sake, but for her own, that she should be of mild disposition. The perverseness and ill-nature of the women only serve to aggravate their own misfortunes and the misconduct of their husbands. They might plainly perceive that such are not the arms by which they gain superiority.[43]

Thus, Rousseau obfuscates his own role in creating fundamental oppositions between men and women by suggesting that nature decrees the hierarchical relation between the sexes and that individual happiness depends upon its preservation. Nature and convention, men's interests and women's happiness become thoroughly merged and virtually indistinguishable in Rousseau's romantic reification of difference.

Taking Rousseau's conception of gender as his point of departure, Immanuel Kant also generates prescriptive arguments about women's nature and role that blur the distinction between what is possible and what is desirable for women. In defining women as the fair sex and men as the noble sex, Kant notes that:

By this is not to be understood, that women want noble properties, or that the male sex must totally dispense with the beauties. It is rather expected, that each sex shall unite both; yet so, that all other excellencies of a woman shall unite themselves but in order to elevate the character of the beautiful, which is the proper point of reference; whereas among the male properties the sublime, as the criterion of his sex, must be the most eximious. To this must refer all judgments of the sexes, as well the commendable as the blameable. This must all education and instruction, and all endeavors to further the moral perfection of both have in view; unless the charming distinction, which nature intended to make between two human sexes, shall be rendered indiscernible.[44]

Kant's point is that the force of convention ought to be deployed to produce women who instantiate the principles of beauty and who understand themselves within the frame of reference set by sentiment, feeling, and emotion, while all the resources available to society ought to be used to produce men who typify the noble principles of fairness, intellect, judgment, and duty.

Intensive socialization and sex-role differentiation are necessary to reinforce a "distinction" so fragile in nature that it stands under threat of extinction. For this reason, Kant identifies mechanisms of social control—strategies of disapproval, contempt, and ostracism—which can be used to engrave gender differences upon a markedly undifferentiated species. To demarcate appropriate sexual spheres, Kant recommends that the symbolism of the Beautiful and the Sublime be accorded institutional manifestations. Intellectual, moral, and political aspirations should be carefully shaped to conform to sex-specified roles:

> Deep reflection and a long continued contemplation are noble but difficult, and are not suitable to a person, in whom ought to appear charms without constraint and a beautiful nature. Laborious study, or painful investigation, though a woman should succeed in it, destroys the excellencies peculiar to her sex, and may because of their singularity render her an object of cold admiration; but it at the same time weakens the charms, by which she exercises her great power over the other sex. Women who have their heads stuffed with Greek . . . or who carry on profound disputes about mechanics . . . might as well have a beard to boot; for this would perhaps express more remarkably the air of penetration to which they aspire. The fine understanding chooses for its objects all that is nearly connected with the fine feeling, and leaves abstract speculations and knowledge, which are useful but dry, to the diligent, solid and profound understanding. Ladies consequently do not study geometry, they know but as much of the position of sufficient reason, or of monades as is necessary, in order to perceive the salt in the satires of the shallow fancymongers of our sex. . . . They should fill their heads neither with battles from history, nor with forts from geography; for it becomes them as little to smell of gunpowder, as men of musk.[45]

Whether one reads this passage as a warning to women of what they will face if they defy conventional sexroles or as advice to men about how to handle a nonconforming woman or as an illustration of the kind of ridicule appropriate for those women who fail to live within the bounds men set for them, it is clear evidence of the social constitution of gender difference. That Kant also invokes the language of nature to justify the gender differentiation he works so diligently to construct may mask—but it does not eliminate—the human agency underlying the reification of difference.

If Rousseau and Kant capitalize upon the stereotype of women as the fair sex in their romantic paeans to sexual difference, Schopenhauer actively takes issue with that depiction, suggesting that the "unaesthetic sex" would be a more appropriate designation: "It is only the man whose intellect is clouded by his sexual impulses that could give the name of the fair sex to that undersized, narrow-shouldered, broad-hipped, and short-legged race. . . . Instead of calling them beautiful, there would be more warrant for describing women as the unaesthetic sex."[46] In addition to decrying their physical appearance, Schopenhauer unabashedly denigrates women's intellect and moral character:

The weakness of their reasoning faculty also explains why it is that women show more sympathy for the unfortunate than men do, and so treat them with more kindness and interest; and why it is that, on the contrary, they are inferior to men in point of justice and less honorable and conscientious. For it is just because their reasoning power is weak that present circumstances have such a hold over them, and those concrete things which lie directly before their eyes exercise a power which is seldom counteracted to any extent by abstract principles of thought, by fixed rules of conduct, firm resolution, or, in general, by consideration for the past and the future, or regard for what is absent and remote. Accordingly they possess the first and main elements that go to make a virtuous character, but they are deficient in those secondary qualities which are often a necessary instrument for the formation of it. Hence it will be found that the fundamental fault of the female character is that it has no sense of justice.[47]

Schopenhauer attributes women's essential inferiority to Nature and suggests that Nature provides women with compensatory faculties to make up for their defective powers of reasoning and deliberation. Women

are dependent, not upon strength, but upon craft; and hence their instinctive capacity for cunning, and their ineradicable tendency to say what is not true. For as lions are provided with claws and teeth, and elephants and boars with tusks, bulls with horns, and the cuttle fish with its cloud of inky fluid, so Nature has equipped women, for her defence and protection, with the arts of dissimulation; and all the power which Nature has conferred upon man in the shape of physical strength and reason has been bestowed on women in this form. Hence dissimulation is innate in women, and almost as much a quality of the stupid as the clever. It is as natural for them to make use of it on every occasion as it is for those animals to employ their means of defense when they are attacked, and they have a feeling in doing so they are only within their rights.[48]

According to Schopenhauer, Nature in its wisdom not only devises sex-specific qualities that enable women to perfect the arts of cunning, subtlety, and dissimulation used in the quest to ensnare a husband, but it also moulds women for their child-care responsibilities:

Women are directly fitted for acting as the nurses and teachers of our early childhood by the fact that they are themselves childish, frivolous and short-sighted; in a word, they are big children all their life long—a kind of intermediate stage between the child and the full grown man, who is man in the strict sense of the word.[49]

Given their moral and mental limitations, their childishness, irresponsibility, orientation toward the present, and complete disregard for anything that lies beyond their immediate sensations, it is not surprising to find Schopenhauer advancing the claim that women must be kept under the constant supervision of a responsible male. Submission to a father, husband, or male guardian is women's natural lot. But Schopenhauer also suggests that Nature programs women to seek out a male protector.

> That woman is by Nature meant to obey must be seen by the fact that every woman that is placed in the unnatural position of complete independence, immediately attaches herself to some man, by whom she allows herself to be guided and ruled. It is because she needs a lord and master. If she is young, it will be a lover; if she is old, a priest.[50]

Thus, Schopenhauer concludes that there is universal agreement concerning male superiority and female inferiority. By their very action in seeking a male's comfort and guidance, women prove they lack the will that defines fully human existence. Men possess this *differentia specifica;* women do not.

Schopenhauer relies upon a particular characterization of women's action—women ensnaring men, women seeking out masters and embracing their subjugation—as proof of his claim that women's inferiority is natural, deeply rooted in instincts, and impossible to change. Should women denounce that construal of their actions or actively renounce all behaviors that could be interpreted along those lines, then naturalistic claims about women's lack of will and autonomy would face formidable counterevidence. In the nineteenth century, women's demands for legal, political, and economic rights raised just such a challenge to naturalistic arguments. Yet, rather than accept women's demands for rights and respect as a validation of their automony and a repudiation of erroneous claims that women are incapable of independent thought, will, and action, philosophers responded with a reaffirmation of the "natural" legitimacy of women's subordinate status. In Nietzsche's diatribes against the women's movement, the tensions between descriptive and prescriptive elements of naturalistic rhetoric become blatantly manifest.

Nietzsche's construal of women's difference bears heavy resemblance to Schopenhauer's in its derogatory tone, its animal imagery, and its depiction of defects: "That which inspires respect in women, and often enough fear also, is her *nature,* which is more 'natural' than that of man, her genuine, carnivora-like, cunning flexibility, her tiger claws beneath the glove, her naïveté in egoism, her untrainableness and innate wildness, the incomprehensibleness, extent and deviation of her desires and virtues."[51] Unlike men—who are imbued with the will to truth, which is the will to power—women are preoccupied with ornamentation, vanity, and appearances: "We may well have considerable doubt as to whether woman really desires enlightenment about herself—and can desire it . . . what does woman care for truth! From the very first nothing is more foreign, more repugnant, or more hostile to woman than truth—her great art is falsehood, her chief concern is appearance and beauty."[52]

In developing his account of women's difference, Nietzsche employs not only the language of nature, but also the language of instinct. To the extent that the traits Nietzsche ascribes to women are rooted in instinct, one would expect images of permanence and immutability to accompany their elaboration. For an instinct is a biologically programmed response that appears upon presentation of the appropriate stimulus, independent of individual will. Rather than suggesting that women's essential nature is involuntary, Nietzsche casts his descriptions in terms of "instincts" that can be learned and unlearned and laments what he perceives as women's choice to unlearn certain womanly charms. Indeed, Nietzsche denounces the notion of "women's emancipation" as a symptom of the "increased weakening and deadening of the most womanly instincts."[53] Denigrating the women's rights movement as "one of the worst developments of the general uglifying of Europe,"[54] Nietzsche notes that the movement is worrisome precisely because the goals lie fully within reach if women are intent upon seeking them:

> Woman has so much cause for shame; in woman there is so much pedantry, superficiality, schoolmasterliness, petty presumption, unbridledness, and indiscretion concealed—study only women's behavior with children!—which has really been best restrained and dominated hitherto out of fear of men. Alas, if ever the "eternally tedious in woman"—she has plenty of it—is allowed to venture forth! if she begins radically and on principle to unlearn her art—of charming, of playing, of frightening away sorrow, of alleviating and taking easily; if she forgets her delicate aptitude for agreeable desires! Female voices are already raised, which by St. Aristophanes! make one afraid:—with medical explicitness it is stated in a threatening manner what woman first and last requires from man. Is it not in the very worst taste that woman thus sets herself up to be scientific?[55]

Underlying the misogynist insults and the mockery of women's bad judgment in casting off the "eternal feminine" is the clear recognition that the character women assume in specific epochs is a matter of convention, not nature. Moreover, in the description of the charms whose loss is worth lamenting is the unmistakable suggestion that some of women's conventional behavior advances men's interests far more than women's. Despite this innuendo, Nietzsche castigates the women's rights movement as inherently "stupid" in that it deprives women of the weapons they have traditionally used to "control" men:

> There is stupidity in this movement, an almost masculine stupidity, of which a well-reared woman—who is always a sensible woman—might be heartily ashamed. To lose the intuition as to the ground upon which she can most surely achieve victory; to neglect exercise in the use of her proper weapons; to let herself go before man, and perhaps even "to the book," where formerly she kept herself in control and in refined artful humility; to neutralize with her virtuous audacity man's faith in a veiled, fundamentally different ideal in woman, something eternally, necessarily feminine; to emphatically and loquaciously dissuade man from the idea that woman must be preserved, cared for, protected, and indulged, like some delicate, strangely wild and often pleasant domestic animal; the clumsy and indignant collection of everything of the nature of servitude and bondage which the position of woman in the hitherto existing order of society has entailed and still entails (as though slavery were a counter-argument, and not rather a condition of every higher culture, of every elevation of culture):—what does all this betoken, if not a disintegration of womanly instincts, a de-feminising?[56]

Nietzsche's language unmistakably reveals the conflation of nature and convention in naturalistic rhetoric. It illuminates the art of mystification in the reification of difference, and it unmasks the interests served by the construction of gender. It also denounces women for asserting their wills, for acting in the world precisely as Nietzsche encourages "great souled men" to do. Truth, will, and action remain the preserve of men in the Nietzschean ideal. For any women who would act in accordance with such human possibilities, Nietzsche offers contempt, ridicule, and warnings. Indeed, Nietzsche exhorts "real" men to refuse to indulge women's autonomy, to turn the clock back to an ancient order in which women's subordination was a matter of course:

> A man who has depth of spirit as well as of desires, and has also the depth of benevolence which is capable of severity and harshness, and easily confounded with them, can only think of woman as Orientals do: he must conceive of her as a possession, as confinable property, as a being predestined for service and accomplishing her mission therein—he must take his stand in this matter upon the immense rationality of Asia, as the Greeks did formerly; those best heirs and scholars of Asia—who, as is well known, with their in-

creasing culture and amplitude of power, from Homer to Pericles, became gradually *stricter* towards women, in short, more oriental. How necessary, how logical, even how humanely desirable this was, let us consider for ourselves![57]

Nietzsche's prescription leaves little room for misunderstanding. That male hegemony constitutes a noble ideal and requires the reification of difference—the dissemination of dehumanizing conceptions of women—can hardly be missed from the tone and content of his texts. From a feminist perspective, Nietzsche's great virtue, like that of Rousseau and Kant before him, lies not in his explicit message, but in his remarkable ability to illuminate the mechanisms by which femininity is constructed. In demonstrating the way that naturalistic rhetoric can be deployed to create women's "inherent" traits within a single process that nurtures and constrains, denigrates and idealizes, cajoles and cautions, rewards compliance and punishes deviance, Nietzsche not only instantiates his owm maxim that untruth is the condition of human existence: he also implants permanent suspicion of the language of nature in human discourses.[58]

Within the twentieth century, despite drastic transformations in the roles of women in society, major philosophers have continued to reproduce reifications of difference markedly similar to those developed in antiquity. Despite his break with many of the classical assumptions concerning ontology and human nature, Jean-Paul Sartre advances a philosophical anthropology that is markedly sex-specific.[59] Sartre identifies the defining characteristic of human existence as the capacity to make of oneself what one will. Denying that there is any fixed, immutable human "nature," Sartre suggests that human beings are entirely what they choose to make of themselves: "As a for-itself one is not man first in order to be oneself subsequently and one does not constitute oneself as oneself in terms of a given essence *a priori*. Quite the contrary, it is in its effort to choose itself as a personal self that the for-itself sustains in existence certain social and abstract characteristics which make of it a man (or a woman)."[60]

Although Sartre presents what at first appears an inclusive conception of human nature, his discussion of the tensions that confront individuals and constrain being for-itself indulges in such a level of gender symbolism[61] that the status of women as free agents becomes suspect. Sartre depicts the human condition as one riddled with angst, alienation, and bad faith. To exist as a free subject (for-itself)—choosing projects from a range of virtually unlimited possibilities and assuming full responsibility for the consequences of one's choices and one's actions—is a burden that humans find difficult to bear. In an attempt to deny such freedom and to escape both the anxiety and the responsibility that absolute freedom entails, many individuals retreat to inauthentic existence, acting as if their choices were predetermined by the situation or social roles in which they find themselves. In Sartre's view, such a retreat to being in-itself is an act of bad faith through which individuals deceive themselves and assume the posture of inert objects—acted upon and incapable of action.

Sartre's discussion of bad faith is peculiarly gendered. Rather than posing the problem of inauthentic existence as one that confronts men and women equally, Sartre consistently refers to being for-itself in stereotypically masculine terms and to being in-itself in markedly misogynous imagery. Sartre's depiction of being for-itself is reminiscent of Aristotle's characterization of essentially masculine qualities. For-itself is a potency, an imposition of form and meaning upon an indeterminate universe, an assertion of primacy in freedom. In-itself is described as a vengeful sweetness, a clinging, sticky slime, a leech-like feminine threat to the for-itself:

> The for-itself is suddenly compromised. I open my hands, I want to let go of the slimy and its sticks to me, it draws me, it sucks at me. . . . It is a soft, yielding action, a moist feminine sucking. . . . I cannot slide on this slime, all its suction cups hold me back. . . . It is a trap. . . . Slime is the revenge of the in-itself. A sickly, sweet feminine revenge which may be symbolized on another level by the quality sugary.[62]

In addition to the threat posed by this "feminine slime," Sartre draws an analogy between holes and female sexual organs in order to capture another ontological challenge to being for-itself. Thus, Sartre moves from the claim that "the hole before all sexual specifications, is an obscene expectation, an appeal to the flesh," to the claim that "the obscenity of the feminine sex is that of everything which gapes open."[63] Within this frame, the feminine is a threat to being for-itself since it carries the ontological imperative of the hole as a form of nothingness that demands to be filled. By imposing demands on being for-itself, female sexuality threatens to narrow the sphere of choice available to men, it threatens to mire men in a fixed agenda:

> In herself woman appeals to a strange flesh which is to transform her into a fullness of being by penetration and dissolution. Conversely woman senses her condition as an appeal precisely because she is "in the form of a hole." This is the true origin of Adler's complex. Beyond any doubt her sex is a mouth which devours the penis. . . . The amorous act is the castration of the man; but this is above all because sex is a hole.[64]

What emerges from Sartre's analysis is not a uniform conception of species possibility, but on the contrary a portrayal of the human condition that is sexually bifurcated. Men confront a world of open possibilities and determinate threats. They are free to create themselves as they will. Mastering challenges or succumbing to bad faith is an equal option. Women on the other hand have certain roles imposed on them by their anatomy. Regardless of individual choice, women are threatening because of their genital configuration. Such bodily immanence implies that being for-itself lies beyond women's reach, not as a matter of bad faith but rather as an ontological limitation. Despite the marked difference in Sartrean terminology, the women conceived in Sartre's imagination remain as inured in the realm of necessity as do those invented by Aristotle. The reification of difference still posits the male *qua* human and the female *qua* privation.

From Plato to Sartre, the reification of difference has been a prominent feature of philosophical anthropology. Although there has been a good deal of variety in the philosophical grounds offered for the assignment of particular traits to particular genders, the form of gender construction has remained fairly constant. The scope of women's difference vacillates from the portrayal of women as lesser men, through the conception of women as a privation of the male and as such an opposite, to the denigration of women as the embodiment of an ensemble of traits that men denounce as unbefitting the species. In recent years it has been suggested that the repetitious construal of masculinity and femininity in terms of a limited number of binary oppositions is not accidental. On the contrary, it has been suggested that fixity in the philosophical construction of gender is inextricably linked to the metaphysics of presence, which operates within the narrow confines of the logic of identity. In this view, the polarization of gender is a predictable manifestation of the philosophical quest for a comprehensive understanding of the totality of existence. In seeking a perspective on the world that encompasses all forms of being in a unified totality, all that differs, all that fails to conform, all that defies incorporation in the whole must be excluded, marginalized, or expelled.[65]

Chief among the critics of the metaphysics of presence as a form of logocentrism or indeed of phallogocentrism is Jacques Derrida, who draws upon conceptions of the feminine as a means to overthrow the logic of identity. Derrida suggests that, precisely because the feminine has been marginalized and displaced in the dominant discourses, it offers metaphors and angles of vision that can break the binary opposition of phallocratic thought. Thus Derrida develops an extended metaphor, a "hymenal fable," to critique the metaphysics of presence, to unfix its imperious imposition of determinate meanings and to unmask the confusions that inform its binary oppositions.[66] Taking the hymen as a symbol of fusion of interior and exterior, veil and unveiling, desire and fulfillment, Derrida suggests that it constitutes a medium in which opposites embrace, defying the linear, unitary, phallocratic will to truth. For Derrida, engaging the imagery drawn from women's sexuality and deploying the metaphors of the hymen, invagination, fake orgasm, *différance*[67] can facilitate the development of a paradoxical logic that defies formalization, defers any fixity of meaning, replaces the unitary with the multiple, and thereby destroys the binary oppositions that inform phallogocentrism.

Given his intent to break with the logic of Western discourse and to illuminate the ironies underlying phallocratic constructions of gender, one might expect Derrida's own analyses to avoid any reification of difference. Derrida expressly repudiates essentialism and adopts irony as his most characteristic deconstructive device. Yet there is still something disturbing in the way images of women surface in Derrida's texts. Too often, the insights Derrida gleans from feminine metaphors merely reproduce thinly-veiled stereotypes of women. Consider, for example, the parallels between Derrida's claim that the feminine constitutes an alternative to phallogocentrism by virtue of the fact that women have no determinable identity, and the more traditional misogynous claim that women lack substance, will, general species characteristics, or indeed that a woman's identity is defined solely in relation to a man.[68] How far removed is his claim that "woman is but one name for that untruth of truth"[69] from the stereotype of women as dissimulators, manipulators, liars? Can the association of women with play escape a legacy of depictions of women as frivolous, childlike, not to be taken seriously?[70] Can the invocation of feminine metaphors to confound and deform traditional logic be kept altogether distinct from the misogynous assumption that women are illogical?[71]

Even if one believes that Derrida's explicit commitment to deconstruction as an emancipatory tactic is sufficient to exculpate him from complicity in misogynous stereotypes, his prescribed alternative to phallogocentrism remains problematic. Derrida recommends the displacement of the metaphysics of presence by the reign of difference/*différance*. He endorses the abandonment of the logic of identity and the adoption of ambiguity, multiplicity, and the free play of signifiers. The merits of this prescription are necessarily dependent upon the validity of the interpretation of the Western canon in terms of the logic of identity, the unrelenting, authoritarian impulse to impose sameness, unity, and totality upon heterogeneous reality. This interpretation takes difference as given, for only when difference is presupposed does it make sense to trace the coercive exclusion of difference from the totality. As an ontological claim designed to encompass the universe of existents, an assumption of difference may not be problematic, for few would deny that stars and sea and camels and humans are markedly different. But if one's scope is narrower and a conception of human nature is one's point of departure, then an *a priori* positing of difference is altogether problematic, for it assumes precisely what needs to be proved. Whether men and women, blacks and whites, rich and poor are fundamentally different is a question that must be philosophically investigated. What meaning is to be assigned to sexual and racial variations in a common species cannot be taken as given, for that is a subject of enormous controversy and of profound political import.

An examination of the treatment of gender in the classic canon suggests that the seminal thinkers of the Western tradition have not "discovered" difference: they have created it. Appealing to an invisible soul, to divine ordination, to nature's intent—that is, to things that are invisible, inaudible, undecidable, or unknowable—great thinkers have freely invented gender distinctions, accredited mystifications and distortions, and endowed them with social and political significance. But if this is the case, then Derrida's embrace of difference is not as radical a break from the great tradition as he suggests. It is just one more manifestation of a discursive process that eclipses species commonalities. Deconstruction may offer a different legitimation for abandoning universal claims pertaining to the human species, but it does not offer an alternative to traditional constructions of gender. In short, an appeal to difference cannot be the solution if the reification of difference is the problem.

Feminism and the Classic Canon

Despite the diversity of the classic canon with respect to conceptions of the good life, explanations of social disorder, criteria of legitimacy, and theories of justice, the great works of the Western tradition are remarkably similar in their treatment of women. Appealing to notions of natural inferiority that are a product of their own reifications of difference, theorists exclude women from the realm of the political. Relegated to the confines of family and household, women are conceived as fit objects of state regulation, but they are depicted as unfit for the power and responsibility accorded to regulators. The pervasive misogyny and astounding lack of critical acuity among traditional theorists in addressing questions concerning the nature of women raise complex problems for feminist theorists, both as a provocation of, and as a determinant of the agenda for, feminist theory.

The conceptions of women advanced in the Western tradition—replete with mystifications, distortions and denigrations—might well be described as the initial provocation of feminist theory, a provocation that produces impassioned although not uniform responses. Taking traditional conceptions of human nature as their point of departure, some feminist theorists have denounced the established constructions of gender as lies, slanders, or simply as mistakes. Others have accepted the validity of certain descriptions of women's character but have challenged the account of how that character is produced, attributing its origin to oppression rather than to nature. Others have attempted to reclaim and revaluate the notion of women's inherent difference, arguing that the denigration of the difference is a consequence of misogyny, but that the difference itself ought to be preserved, free from all punitive social and political limitations previously associated with it. The difficulties that these various responses encounter and the implications of these alternative prescriptions for feminist politics will be explored in Chapters 3, 4, and 5. But it is also important to consider the problems the reification of difference poses for feminists who must situate themselves in relation to the classic canon.

The issues of equality, justice, and the good life central to feminist theory acquire their meaning in the context of the classic tradition. Moreover, the terms of discourse, the techniques of analysis, the strategies of argumentation, and the dynamics of critique available to feminists draw heavily upon the legacy of Western philosophy. Thus, feminist theorists must develop a sophisticated stance toward a tradition, at once the target of their criticism and the source of techniques essential to the success of the critical project. If feminists are to challenge sexism in traditional accounts of gender, society, and politics, must the classic theories of human nature and political life be rejected *tout court*? Are certain conceptions salvable? If so, which ones and by what means?

The remaining sections of this chapter will consider three alternatives feminists have developed for dealing with the problem of gender in classic texts: 1. corrective emendation; 2. critique of malevolence; and 3. historicist excuse. Although each approach has certain advantages and disadvantages, none succeeds in fully escaping the "straight-jacket of gender,"[72] established by the reifications of difference in the classic canon. For this reason, the uncritical adoption of these strategies tends to trap feminists within a negative dialectic that is only imperfectly understood. Reflection upon the dilemmas each of these alternatives confronts, however, illuminates the importance of feminist theory as a correction of traditional philosophical discourses.

Corrective Emendation

Traditional conceptions of human nature raise important questions about the nature of individual existence, social relations, and political possibility. Whether human beings are primarily rational and as such capable of making wise decisions about the structure and direction of collective life or whether they are creatures of passion motivated solely by self-interest has important ramifications for the character of political life. Whether conflict is inherent in the human psyche, a function of ignorance, or a result of particular situational variables has important implications for the role of government in regulating human behavior. Whether political institutions are capable of achieving order, liberty, or justice is a significant consideration for those who would design political institutions. What character of citizenry and what social institutions are necessary to sustain a just political system are central issues for those who would transform contemporary political affairs. Feminist theorists must consider such questions in detail if they hope to devise recommendations for a sexually egalitarian political order.

In advancing prescriptions for a just polity, some feminists have sought to reconstruct traditional arguments about the relations of individuals and states, draw out their insights, and assess the evidence adduced to sustain their positions with one major emendation. In place of the reification of difference, the feminist theorist constructs a "generic" human.[73] The strategy of corrective emendation suggests that the feminist theorist can and should overlook the misogynous myopia of the classic theorists. Indeed, this strategy requires that the feminist correct the omissions, distortions, and limitations introduced by sexism. By using inclusive language and treating universal claims as universal, the feminist can provide a corrective emendation of the canon, a reading of the classics in which human beings are male and female, black and white, rich and poor. The competing prescriptions for political life can then be assessed free of the taint of unnecessary bias. In addition, feminists then can draw upon the tradition's legitimate insights in their own theorizing.[74]

The strategy of corrective emendation has certain advantages. It enables one to focus upon a specific problem, compare contradictory diagnoses of and remedies for the problem, consider the implications of alternative views for political life, weigh the arguments and evidence, and arrive at a considered judgment concerning the merits of contending accounts. It also fosters an understanding of political life in which sex is irrelevant to citizenship and leadership. When men and women are depicted as rational and self-determining, as self-interested and contentious, as wild rather than wicked, when rulers and citizens are conceived as male and female, an assault is launched against the notion that politics is uniquely a male preserve.

Corrective, nonsexist emendations of the canon also raise certain problems, for however scrupulous the feminist theorist is in constructing inclusive versions of specific conceptions of the polity, the original texts remain markedly misogynous. Corrective emendation requires a benign neglect of the reification of difference in the originals. In inventing a "generic" human, the feminist theorist must intentionally falsify the theorists' real position on women.

Why should a feminist mask the misogyny of male supremacists? Benign neglect of the sexist claims of traditional theorists may provoke charges of duplicity and deceit, charges that the feminist is abandoning crucial aspects of the feminist project. That benign neglect could be construed as betrayal of the feminist project illuminates a major flaw in the strategy of corrective emendation. By ignoring the sexist bias of the dominant tradition, the feminist renders women's oppression invisible. A charge of complicity and collusion in the oppression of women is not altogether without merit, for in masking the marginalization of women in the classic discourses on political life, the feminist may erase centuries of exploitation and discrimination. Corrective emendation heightens sensitivity to the possibility of a sexually egalitarian future by producing a fictive and unrecognizable past. In the service of future equity, it eradicates a legacy of offenses and transgressions.

Critique of Malevolence

In contrast to corrective emendation's implicit suggestion that erroneous beliefs about half the human population do not contaminate otherwise legitimate visions of political possibility, a second strategy for feminist theorists involves the deployment of gender as an analytic category. The critique of malevolence starts with the conviction that extant political theories cannot be treated as if they were sexually neutral because the ideals of the Western philosophical tradition are premised upon the exclusion of the female. In this view, "Women cannot be easily accommodated into a cultural ideal which has defined itself in opposition to the feminine."[75] Use of inclusive language is inappropriate, therefore, because the classic discourses on politics "constitute men and women as radically different and often incommensurable creatures."[76] Traditional political theorists envision a world "both gender divided (masculine vs. feminine) and gender dominated (masculine)."[77]

The critique of malevolence suggests that the Western tradition constitutes the feminine as a denigrated category. Thus, the suppression and exclusion of womankind is neither accidental nor unintentional. On the contrary, androcentrism in the tradition is a necessary component of the consolidation of male power in the world. Valorization of all things masculine constitutes a strategy of legitimation used by men in the struggle to vindicate male supremacy.

When understood in these terms, adoption of gender as an analytic category is designed to stimulate critical awareness of the malevolent uses of gender in classic texts.[78] In investigating the means by which gender differentiation and gender symbolism are used to legitimate hierarchy, justify inequities, and consolidate power, a far more sophisticated understanding of the dimensions and techniques of politics is generated. In analyzing traditional works, the feminist theorist strives to illuminate the mechanisms by which conceptions of gender are harnessed to notions of natural or divine order, thus circumscribing politics by eliminating certain relations and issues from the sphere of human action and alteration. The feminist demonstrates how notions of hierarchy dependent upon assumptions concerning "natural" relations between the sexes are displaced onto other oppressed groups, such as colonial subjects, in order to legitimate their subjugation. The feminist emphasizes the use of analogies drawn from gender relations to justify or criticize entrenched power and to express the relationship between ruler and ruled.[79] In addition, the feminist draws attention to instructions for the art of ruling rooted in sexual stereotypes.[80] Moreover, the feminist investigates historical connections between legitimations of regimes that appeal to the inherent authority of males and the institutionalization of legal codes that forbid women's political participation, outlaw abortion, prohibit wage-earning by mothers, impose female dress codes, and generally restrict women's freedom.[81]

The critique of malevolence is a particularly good strategy for heightening awareness of inequalities of power, the use of naturalistic rhetoric in masking the social construction of domination, and the questionable character of popular assumptions concerning women's inferiority. By turning attention to the manner in which implicit understandings of gender are invoked and reinscribed in diverse social contexts having nothing to do with relations between the sexes, the critique of malevolence encourages the exploration of modalities of power that are too frequently overlooked. The critique of malevolence also has certain drawbacks. The use of gender as an analytic category may tacitly suggest that sex oppression is the primary or only oppression. Focus on the battle of the sexes may eclipse all other theoretical questions and thereby diminish the richness of the social, psychological, and political issues addressed in the philosophical tradition. Mistaken views about women may be taken as an indicator of generic flaws in a theorist's work and advanced as grounds for rejecting the entire project without fully engaging the diverse arguments included in the text. Moreover, using gender as an analytic category to illuminate how systems of power operate does not explain why they operate as they do. In the absence of sophisticated causal explanations, unwarranted inferences about the "nature of men" may degenerate into a form of biologism that undermines the possibility of sexually egalitarian politics.

The Historicist Excuse

To avoid the pitfalls of corrective emendation and the critique of malevolence, a third strategy suggests that the feminist theorist include an examination of conceptions of womanhood as one element in the analysis of a theorist's work. Thus, consideration of each theorist's conception of woman's nature supplements analysis of the theorist's arguments concerning human nature, freedom, law, community, the nature and organization of political life, and the institutions and objectives of government. Analyzing traditional theories in detail, the feminist theorist indicates the inconsistencies between the conception of human nature and the conception of women advanced by the theorist, suggests that an adequate understanding of human beings requires the inclusion of both sexes, and explains the theorist's insensitivity to the issue in relation to the limitations of sexism characteristic of earlier historical periods. The strategy of historicist excuse recommends that feminist analysts forgive the theorist's misogyny as a predictable artifact of less enlightened ages, reconstruct the account of human nature on the basis of contemporary knowledge of sexual equality, and assess the theorist's political vision in light of this additional information.

As an analytic strategy, the historicist excuse has a number of virtues. It ensures that distorted conceptions of women's nature are addressed directly. It guarantees that the question of gender is subject to systematic examination without overshadowing other important issues raised by philosophical texts. In addition, it stresses the importance of treating sexist bias as an error that must be corrected. But the historicist excuse also suffers from certain defects. It fails to consider the possibility that distorted conceptions of gender may permeate theoretical visions of political life far more profoundly than is commonly suggested. It does not seriously engage the possibility that the forced exclusion of women from political life has produced an overly restricted conception of politics, that the demarcation of the political may be skewed toward the priorities of men. By failing to question such a narrow construal of political life, the historicist excuse may perpetuate the assumption that "the only human excellence and virtues which deserve to be taken seriously are those exemplified in the range of activities and concerns that have been associated with maleness."[82]

There are additional problems with the historicist excuse as a mode of feminist analysis. The optimistic notion that misogyny is a relic of outmoded understandings, which our age has relegated to the dustbin of history, is altogether at odds with the institutions and ideas of contemporary cultures that continue to be pervaded by pernicious forms of sexist bias. Moreover, the historicist excuse for androcentrism is incompatible with any effort to address theoretical arguments on their merits. Excusing conceptions of gender on the basis of particular limitations of determinate historical epochs can easily be extrapolated to theorists' other arguments with a predictable result. Rather than grappling with the adequacy of specific arguments, historicist excuse fosters the unwarranted conclusions that all theories must be understood only in relation to the conditions of their genesis, that they must be understood simply as reflections of historical worldviews, and that they shed little light on contemporary political problems. Thus, the historicist excuse provides grounds for a summary dismissal of alternative theories of political life by negating the power of theoretical insights and denying their relevance for current political debates.

Problematizing Gender

Even this brief depiction of the advantages and disadvantages of alternative feminist stances towards the classic canon reveals that the reification of difference raises a problem. In attempting to situate themselves in relation to the philosophical tradition, feminist theorists quickly discover that rather than being a simple problem with clear solutions, issues pertaining to gender are deeply problematic. In deciding whether to pursue a strategy involving corrective emendation, critique of malevolence, or historicist excuse, feminists confront crucial theoretical questions ignored by traditional philosophical discourses. How important is gender? What is the relation between gender and individual identity? What are the implications of the systematic oppression of half the species for our contemporary understanding of politics? How are conceptions of justice influenced by notions of natural sex differences? What relation should sexual dimorphism have to the assignment of benefits and burdens in society?

Feminist theory begins with the insight that any construction of gender must be treated as problematic rather than given, for construals of sexual difference have far reaching political implications. In problematizing gender, feminist theory makes an important contribution to traditional and contemporary philosophical discourse, for it identifies a field of investigation that raises critical issues in relation to claims of truth, justice, equality, and liberty. It accords visibility to a range of theoretical problems that remain hidden in traditional analyses. In bringing the problem of gender to light, feminist theory challenges theorists both to transcend a history of political organization that affords rights and immunities only to men and to design a set of political relations and institutions worthy of the allegiance of men and women.

In attempting to devise an adequate stance toward the classic canon, feminist theorists have also learned a great deal about the practical implications of various theoretical positions. The strategy of corrective emendation teaches that adoption of gender-neutral language and universal claims, in the absence of any systematic efforts to redress sexism, merely renders women's oppression invisible. It masks rather than eliminates continuing sex discrimination. The critique of malevolence teaches that an unrelenting focus on gender may produce prescriptions for political life insensitive to injustices rooted in race, class, religion, age, and ethnicity. It may unwittingly suggest that gender injustice is the result of inherent male impulses. And it may foster the erroneous impression that the marginalization and exclusion of women are basically women's issues, of little interest to men who have "more important" questions on their minds. The historicist excuse teaches that it is far too easy to dismiss misogyny as an artifact of ancient cultures and to allow this conviction to blind theorists to the multiple manifestations and destructive consequences of sexism in contemporary societies.

Taking lessons from their own attempts to relate to the classic canon, feminists have learned that sophisticated prescriptions for a political system characterized by liberty, justice, and equity require detailed analysis of the social construction of gender and the range of gender symbolism within contemporary cultures. The lessons of feminism are not for feminists only.

To avoid reproducing a system of power that privileges men, political and philosophical discourses must engage questions concerning the causes of and find solutions for all forms of sex discrimination. If the life-constraining errors of the past are not to be repeated, the problematics of gender must become a focal point of philosophical and political analysis. Designs for the reconstitution of political life must take the problems that confront women seriously: feminist theory serves as a constant reminder of this.

Chapter Two

Social Consequences of Gender Misconceptions

Beliefs have social consequences. When it is widely believed that women are inherently different from men, social practices will reflect that conviction. Whether the nature of that difference is conceived in terms of natural inferiority or moral superiority, social expectations, social roles and social institutions will be shaped in conformity with the contours of the presumed gender distinctiveness.

Differential treatment for people who have differing capacities can be justified on rational and moral grounds. It makes good sense to treat heterogeneous individuals differently, for if individual talents and interests can be linked to determinate social roles, then both individual happiness and social efficiency can be maximized. Moreover, elementary conceptions of justice suggest that treating people fairly is inextricably connected to giving them their due—a notion that necessarily requires differential treatment in accordance with various degrees of excellence and achievement.

Virtually every known society is characterized by social practices that treat men and women differently. As the legacy of traditions whose origins are often unknown or only imperfectly understood, these practices are typically vindicated as natural, reasonable, moral, and proven by having withstood the test of time. In problematizing gender, feminists have subjected these practices and their legitimations to close scrutiny. By doing this, they frequently discover patterns of interpersonal and institutional relations that do far more than simply treat men and women differently. Rather than enshrining a policy of different but equal, numerous social practices privilege men. Recognition of such privileging leads feminists to a basic question: Are women treated differently because they are different, or are women different because they have been treated differently from birth? This chapter will survey patterns of social interaction that advantage men and disadvantage women with the aim of tracing the social consequences of beliefs about gender.[1] It will begin with an examination of subtle sex bias in expectation and evaluation that influences not only how men and women perform their responsibilities, but also how they are perceived to perform them. Then it will consider consequences of subtle bias for the occupational prospects of women, focusing on the issues of underrepresentation, underutilization, pay differentials, and job segregation by sex. In addition, it will explore the systematic effects of gender expectations in relation to a range of harms that women experience far more often than men: poverty, sexual harassment, rape, and domestic violence.[2] Finally, this chapter will analyze traditional explanations of these phenomena in order to demonstrate their deficiences and to illuminate the importance of feminist analysis for an adequate understanding of critical features of contemporary life.

Undervaluing Women

A number of psychologists have devised experiments designed to tap social expectations related to gender. Some of these studies investigate sex bias in evaluation of particular works, some explore how competent performance is explained in relation to internal and external factors, and some measure selection bias in hiring and promotion situations. Taken in consort, these studies suggest that both men and women consistently attribute greater competence to men than to women.

The research design for tests of sex bias in evaluation typically consists of the selection of two groups of matched subjects who are given identical articles from professional journals or identical paintings to evaluate. One group is told that the work was done by a man; the other group is told that the work was done by a woman. In these studies, the products attributed to male authors/painters are consistently rated higher than the identical works attributed to female authors/painters.[3] Comparable studies of performance have found that male performance on perceptual discrimination tasks is perceived to be more skillful than equivalent female performance, both when the perceptual discrimination involves household items stereotypically associated with women and when it involves mechanical objects traditionally associated with men.[4] Similar results were also found in the evaluation of responses to emergencies. When identical responses were ascribed to men and women, subjects evaluate the men's performance as more logical and helpful than the women's.[5]

Social psychologists have also investigated differing explanations of competent and incompetent performance by men and women. The factors that are usually cited to explain performance include individual characteristics such as ability and effort, and situational determinants such as level of task difficulty and luck.[6] Investigators have discovered that both success and failure are explained differently depending on the gender of the individual who succeeds or fails. Women's achievements, especially in nontraditional activities, tend to be attributed to luck; men's achievements are attributed to skill and intelligence.[7] Excellent performance by women is also explained in terms of a one-time, extraordinary effort; similar male achievement is attributed to unwavering levels of superior ability.[8] Moreover, unsuccessful performance by women is readily attributed to lack of ability; unsuccessful performance by men is explained in terms of bad luck or the insuperable difficulty of the task.[9]

Given such tendencies to overvalue male performances and to undervalue women's performances, and to attribute male achievement to inherent characteristics while attributing women's achievements to external variables like good fortune or family connections, it is not surprising to find considerable pro-male bias in research on selection preferences. Within such experiments, subjects are presented with hypothetical hiring or promotion situations. Male and female candidates with identical records are presented for evaluation. Despite the fact that the records of the hypothetical applicants are identical in all respects, the male applicants are selected far more frequently than female applicants for managerial, scientific and semiskilled positions.[10] In addition, although their qualifications are literally indistinguishable, the male candidates are rated more positively than their female counterparts in terms of personal acceptability as well as potential for service and career longevity.[11] A similar study of 228 department chairpersons in universities revealed not only that the vast majority of department chairs rated male candidates more highly, but also that when they decided to hire women candidates, it was at the assistant professor level; yet the male candidates with identical *curriculum vita* were offered positions at the associate professor level.[12] Several other studies have documented the tendency to hire men and women with identical records at different levels of pay: men are far more likely to be hired with higher starting salaries, and women with lower starting salaries in these experiments.[13]

The differences in expectations, perceptions, and appraisals of male and female performance documented in these psychology experiments have also been corroborated in real life situations when systematic investigations have been undertaken. Court cases and investigations by regulatory commissions—such as the Equal Employment Opportunity Commission, the Office of Civil Rights, and the Office of Federal Contract Compliance—have proven the existence of sex discrimination in hiring, promotion, and pay in both private and public sectors in numerous specific instances. In addition, widespread pro-male bias has been observed in the schools and the courts. A joint study conducted by the Council of Chief State School Officers and the National Association of State Boards of Education discovered that teacher expectations concerning boys' and girls' performances had palpable effects in the elementary school classroom. Sustained observation of teacher-pupil interactions indicated that boys receive more teacher attention than girls in every category of classroom interaction: active instruction, listening, praise, and punishment. Noting that boys are more likely to receive criticism for their deportment and praise for their academic performance and that girls are more likely to receive praise for their appearance and criticism for their academic work, the study suggested that different patterns of teacher-student interaction may be responsible for students' internalized assessments of their capabilities. Indeed, the study suggested that girls' tendency to attribute their failures to lack of ability and their successes to hard work, in contrast to boys' tendency to attribute their failures to lack of hard work and their successes to native abilities, might well be traced to patterns of praise and blame first established in the primary grades.[14]

Within educational institutions, the tendency to undervalue women is not the sole preserve of teachers. On the contrary, students also show a marked propensity to accredit the performances of their male teachers and to discredit the performances of their female teachers. In a survey of 16,000 teacher evaluation forms completed by students at the University of California, Norma Wikler found that students routinely discounted assessments of their woman professors' superiority on particular questionnaire items in arriving at overall judgments of performance. Both men and women students rated their women professors superior to their male professors in level of preparation, mastery of material, and responsiveness to students: "But they gave significantly more weight to the views of their male professors, evaluating them as more credible, more believable, more authoritative and more persuasive than their female professors. Moreover, male students were much more dramatically prejudiced in favor of the male teachers than were the woman students."[15]

A number of studies have also documented gender bias in the courts—on the parts of judges, attorneys and juries. Defining gender bias as "the predisposition or tendency to think about and behave toward others primarily on the basis of their sex,"[16] task forces on women and the courts in New Jersey, New York, Rhode Island, and Arizona have investigated court proceedings for traces of gender bias in the relations among judges, lawyers, litigants, witnesses and jurors. Their findings reveal that stereotypical beliefs about women permeate court interactions to a degree that impairs women's credibility as judges, lawyers, witnesses, and jurors. The task force reports have noted that women lawyers are often subjected to offensive remarks concerning their physical appearance or sexuality. The testimony of women witnesses is frequently impugned by references to women's notorious unreliability, their tendency toward exaggeration, their poor memory for facts, and their indecisiveness. Even the ability of women judges' to cite the law and instruct the jury has been questioned by male defense attorney's during concluding arguments. In the aftermath of a two-year study of sex bias in the New York court system, the New York State Task Force on Women in the Courts concluded that women lawyers were so routinely demeaned and treated patronizingly by male judges and attorneys and that the credibility of women witnesses was so frequently impugned by counsel, that women were effectively denied equal justice.[17]

Whether incorporated in tacit expectations that subtly affect perception and appraisal of women's capacities and performance or institutionalized in educational and legal practices, the tendency to undervalue women advantages men. If internalized by women, tacit pro-male bias may curb their ambitions and aspirations and thereby circumscribe their life choices. If internalized by teachers, counselors and employers, pro-male bias may make it far more difficult for women to demonstrate their talents. Indeed, to the extent that women's achievements are attributed to luck, extraordinary effort, or family connections rather than to ability, women may never be able to prove their competence. Explanations for their successes, which emphasize external factors over which women have little or no control, ensure that women's achievements vanish as the link between ability and performance is severed.[18] Thus in hiring and promotion situations, women find themselves confronting a burden of proof that is close to insurmountable. Men benefit from this situation, in part because they face no comparable burden of proof. On the contrary, pro-male bias ensures that men are given the benefit of the doubt. In addition, subtle pro-male bias in expectation and evaluation guarantees that men have an advantage in any competition for educational, occupational, or economic opportunities.[19] The tendency to perceive women as less capable, less creative, less meritorious, less credible, and, hence, less deserving of serious consideration, ensures that women cannot compete on precisely the same terms as men: women are judged in relation to standards—drawn from an array of gender stereotypes—irrelevant to the competition and not applied to men. Assumed superiority affords men a sizable competitive advantage.

Illusory Equality

Women constitute 51 percent of the population of the United States and 44 percent of the paid laborforce, yet the roles they fill in the economic and political life of the nation vary markedly from those filled by men. Women hold only 5 percent of the seats in the United States Congress, 16 percent of the seats in state legislatures, 2 percent of the state governorships, and 17 percent of the elective offices at the local level.[20] In short, women are markedly underrepresented in positions of political power.

Within the economic sector, estimates of women's share in positions of power and prestige vary from one statistical source to another. The Women's Bureau of the United States Department of Labor presents the most optimistic statistics, indicating that 33.6 percent of all executive, administrative, and managerial workers are women.[21] Yet, in calculating this figure, the Department of Labor includes a wide range of jobs within this category—executive, administrative, and managerial—without distinguishing top executive positions from those of middle or lower management, thereby inflating the numbers of women in leadership positions.[22] Other sources afford far more conservative estimates of the percentage of women in upper management. A 1982 study conducted by *Time* magazine indicated that women held only 5 percent of the executive positions in the fifty largest companies in the United States; a more recent study by the executive recruiting firm Korn/Ferry International reported that women held only 2 percent of the top executive positions.[23] Another way of considering the comparative underrepresentation of women in the upper echelons of the corporate sector in the United States is by noting that, of all working women, only 8.5 percent are employed in managerial positions, while 19 percent of all male workers hold such executive/administrative jobs.

Statistics demonstrating the underrepresentation of women in positions of power and prestige in the public and private sectors do not of themselves explain why women are underrepresented. This is due to inherent limitations of statistical correlations. As a quantitative technique devised to systematize inductive observations, statistics present descriptive not explanatory accounts. Statistical correlations cannot prove causation either in principle or in practice. In taking the underrepresentation of women to be problematic, feminists do not mean to attribute greater explanatory power to statistics than they can possibly convey. Rather, their goal is to raise an open question. Why are women so patently absent? By rendering that absence visible, they illuminate an area in need of investigation.[24]

To shed light on the issue of underrepresentation, feminists have also investigated the phenomenon of underutilization of women. Underutilization involves a comparison of the number of women in particular career positions with the number of women in the laborforce who possess all the relevant qualifications for the job. Studies of underutilization compare, for example, the number of women faculty hired in specific disciplines with the number of women Ph.D.s in that discipline who are on the job market in a given year.[25] What investigations of underutilization seek to explain is not the dearth of women professionals or women in skilled craft positions per se, but the dearth of women in these fields given the availability of qualified women candidates. Investigations of employment trends in banking, law firms, universities, construction companies, elementary and secondary school administration, and a wide range of skilled craft occupations have revealed widespread underutilization of women. Although qualified women candidates are available in these diverse fields, they do not tend to get hired. Within the past two decades, the underutilization of women has been demonstrated so frequently in litigation that the United States Supreme Court has ruled that a demonstration of underutilization is sufficient to establish a *prima facie* case of discrimination.[26]

Underrepresentation and underutilization of women in executive and administrative positions are symptomatic of occupational segregation by sex. In the contemporary United States, 80 percent of all women workers are employed in only twenty-five job categories. Indeed, 60 percent of all women workers are employed in clerical and service sectors (compared to 15 percent of all male workers).[27] Job segregation by sex is apparent in most contemporary occupations. Some jobs have come to be associated with "women's work," while others are seen as the fit preserve of men. Thus, women constitute 98 percent of all secretaries, 97 percent of all nurses, 95 percent of all household workers, 94 percent of all typists, 75 percent of all clerical workers and 64 percent of all service workers; men comprise 97 percent of all engineers, 91 percent of all skilled craftworkers, 85 percent of all lawyers, 74 percent of all university faculty, 70 percent of all computer systems analysts, 60 percent of all computer programmers, and 55 percent of all accountants and auditors.[28]

Although job segregation by sex has been a fairly constant feature of the American laborforce in the twentieth century, economist Francine Blau has charted some change in the past forty years by constructing an "index of segregation" based on the number of women or men who would have to change jobs in order to achieve equality in the occupational distribution of men and women. Blau notes that the

> degree of occupational segregation actually increased slightly between 1950 and 1960 as predominantly female clerical and professional jobs grew in relative size. Between 1960 and 1970, an inflow of men into female professions and of women into male sales and clerical jobs produced a drop in the segregation index of 3.1 percentage points. Between 1972 and 1981, the index declined by 6.6 percentage points, as women increased their share of traditionally male managerial and professional jobs.[29]

Despite a decline of approximately 10 percent in the level of occupational segregation by sex in the past thirty years, the magnitude of segregation remains substantial among all age groups. "More than 60 percent of the women (or men) in the labor force would have to change jobs for the occupational distribution of the two sex groups to be the same."[30]

Some insight into the reasons for the relatively small decline in sex segregation in the workplace and for the exceedingly slow pace at which such change has occurred can be gained by considerating the extrinsic rewards associated with traditionally male and female occupations. Typically male and typically female jobs do not receive equal remuneration. On the contrary, women's jobs afford lower pay and fewer opportunities for career advancement than men's. According to the Bureau of the Census, women's salaries in 1986 were only 64 percent of male salaries, a percentage that has remained fairly constant since 1955.[31] When considered in terms of lifetime earnings, this constitutes a significant difference. Census Bureau projections suggest that a male who completes a Bachelor's degree within the next decade can expect to earn 50 percent more over the course of his lifetime than a woman with the same degree. A college-educated male can expect lifetime earnings of $1,190,000; but a college-educated woman can expect lifetime earnings of only $523,000—about the equivalent of a man who completes only a gradeschool education.[32]

It would be a mistake to attribute all pay differentials to occupational segregation of the workforce along sex lines. Although some of the disparity in men and women's wages can be attributed to the different kinds of work that men and women do, several other variables are relevant to a full account of pay inequity. Numerous studies have noted that even in cases in which a man and a woman perform exactly the same job, have the same years of experience, the same educational background and the same evaluations of their job performance, the woman employee will earn 75–82 percent of her male colleague's salary.[33] Other studies, which evaluate jobs on the basis of the knowledge, skill, mental demands, accountability, and working conditions they require, indicate that predominantly female jobs are paid roughly 20 percent less than predominantly male jobs that require comparable levels of skill and responsibility. When researchers investigating pay-inequities control for an array of productivity-related factors—including formal education, work history, laborforce attachment—as well as for occupational segregation by sex, they find that significant pay differentials still remain to be explained. For this reason, economists have suggested that discrimination against women in the labor market accounts for a significant proportion of the gap between men and women's salaries. They estimate that approximately 50 percent of the pay differentials between male and female workers is related to subtle forms of sex bias.[34]

Proponents of a free market economy often defend open competition for employment in terms of individual rights and meritocratic principles.[35] Competition is supposed to establish equality of opportunity by ensuring that all individuals start on an even footing, are considered solely on the basis of merit, and are awarded jobs on the basis of demonstrated superiority over all other candidates. Job segregation by sex and a wage gap of at least 20 percent between male and female workers who perform the same job, on the basis of the same education and experience, and with the same degree of excellence suggests that equality of opportunity remains largely illusory for most contemporary women workers in the United States. Subtle sex bias advantages men by granting them easier access to most occupations, affording them preference in hiring and promotion, and according them higher rates of pay in every field starting at entry level and continuing through retirement. Despite the Equal Pay Act of 1963 (which mandates equal pay for equal work), Title VII of the Civil Rights Act of 1964 (which prohibits discrimination in employment on the basis of race, sex, ethnicity, or national origin), and thirty years of affirmative action programs, men and women remain markedly unequal in the work place. The underrepresentation and underutilization of women, the sex-segregated workforce and significant pay differentials remain as persistent and problematic now as they were thirty years ago.

Persistent Harms

Certain harms are uniquely associated with women. Poverty, sexual harassment, rape, and domestic violence are far more likely to befall women than men. Feminists have sought to illuminate the prevalence of these harms, to investigate the physical, emotional, and psychological risks that such harms pose for women, and to identify strategies for the eradication of these afflictions. Even the most cursory review of the research in these fields suggests that women inhabit a world on terms markedly different from those of men. Within existing institutions, their interests are not promoted and their bodies are not protected as fully as are men's nor are their concerns accorded the same degree of consideration as men's.

The Feminization of Poverty

Poverty is not a sex-neutral phenomenon. Two out of every three poor adults in the contemporary United States are women.[36] Although the number of male-headed households living in poverty declined from 3.2 million in 1969 to 2.7 million in 1979, the number of female-headed households living in poverty grew dramatically during this same period, from 1.8 million in 1969 to 2.6 million in 1979.[37] The addition of 10,000 families headed by single women to the ranks of the poor each year during the 1970s has been labelled the feminization of poverty. As the 1980s draw to a close, women and their children constitute 80 percent of the nation's 34.4 million people living below the official poverty line. Of all families with children under 18 years old, 43 percent of those maintained by single women are in poverty, compared to 8 percent of families headed by men.[38] More than 50 percent of the black and hispanic female-headed households live at or below the poverty level, a percentage that has been growing since 1980. Moreover, women constitute 73 percent of the nation's 3.8 million elderly poor.

The feminization of poverty has three main sources: the increase in households headed by single women as a result of death, divorce, desertion, or pregnancy outside of marriage; women's wages that are insufficient to support their dependents; the growing number of elderly women who are not adequately protected by social security, pensions, or insurance.[39] There has been a 34 percent increase in the number of single, widowed, and divorced adult women in the United States since 1970.[40] The risk of poverty faced by married women upon loss of a spouse has become increasingly clear in the past two decades. A California study of 3,000 divorced couples revealed that one year after the divorce, the wife's standard of living (measured in terms of income in relation to needs) declined by 73 percent, while the husband's rose by 42 percent.[41] Contrary to popular stereotypes, judges award alimony in only 15 percent of divorce cases; men pay alimony in only 4 percent of these cases; the mean award of alimony is $3000 per year.[42] Child support is awarded in only 59 percent of the divorces involving families with children under 21 years of age; only 22 percent of divorced mothers actually receive child support payments; and the average amount of child support received was $2,110 per year per family, not per child.[43]

Sixty-two percent of the women who head households work outside the home. But employment is not sufficient to prevent poverty. Three of every five working women earn less than $10,000 per year, a sum that is simply not large enough to support a family at a very high standard of living. At a time when the federal poverty level is $9,120 for a family of three, one-fourth of the families headed by working women have incomes below the poverty level.[44] For those women heads of household who do not work outside the home, welfare benefits fall far short of providing a means to escape poverty. Benefit levels vary from state to state. At the low end of the scale, some states provide benefits that afford recipients an income equivalent to 25 percent of the federal poverty level.[45] No state provides benefits that raise recipients' incomes above the federal poverty level.

Males are at greatest risk of being poor when they are under 21 years of age, that is, when they are most likely to be dependent upon a woman head of household for support.[46] Women, on the other hand, confront the greatest likelihood of being poor in old age. Twenty-seven percent of women over 65 years of age live on incomes below the poverty level. Indeed, the median income for single women over 65 is only $6,000. As a result of low wages in predominantly female occupations, women's life-time earnings and, hence, their social security benefits, tend to be much lower than men's. Women constitute 75 percent of those who receive the minimal social security benefit.[47] Of those who receive more than the minimum, the average monthly social security payment for retired women workers is approximately $100 less than the average benefit for retired men.[48]

At the close of the twentieth century, women are far more vulnerable to poverty than men. Inequitable allocations of resources in divorce settlements, as well as inadequate wages, pensions, and social security benefits leave women far more exposed to impoverishment than men. The contraction of the welfare state—marked by cuts in level of federal assistance to the poor and coupled with imposition of work requirements for welfare recipients—imposes an onus of mandatory menial labor on poor women in return for benefits that fall far below the level of subsistence.[49] Should present trends continue, the National Advisory Council on Economic Opportunity has warned that by the year 2000 virtually all the poor will be women and their children.[50]

Sexual Harassment

Within the workplace and in educational institutions, gender stereotypes can foster unwarranted expectations of women. Rather than being accepted as a co-worker, colleague, professional, or student like any other, women are often singled out for a special form of treatment that has been compared to "psychological warfare."[51] They are exposed to verbal, nonverbal and physical behavior that objectifies and exploits them as sexual objects and that makes it difficult for them to perform their assignments. Within the past decade, feminists have labelled this phenomenon sexual harassment. They have investigated the prevalence and consequences of such harassment, and they have fought to have the behavior condemned as unethical conduct and as a form of illegal sex discrimination.[52]

Unwelcome sexual advances, requests for sexual favors, and other verbal or physical conduct of a sexual nature constitute sexual harassment when (1) submission to such conduct is made either explicitly or implicitly a term or condition of an individual's employment or academic achievement; or (2) submission to or rejection of such conduct by an individual is used as the basis for employment decisions or academic decisions affecting such individuals; or (3) such conduct has the purpose or effect of unreasonably interfering with an individual's work or academic performance or creating an intimidating, hostile, or offensive working or academic environment.

In contrast to the stereotype that conflates sexual harassment with overt sexual propositions as a condition for employment or successful completion of a course, sexual harassment includes a range of verbal and nonverbal, as well as physical behaviors. Physical harassment may range from leering, fondling, and pinching to rape. Verbal harassment occurs in the form of persistent derogatory comments pertaining to a person's sex (for example, "There never was a woman who could do a man's job" or "I didn't expect you to follow what I said. It's well known that women are incapable of higher reasoning" or "You really ought to switch your field of study to literature. A woman trying to master mathematics might as well try to grow a beard" or "You'll have to face the facts—there's no room for women in the world of engineering. The demands for strength, rigor, and precision are simply more than any woman can muster"). Verbal harassment may also take the form of sexist remarks that draw attention to a person's body, clothing, or sexuality (for example, "With a body like that, you shouldn't have to work" or "I bet you know how to keep your man warm at night" or "Your presence in this classroom is unnecessary. Nature has ordained that women's fundamental role is that of reproducer of the species; any other undertaking is purely superfluous"). In addition to verbal and physical harassment, a variety of nonverbal behaviors can also harass women. The circulation of *Playboy* centerfolds attached to biographies of new women employees and the inclusion of photos of nude women or pornographic films in training programs that women employees are compelled to attend are recent examples of such harassment.[53] Behaviors and utterances of this sort constitute sexual harassment precisely because they create a hostile and intimidating environment that impairs women's work or academic performance.

Sexual harassment in the workplace can have severe economic conseqences. Many women who refuse to comply with sexual propositions or who complain of sexual harassment in the office are fired or denied promotions and raises. Others are transferred to jobs that are less lucrative and offer fewer career opportunities. Women in sales lose important commissions when they resist sexual harassment by clients. In addition, women who leave jobs as a result of sexual harassment may be labelled "trouble-makers" and blackballed from their profession, or they may be denied positive recommendations necessary to secure other employment. In all such instances, women suffer financial injury. They lose jobs and income that are essential to their maintenance and well-being.

A number of studies have also documented that sexual harassment—whether in the form of graphic commentaries on the victim's body, degrading descriptions of the victim's sex, or overt sexual propositions—adversely affects the victim's mental and physical health and undermines the victim's self-esteem.[54] Women exposed to sexual harassment on the job suffer insomnia, head-, neck-, and backaches, stomach ailments ranging from nausea to ulcers, decreased concentration, diminished ambition, depression, and anxiety, none of which is conducive to superior job performance. In addition, sexual harassment exacts an enormous toll on the victim's self-esteem. Rather than feeling competent and in control of their work life, victims of sexual harassment feel powerless and frustrated as a consequence of being unable to fend off the harasser. Moreover, when harassment impairs their work performance, victims of harassment often begin to doubt their own competence and blame themselves for failing in their work.

The consequences of sexual harassment upon an individual's academic aspirations and educational achievements are just beginning to be investigated.[55] One study at the University of Illinois indicated that 18.7 percent of the students who had experienced sexual harassment on campus suffered a marked deterioration in academic performance; 23.4 percent altered their course selections in order to avoid the harasser; and 13.9 percent of the victims changed their major area of study and their career plans in order to escape further harassment. A similar study at Harvard University revealed that 12 percent of the undergraduate students and 15 percent of the graduate students who experienced sexual harassment altered their academic objectives as a result of the harassment.[56] A ten-year study of eighty high-school valedictorians also indicated that universities afford a far less hospitable environment to women students than to men and that this difference has palpable effects on women's career choices. Although female valedictorians typically outperformed their male counterparts academically throughout their college years, as early as the second year of university "two-thirds of the women began reporting lower levels of intellectual self-esteem and less ambitious career aspirations than they did when they graduated from high school."[57]

As a form of sex discrimination, sexual harassment ensures that women do not experience employment or educational opportunities on the same terms as men. They confront obstacles, exploitation, and insult solely because of their sex. The perniciousness of sexual harassment is matched by its pervasiveness. Estimates of the prevalence of sexual harassment in the workplace vary from one study to another. In a study conducted by *Redbook* in the mid-1970s, 88 percent of the 9,000 respondents reported that they had experienced sexual harassment on the job. In a study conducted by the United States Navy, 81 percent of the enlisted women reported that they had been victims of sexual harassment. A survey of state employees in Kentucky indicated that 56 percent of the women respondents had experienced sexual harassment at work; of these 79 percent noted that they had been sexually harassed more than once. A study at Harvard University indicated that 32 percent of the tenured women faculty, 49 percent of the untenured women faculty; 41 percent of the female graduate students and 39 percent of the female undergraduates had experienced sexual harassment at Harvard. When the data from numerous studies are combined, it is estimated that 20–30 percent of women workers are subjected to sexual harassment during their careers and a comparable percentage of women students are sexually harassed during their university studies.[58]

Rape

Rape is a markedly misunderstood phenomenon. When adult women are asked if they have been the victims of an attempted or completed rape, 22 percent respond positively. When the same women are asked if they have ever been in a situation where force or threat of force has been used by men to obtain intercourse, 56 percent report that they have been in such situations.[59] Among women college students, survey results are equally puzzling. When asked "Have you ever been raped?" only 5 percent of the respondents said "Yes." But when asked "Have you ever had sexual intercourse without your consent?" 21 percent of the respondents said "Yes." In the same study, 25 percent of the women students reported that they had been "subjected to forms of restraint to get sex" and 25 percent reported they had been slapped, hit, beaten, or threatened with a knife to get sex.[60]

Rape is a crime. The Universal Crime Reports published by the FBI define rape as "the carnal knowledge of a female forcibly and against her will."[61] Yet, large proportions of male undergraduate students who do not understand themselves to be engaging in criminal activity report that they do use force in sexual situations. In one study, 15 percent of the male students surveyed reported they "had used force to get sex"; 50 percent noted that they had taken a woman's clothes off against her will; 37 percent reported that they had engaged in genital petting against a woman's will.[62] In another study, only 43 percent of the males surveyed reported that they had *never* used force in any sexual encounter.[63]

Survey research has also revealed that there are certain conditions under which it is perceived to be acceptable to rape a woman. In a survey of high school students in Los Angeles, 54 percent of the male students agreed that "it is okay to rape a girl if she teases you"; 42 percent of the female students agreed that "A girl cannot get raped if she leads a boy on."[64] A survey of 1,700 junior high school students who attended assault awareness programs sponsored by a Rhode Island Rape Crisis Center revealed even greater tolerance for rape. Fifty percent of these students said that a woman who dresses "seductively" and walks alone at night "is asking to be raped." Sixty-five percent of the boys and 47 percent of the girls noted that it is acceptable for a man to force a woman to have sex if they have been dating more than six months; 31 percent of the boys and 32 percent of the girls believed it is not improper for a man to rape a woman who has had previous sexual experiences; 87 percent of the boys and 79 percent of the girls said that "rape is okay if a man and woman are married."[65] Another study of male college students found that 51 percent of the students reported that they would rape a woman if they were certain that they would "get away with it."[66]

Confusion about the nature of rape is not restricted to any particular age group, to one sex, or to the lay population. On the contrary, judges in sexual assault cases have also manifested deeply ingrained misunderstandings of rape. In the early 1980s, a Wisconsin judge suggested that a rapist was really a victim of a permissive society and a teenager's provocative dress (blue jeans). Raping a young girl in a high school stairwell was, according to this judge, merely a "normal reaction" to the girl's seductive charms.[67] A judge in California informed a rape victim that by hitchhiking on a city street, she had "invited" a sexual attack; a judge in Connecticut dismissed charges against a man who had attempted to rape a woman with the quip, "You can't blame a man for trying."[68]

The American public is not equally confused about any other major crime. No similar ambiguity surrounds murder, burglary, theft, or assault. The problem with rape is that it does not conform to popular stereotypes. In contrast to the image of the psychotic stranger who stalks a woman in a public place and brutally attacks her using a knife, a gun, or sheer physical force, most rapists are quite average men who hold respectable jobs and who know their victims. Seventy percent of all rapes are committed by men who know and are known by their victims. Fifty percent of all rapes occur in the victim's home. In contrast to the belief that rapes are impulsive responses to a woman's seductive charms, most rapes are premeditated and planned. One-third of all rapes are committed by two or more men; 90 percent of these "trains" or "gang rapes" are planned. In cases in which rapists act alone, 70 percent of their attacks are planned. Whether acting alone or in consort with other men, rape has nothing to do with spontaneous and uncontrollable responses to the lures of beautiful young women. Although women are at greatest risk of being raped between the ages of 18 and 24, rape respects no age limitations: 10 percent of all rapes involve victims who are over 65-years-of-age and 15 percent involve victims who are younger than 15. Nor is rape associated with particular styles of dress or standards of beauty. One in four women is raped at some point in her life.[69]

Most rapes are acquaintance rapes, which do not conform to conceptions of force that feature knives, guns, or massive physical abuse. They do involve intimidation, physical force, and various forms of constraint by men to obtain intercourse without consent. Yet, because the rapist is known to the victim, because the victim often admitted the rapist to her home, because the level of force is not as brutal and the physical scars not as visible, many assailants, victims, and law enforcement officers do not accredit this form of sexual assault as "real" rape. This refusal to acknowledge intercourse that occurs against the will of the woman partner as real rape is compounded by a number of gender stereotypes that question women's ability to know their own will in sexual situations. That in the case of women "no" means "yes," that physical resistance serves only to prove her virtue not to signify her dissent, and that tears and protestations are insufficient to prove nonconsent, are claims frequently invoked by defendants in rape trials to demonstrate a reasonable mistake regarding consent and thereby to secure acquittal.[70]

Rape is an extremely traumatic experience that has lifelong consequences for the victim. Long after the bruises have healed and the evidence of the physical harm has vanished, victims must grapple with the psychological consequences of having been terrorized, intimidated, and physically subdued, of having had their trust as well as their bodies violated, of having been treated as non-persons—undeserving of concern or respect, of having been used as objects devoid of will, objects whose words carry no weight and whose gestures of pain, refusal and resistance have no effect. Rape is no less traumatic when perpetrated by an acquaintance. The serious confusion about rape in contemporary culture masks the harm to victims and imposes upon them a legacy of guilt and shame. This confusion affords great advantages to men, for to the extent that victims are blamed for the crime, rapists are freed from any pressure to assume responsibility for their actions. Imposing the burden of guilt and shame on the victim makes them far less likely to report the crime, much less likely to press charges.[71] Thus, the widespread cultural confusion about rape affords a certain immunity to men against prosecution. Men can rape with impunity, knowing that the 3 percent conviction rate in rape cases and the general proclivity to hold women rather than men accountable for rape will place their action well beyond the pale of ordinary crime and punishment.

Domestic Violence

The belief that violence against women is rare, sporadic, and typically perpetrated by strangers is dramatically contradicted by existing evidence about domestic violence.[72] Women confront the greatest threat of physical abuse from the men with whom they live. Studies by the Law Enforcement Assistance Administration indicate that in the United States one woman in ten is beaten by her husband or lover in any year and that one woman in five is beaten in any ten-year period.[73] It is estimated that 1.8 to 3.3 million women experience some form of intraspousal violence every year.[74]

A number of traditional assumptions have insulated domestic violence from routine treatment by the criminal justice system. Although the absolute right of the husband/father over the life and liberty of all members of the household has long since been abolished, in contemporary homes there lingers a notion that the man is the head of the household and as such has a responsibility to mete out justice, including corporal punishment, within the home.[75] The assumed link between punishment and physical abuse is important, for it accords a *prima facie* legitimacy to the man's action, just as it suggests that women are fundamentally at fault: wives have done something to precipitate their husbands' anger and retribution. The problem is not the punishment per se, but that the husband gets carried away, his punishment is excessive. The image of a provocative victim who has done something to incite her aggressor complicates the state's relation to domestic violence, for it suggests mutual culpability. If both the husband and wife are at fault, then it would be patently unfair to take action against the husband.

Conceptions of privacy also mitigate the state's response to domestic violence. When the home is understood as a space that must be sheltered from unwarranted intrusions from the public, either in terms of the prying eyes of neighbors or the meddling interventions of police, then reluctance to transgress privacy becomes the norm.[76] The institutionalization of such reluctance is manifested in official nonresponse to the problem of domestic violence. Public officials routinely deny that violence is a problem in the home. When violent disagreements erupt between spouses, they are construed as the "normal" give-and-take of marriage, which must be dealt with privately by the parties involved. Consequently, no public monies are allocated for shelters or services for victims of violence.[77] Moreover, police are unwilling to intervene.[78] Their reluctance to intrude upon a family dispute results in the protection of men's privacy at the expense of women's physical safety.

As in the case of rape, the pattern of expectations about domestic abuse favors the male perpetrator of violence. Tacit assumptions about the husband's role as guardian, the wife's need for benign correction, and the inviolability of the private realm subtly expand the sphere of male authority. A certain level of violence is deemed man's right, a certain degree of punishment is conceived as a woman's just desert. Within such a constellation of assumptions, an accurate understanding of the severity of the problem of domestic violence, either in terms of its prevalence or its physical and emotional toll on its victims, is precluded. The normal mechanisms that might stimulate efforts to thwart brutal beatings of women are confounded. Individual conscience, social norms, and official channels of social control are all obstructed by a cluster of presuppositions that exculpate men and blame women.

Explanation or Legitimation?

In calling public attention to practices that privilege men, feminists have multiple objectives. They seek to challenge the view that sex discrimination no longer exists. They hope to sensitize the public to the severe constraints that circumscribe women's daily lives. They also aspire to transform social institutions in order to eliminate pro-male bias. Central to these objectives is a demonstration that such practices are palpably unfair.

Those who defend "traditional values" do not deny that men and women are treated differently in innumerable public practices; they simply deny that different treatment is unfair. Indeed, they insist that differential treatment is perfectly consonant with the determinate needs of men and women. To adjudicate the debate between feminists and traditionalists, then, it is important to consider the evidence that traditionalists introduce to support differential treatment. Can their explanations of existing institutions and practices withstand scrutiny?

Traditionalists suggest that there are ways to explain underrepresentation, job segregation by sex, and pay differentials without appealing to vague notions of sex discrimination.[79] In this view, the underrepresentation of women does not result from intentional discrimination against qualified women applicants, but rather from the fact that women lack the requisite qualifications for certain positions. As a consequence, women often do not apply for such jobs; but they are rightly rejected when they do. Since the cause of underrepresentation is primarily an inadequate supply of qualified women, it would be patently unfair to qualified men and devastating to the efficiency of the economy to hire unqualified women.[80] Should such unfairness be indulged and women be hired, then it is perfectly predictable that women will earn less than their male counterparts. Pay differentials can be explained by women's inferior qualifications, their propensity to interrupt their careers for childbearing, and their preference for part-time work.

To explain why women lack the requisite qualifications for so many jobs, traditionalists typically suggest that individual women make free career choices based on inherently different interests and aspirations. Empirical evidence is said to indicate that women freely choose career patterns that differ from men and "this crucial element of choice is routinely ignored in syllogistic arguments that go directly from statistical 'underrepresentation' to 'exclusion' or 'discrimination.' "[81] Women prefer the "caring professions," the service sector and support roles in organizations, which require the same kinds of skills that they have perfected in their interpersonal relations.[82] In this view, any effort by government to attempt to control or alter individuals' natural inclinations and the occupational choices that accrue therefrom is undesirable, unacceptable, and in all probability, futile.

Traditionalists' claims concerning women's voluntary choices and their preference for sex-specific career paths have a certain intuitive appeal. For everyone can point to several women who do prefer nurturing to competitive activities, child-rearing to career-building, part-time to full-time work. Yet, the traditionalist account entirely overlooks the problem of underutilization. It cannot explain why women who possess all the requisite qualifications for certain positions do not get hired or promoted. It stretches credulity a bit too far to suggest that women who consistently outperform men in their educational achievements are somehow thoroughly inferior job candidates. Claims of inferior qualifications cannot explain the underutilization of women or pay differentials for women who have records and performance ratings identical to their male colleagues. They instantiate rather than explain the pervasive tendency to accredit male performance and to discredit identical performance by women.

The failure to explain underutilization raises certain questions about the adequacy of the traditionalist explanation of underrepresentation. The argument that women choose to be different—advanced in a context where difference signifies inferior qualifications and significant power and pay differentials—is pervaded by the logic of blaming the victim. It seems a bit too facile to assume women always prefer subordination, self-abnegation and impoverishment. When the only evidence offered in support of such alleged preferences relies upon women's "natural" inclinations or "traditional" roles, there is good reason to suspect circularity in reasoning. The "naturalness" of women's proclivity for support positions and the "voluntariness" of their choice of subordinate occupational roles may be more a matter of traditionalists' imaginings than of women's autonomous preferences. In claiming that differential treatment merely conforms to what women want and to what they deserve, traditionalists offer a legitimation not an explanation of the status quo, for naturalistic rhetoric cannot explain the social construction of desire in contemporary cultures. It merely conflates women's "natural propensities" with that which is most likely the consequence of the institutionalization of practices that advantage men.

Traditionalist accounts of practices that treat men and women differently invoke a number of gender stereotypes that become increasingly problematic as one moves from explanations of underrepresentation and job segregation by sex to explanations of sexual harassment, rape, and domestic violence. The image of women who prefer to work behind the scenes, to fill research and support positions rather than to assume leadership or management positions is a harmful fiction that may be invoked to legitimate gender inequality in the workplace. Images of women whose sexuality ensnares men, who seduce and then cry rape, who incite aggression, who masochistically seek out violence perform a similar legitimating function in relation to sexual violence. Traditionalists depict a world populated by two markedly different kinds of women. Good women know their place, are deferential to men, need male protection and guidance, and devote their energies to satisfying the emotional needs of their loved ones. Evil women seduce men, arouse their passions, provoke their lust, tantalize with their wickedness, and divert men's attention from the important projects of civilization.

This familiar pattern of idealization and demonization is central to traditionalist explanations of sexual harassment, rape, and domestic violence. Virtuous women escape such ills; evil women precipitate them. Precisely because evil women provoke sexual aggression, they deserve whatever they get. These notions posit a rudimentary justice in social relations: people reap what they sow. The virtuous are rewarded and the evil punished as a direct consequence of their own actions. To refute such a simple vision, one might note that most human relations seem to evade this retributive scheme. The world is rife with instances in which the wicked flourish and the saintly perish. But that would largely miss the point of the traditionalist's good woman/evil woman fable. For within the traditionalist vision, the acts of rape and violence prove that some are punished, and the fact of punishment proves that some are guilty. Guilt is inferred from the fact of victimization. But if this is so, the good woman/bad woman dichotomy breaks down. Rather than being mutually exclusive categories that capture actual distinctions in the fixed characters of different human beings, the good woman/evil woman opposition is situationally defined. A good wife becomes an evil woman in the process of being beaten; a virtuous teenager becomes a seductress in the process of being raped. Brutal aggression estab-lishes their true nature.

What the good woman/evil seductress model offers is neither an expla-nation of sexual harassment, rape, or domestic violence, nor a drama of salvation in which punishment redeems the evildoer. For evil women lie beyond redemption. What it offers is a sophisticated vindication of men's innocence in the face of overwhelming evidence that many men engage in brutal acts. Rather than requiring them to confront their depredations, the good woman/evil woman dichotomy allows men to displace responsibility from the perpetrator onto the victim. As explanations of the high inci-dence of sexual harassment, rape, and domestic violence, accounts that blame the victim have no intellectual integrity, but as rationalizations of intolerable behavior, they are unparalleled. In trading on misogynous ste-reotypes to confound causal agency, they sentence victims to a lifetime of guilt and remorse while they allow the perpetrators to roam free with an easy conscience.

Feminist research has illuminated a range of social practices that privi-lege men, by attributing greater competence and authority to men, by re-warding presumed superiority with social positions of power and wealth, and by forgiving men the violence they perpetrate against women. Efforts to defend such practices as differential treatment based on legitimate gender differences must either ignore the palpable harm that women suffer from such pro-male bias, impose reified conceptions of difference upon women under the guise of "natural" preferences, or indulge fallacious arguments that blame the victims for the evil that befalls them. Whichever strategy is adopted in a particular case, it cannot adequately explain the empirical phenomenon under investigation.

At this stage in feminist scholarship, no consensus exists concerning the causes of all the social practices identified in this chapter.[83] But feminists do agree that much more research must be done if these practices are to be fully understood and if unwarranted male advantages are to be eradicated. Moreover, feminists agree that if research is to shed light on these problem-atic social practices, it must be conducted by individuals who have aban-doned the presumption of female inferiority. Those who begin with the premise of women's inferiority will simply reproduce the legitimations of differential treatment that have been the stock-in-trade of traditional dis-courses on women. These intellectually bankrupt accounts can shed no light upon the pressing issues of sexual inequity confronting contemporary societies. They merely reproduce legitimations of male dominance that sac-rifice individual talent and freedom to ill-fitting notions of natural function or social convenience. If creative solutions are to be found for the host of problems that truncate women's life-prospects, then feminist research must continue. Without continuing efforts to problematize received views of women and to challenge traditional gender assumptions, sexual equality will remain illusory.

Part Two

Feminist Problematics

Chapter Three

Explaining Oppression: Matriarchy, Patriarchy, and the Defeat of the Female Sex

Feminist theory offers more than a perceptual lens that problematizes social beliefs and practices advantaging men. It suggests that the persistent gender asymmetry characteristic of such diverse ideas and conventions can be understood as a system of oppression. The imbalances of power in the family, in the schools, in the workplace, in the churches, temples, and synagogues, and in the official institutions of government are interrelated. Male control over myth and ritual, over women's sexuality and the technology of reproduction, over the sexual division of labor in the domestic and in the public realms, and over the very conceptions of masculinity and femininity constitute the means by which men impose unjust constraints upon women's freedom.[1]

Feminist discourses are rich in descriptions of the dimensions of women's oppression.[2] Within a system of male domination, Iris Young defines gender oppression as a pattern in the institutional organization of society "in which men have some degree of unreciprocated authority or control over women, and/or men have greater control than women over the operations of institutions."[3] In this view, women are oppressed when

> (a) men have power to control aspects of women's lives and actions and the means to enforce their will, and women do not have complementary control over men's lives; (b) men occupy institutionalized positions of social decision-making from which women are excluded, and women do not have their own spheres with comparable privilege or control over men's lives; (c) men benefit from the labor and other activity of women to a greater degree than women benefit from that of men.[4]

Manifested in "women's lesser access to money, power, status, leisure, and sense of self-worth,"[5] gender oppression resonates in conceptions of masculinity defined in terms of characteristics valued by society and in conceptions of femininity defined in terms of whatever is useful or pleasing to men.[6] It is apparent in "a system which takes a physical characteristic, sex, and builds on it divisions of labor, ability, responsibility and power which are then called 'natural'."[7] It is most visible in systems that define women's existence solely in terms of the roles of wife, mother, domestic laborer, and consumer; but it is no less pernicious when it surfaces in societies that encourage men and women to be active, independent agents of their own destinies, while subtly affording women fewer opportunities for self-realization than men.[8] Whether embodied in absolute prohibitions, paternalistic legislation, or informal mechanisms of social control, gender oppression includes both a sexual division of labor that assigns noncreative, isolating, and alienating tasks to women, and a set of arguments concerning women's nature and the character of women's work that can be used to justify lower wages and fewer rights for women, thereby exacerbating women's economic and political dependence upon men.[9]

In addition to external restrictions upon the appearance, movement, occupations, and public roles of women, the cultivation of internalized constaints upon women's action is central to gender oppression. Through negative sexual stereotyping and systematic sexual objectification, women's desires and aspirations are circumscribed. Operating on the individual psyche, such oppression

> does not inhere in any isolated and measurable set of omnipresent facts. Rather, it seems to be an aspect of the organization of collective life, a patterning of expectations and beliefs which give rise to imbalance in the ways people interpret, evaluate and respond to particular forms of male and female

action. We see it not in the physical constraints on things that men or women can or cannot do, but rather in the ways they think about their lives, the kinds of opportunities they enjoy, and in their ways of making claims.[10]

Psychological oppression is the logical consequence of a system of cultural practices that places women in a "double bind" situation—simultaneously affirming their human status while condemning them to the immanence of mere bodily being, devoid of autonomy, cultural expression, and opportunities for transcendence. Because psychological oppression operates through the internalization of debilitating norms, it produces women who are convinced that they are incapable of autonomy, who doubt that they have the abilities to excel in the full range of human activities.[11] By truncating women's sense of possibility, psychological oppression produces women who are the agents of their own constraint.

Gender oppression involves a system of power in which "the vast majority of opportunities for public influence and prestige, the ability to forge relationships, determine enmities, speak up in public, use or forswear the use of force are all recognized as men's privilege and right."[12] Within such a system, women are "burdened in some unnecessary and systematic way that prevents or makes difficult full human development."[13] By casting these unequal power relations in the language of oppression, feminist theorists emphasize human agency, insisting not only that these systems are humanly created, but also that they are amenable to human transformation. But if the subordination of half the species is a product of human choice and will, then a straightforward question ineluctably arises: Why? The genesis of women's subordination becomes an issue of some urgency, for "the analysis of the causes of women's oppression forms the basis for any assessment of just what would have to be changed in order to achieve a society without gender hierarchy."[14] Feminist theorists move from a perception of the manifold symptoms of women's oppression to a diagnosis of its fundamental causes both to identify the precise nature of the disease and to prescribe an appropriate remedy.

This chapter will consider the major explanations of women's oppression advanced by feminist theorists. It will examine explanations that tie women's subordinate status to biology, to the use of physical and technological force, to the sexual division of labor in producing the necessities of life, and to certain psychological predispositions of men and women.[15] It will explore these explanations in order to assess the merits of explicit etiological claims concerning women's oppression, to identify and evaluate tacit assumptions that sustain these strategies of explanation, and to identify points at which both explicit claims and tacit assumptions lose plausibility. The final section of this chapter will consider general presuppositions that inform the feminist quest for the origins of oppression—assumptions about the philosophy of history, the nature of justice, and the role of myth in social transformation. By differentiating unwarranted from legitimate concerns and by identifying alternative modes for resolving legitimate issues, this chapter will attempt to free feminist theory from certain implausible and self-defeating arguments that have been seized upon by critics as reasons to dismiss feminism *tout court*.[16]

The Tyranny of Biology

Claims that the relations between the sexes are ordained by nature are a staple of traditionalists and sociobiologists. That all differences in inclination, outlook, ambition, and behavior are rooted in human biology and as such are immutable (or mutable only at unacceptable costs) is the foundation of most antifeminist arguments for the preservation of traditional gender relations. Thus, it seems surprising that feminists should turn to biology for an account of women's oppression. Yet, there are several reasons that feminists may be drawn to biological determinism as the ground of women's oppression.

In contrast to explanations of women's inferior status that depend upon postulated differences between men and women, which exist in the unobservable realm of the psyche or the intellect, some biological differences are immediately observable.[17] Differences in height, body shape, genitalia, and certain secondary sex characteristics are visible and hence provide a "material base" for women's subordination that has an intuitive appeal. In addition, arguments drawn from nature promise a universal explanation for women's condition that transcends cultural and historical specificity. Finally, feminists may be attracted to biological arguments in order to develop an internal critique of traditionalists' claims. By accepting the premises of biological determinism, but demonstrating that the social and political conclusions do not follow, feminists may hope to win a decisive victory in an age-old debate, offering a definitive refutation of what seems to be the strongest case for male dominance. Whatever the specific rationale, arguments concerning biological differences have surfaced regularly in feminist debates.[18]

Perhaps the most famous analysis of women's oppression in terms of biological determinism is that developed by Shulamith Firestone in *The Dia-*

lectic of Sex.[19] According to Firestone, "Nature produced the fundamental inequality—half the human race must bear and rear the children of all of them."[20] By imposing upon women the "barbaric" ordeal of pregnancy, "the temporary deformation of the individual for the sake of the species,"[21] nature created a situation in which women would necessarily become dependent upon men. Depicting the situation of women in dire terms, Firestone suggests that throughout history "women were at the continual mercy of their biology—menstruation, menopause, and 'female ills,' constant painful childbirth, wetnursing and care of infants, all of which made them dependent on males (whether brother, father, husband, lover, or clan, government, community-at-large) for physical survival."[22]

Women's reproductive capacity created a "structural imperative" with profound emotional, psychological, cultural, and institutional consequences: "Women were the slave class that maintained the species in order to free the other half for the business of the world—admittedly often its drudge aspects, but certainly all its creative aspects as well."[23] The bulk of Firestone's work is devoted to a demonstration of the pervasive effects of this "natural division of labor." Modes of social organization that carve the world into public and private spheres and allocate the public realm to men while restricting women to a stultifying domesticity, modes of political organization that accord power and privilege to men, modes of psychological development that capitalize upon the association of men and power to facilitate a devaluation of the feminine, modes of culture that institutionalize a dichotomy between reason and emotion—circumscribing intellect, science, and technology within the male preserve while relegating beauty and feeling to women, promoting childrearing practices that retard development and a cult of romance that enslaves the mind: all this can be traced to the reproductive differences between men and women.

In Firestone's view, the cause of women's systematic oppression lies within each woman's body. The capacity to bear children is the source of women's enslavement. But rather than resign herself to the perennial limitations of nature, Firestone suggests that the conditions for the transformation of human nature are at hand. Technology creates the means by which biological tyranny can be abolished. The effects of reproductive differences can be negated with the elimination of the sex distinction itself. The technology of birth control in conjunction with artificial reproduction can free women from biological determinism and free humanity from the social and psychological consequences thereof.

If Firestone locates the cause of women's oppression within the female body, several other feminists link women's subordination to men's anatomy.[24] In *The Politics of Reproduction*, Mary O'Brien offers the most sophisticated version of this argument.[25] According to O'Brien, women's oppression has less to do with women's capacity for and experience of reproduction than with the unique contradictions experienced by men in relation to the reproductive process. The fundamental problem originates with "the alienation of the male seed in the act of ejaculation."[26] Unlike the experience of continuity in menstruation, ovulation, pregnancy, and birth that characterizes women's relation to reproduction and constitutes the "integrative potency of all women,"[27] in the act of ejaculation, men experience a negation of self: "We are not speaking here about some kind of psychological process, a sense of loss or something like that. Alienation is not a neurosis, but a technical term describing separation and the consciousness of negativity."[28]

Like Firestone, O'Brien suggests that the physiological fact of alienation of the male seed in ejaculation has profound social and psychological consequences. "For men, physiology is fate"[29] precisely because the physical loss of their seed in copulation creates needs that structure male action in history. The quest for potency, "a masculine triumph over men's natural alienation from the process of reproduction,"[30] gives a determinate and predictable form to male behavior. In the effort to resist the alienation of their seed, men create theories of reproduction that depict women as the raw material for, the mere receptacle of, or the incubator for the male seed, which contains the real principle of life. In addition, men attempt to offset the experience of alienation in reproduction by "appropriating" the child. O'Brien notes that such an appropriation requires the cooperation of other men in structuring supportive institutions and relations. In order to appropriate the child, men agree to limit their physical access to women by creating a spatial separation between public and private realms, thereby limiting the interactions among men and women. The institution of monagamous marriage guarantees each male exclusive sexual access to one woman. The definition of paternity in a nonbiological way, that is, in relation to the social role of the husband, further enhances the husband's right to his wife's offspring. Moreover, the experience of alienation creates in men a need for principles and structures of continuity, which underlies male efforts to create "order in history" whether in the form of hereditary monarchies, primogeniture or state constitutions.[31] Indeed, O'Brien suggests that the "huge and oppressive structure of law and custom and ideology is erected by the brotherhood of Man to affirm and protect their potency, and it is a structure which must be actively maintained, because at the heart of male potency lies the intransigent reality of estrangement and uncertainty."[32]

That human history to date has been fueled by men's efforts to transcend the alienation they experience in the reproductive process does not imply that the future must be so constrained. O'Brien, like Firestone, believes that the objective conditions necessary to cancel "the dualism which is embedded in the theory and practice of male dominant history"[33] now exist. These conditions include "the technological capacity to control the process of reproduction," and "evidence that man's definition of the human condition as the endless struggle with nature leads not to the subjection of the natural environment but to its destruction."[34] The technological capacity to control reproduction creates the conditions in which women can transcend the experience of continuity that has characterized their reproductive consciousness; they can then develop theoretical accounts of their experience that can ground a new feminist praxis.

> The social relations of reproduction are now increasingly displaying evidence of transformation, evidence which permits a clearer understanding of the historical forces at work. This understanding will come from women who, as the dehumanized people of this dialectical struggle, are at the same time a progressive social force in the restructuring of the social relations in question.[35]

According to O'Brien, the emerging feminist praxis will offer an alternative to male dominance, an alternative informed by "the feminist principle . . . which upholds the value of individual lives against collective death, of integration with the natural world against the 'masterful' destruction of that world, of the abolition of the phoney wall between public and private, first nature and second nature, continuity and discontinuity."[36]

What is one to make of such claims concerning biological determinism? Can physiological characteristics carry the explanatory force that these theorists assign them? Can either men's or women's relation to the reproductive process explain the social subordination of women?

Feminists have rightly challenged explanations that attribute the cause of women's oppression to women themselves as a form of ideological mystification that blames the victim. Shifting the site of oppression from the female to the male body avoids the problem of victim blaming, but it does not deal adequately with the questions of power and human agency that are central to a full understanding of the relation between cultural practices and physiological capabilities. Whether male or female anatomy is invoked as the explanation, biological determinism fails to explain oppression for a number of reasons. It posits an unmediated experience of the body that is untenable; it erroneously suggests that physiological fact dictates social role; it mistakenly assigns responsibility to Nature for the design of human institutions. And it rests upon a logic that is both circular and self-defeating. The suppositions that underly biologistic explanations of women's subordination will not withstand scrutiny.

In describing the "barbarism" of pregnancy and the "alienation of the male seed," Firestone and O'Brien, respectively, suggest that there is a universal, sex-specific experience of the body. The posited universality is the key to an explanation of oppression that transcends history and culture. Yet the posited universality is altogether implausible. Neither men nor women have an unmediated experience of the body. Human reproduction is not a matter of instinct, a function of a preprogrammed biological response that occurs upon presentation of the appropriate stimuli. Understandings of sexuality and reproduction, of menstruation, pregnancy, parturition, lactation, and menopause are socially constructed and culturally variable. What biological determinists fail to grasp is that culturally mediated understandings influence how physiological processes are experienced. The meanings accorded to experience, even the most personal experiences of sexuality and reproduction, are socially constituted. When the cultural contribution to the constitution of individual experience is taken seriously, there are strong theoretical reasons to doubt that women in all cultures experience their bodies in the way Firestone suggests and that "alienation of their seed" is the invariant male experience of sexuality. When such theoretical suspicions are combined with anthropological evidence concerning the experience of the body in distinct cultures, the grounds for the rejection of biological determinism become overwhelming.[37]

One tactic employed by traditionalists, sociobiologists, and Firestone to support biologistic explanations is to introduce data from animal studies, suggesting that physiological imperatives transcend species boundaries.[38] But this strategy meets insuperable evidentiary and epistemological problems. To claim that human reproduction conforms to patterns in the animal kingdom requires very selective use of evidence. Detailed study of animal behavior reveals a wealth of diversity in the roles of males and females in reproduction that precludes any hope for identifying any particular human propensity as *the* dictate of biology.[39] If nature imposes no uniformity on animal reproductive practices, then those who rely on the behavior of particular animals as a guide for human action must justify their selection of the species worthy of emulation. Why should humans choose to model their reproductive practices on those few species in which male dominance is prevalent? The need for such justification demonstrates that far more is at issue in biological determinism than a mere discovery of unalterable physiological mandates.[40]

At issue is the process through which social significance is assigned to physiological fact. There are a number of biological differences between men and women: chromosomal, hormonal, and anatomical. But the oppression of half the species cannot be explained by the mere fact that such differences exist. What must be explained is how these physiological differences come to have such extraordinary social significance. The animal kingdom affords no insights here because the complex relationships through which meaning is created, fixed, and transmitted fall within the realm of culture, a realm which distinguishes human from animal existence.

Proponents of biologism insist that physiological differences dictate cultural practices, hence the uniformity of sex roles across cultures. But the uniformity posited may be more an artifact of method than a reflection of empirical reality. To make their case concerning physiological imperatives, biological determinists suggest that basic biological "traits" can be abstracted from the multiplicity of cultural practices in which they are merely expressed.[41] The process of "abstracting" essence from appearance requires that all cultural diversity must be discounted. The notion of a universal biological essence is constructed by intentionally neglecting all cultural specificity. But if humans are beings whose experience gains meaning only within cultural contexts, then the quest for a biological essence rests on a mistake, a mistake that undermines biological explanations of human behavior. In methodically neglecting cultural differences, that which differentiates human from animal life is eclipsed; human agency is masked. The abstract universal is purchased at the cost of historical accuracy and species possibility.

To claim that human anatomy dictates an invariant set of social relations and institutions is to misconstrue both the nature of humans and the nature of social organization. Humans have the capacity to choose how they wish to live. The evidence of markedly diverse cultures suggests that the range of choice in ordering social institutions and practices is wide. Thus, the "facts about the nature of men and women do not on their own make it clear what the institutions governing their relationship and social position ought to be."[42] Other factors contribute profoundly to such determinations. By ignoring the diverse ways in which sexual, familial, productive, and political relations have been structured in history, biological determinists mistakenly reduce all considerations relevant to social organization to biology, on the assumption that biology has organizational lessons, which humans can ignore only at their peril. But once reductionist biologistic assumptions are jettisoned, there is no reason to believe that there is only one form of social organization consonant with human potential. The wealth of cultures that have fostered human growth, development, and creativity provide strong grounds for rejecting any effort to impose uniformity upon the species in the guise of a misguided natural teleology.

Claims that male dominance is rooted in nature suffer from a problematic circularity as well. Biological determinists seek an explanation of social experience. They attempt to explain an imbalance of power between men and women in terms of biological differences between the two sexes. But if biology is to explain social hierarchy, then biological determinists must draw upon more than mere claims of physiological difference. What is needed if anatomical differences are to sustain social hierarchy is not a notion of difference, but notions of superiority and inferiority. For sexual differences to impose a hierarchical structure upon social relations, they must themselves be hierarchically ordered. Firestone's discussion of women's biology, for example, does not merely suggest that men and women are different. On the contrary, it suggests that women's susceptibility to pregnancy and other "female ills" renders them dependent on men.[43] The implication is clear: women's dependency is a function of an inferior biology, but that inferiority is posited, not given in nature.[44] Men and women do have different reproductive systems, but there is no natural order that ordains one superior to the other. To perceive physiological differences in terms of natural superiority and inferiority is to impose social valuations upon natural phenomena. The question that must be answered then, is why posit hierarchy as natural? The answer illuminates the ultimate circularity of biological determinism. The socially created structure of gender hierarchy is superimposed upon nature. Tacit presuppositions concerning the natural superiority of men, shaped by evidence drawn from male dominant societies, provides the theoretical framework that shapes perception of the natural world.[45] What masquerades as neutral biological description is subtly, but unmistakeably, "culturally freighted."[46]

When feminists put the body (whether the male or female body) at the center of their explanations of women's oppression, they give ammunition to proponents of male domination by suggesting that "natural" differences are the basis of women's oppression. Efforts to show that the social and political consequences of "natural" gender hierarchy can be altered due to changes in technology or human consciousness are undercut by the logic of naturalistic discourse. By incorporating assumptions about a natural gender hierarchy, biological explanations of women's oppression fall prey to a vicious and self-defeating circularity. They absolve humans of responsibility for their social institutions and practices by invoking a conception of Nature with determinate designs for human life. In so doing, they mask the anthropomorphism that supports this notion of Nature—for a conception of Nature possessing intentionality and will is extrapolated from human characteristics, just as notions of a "natural" sex hierarchy are drawn from social experience. Within the trope of naturalism, the powers projected onto Nature are literally taken from humans: when Nature has designs for human life, intelligent humans conform to them. Feminist efforts to appropriate the rhetoric of biologism for emancipatory ends ultimately fail because the logic of biological determinism breeds pessimism, resignation, and a tacit denial of human authority over social relations. Within such parameters, claims that technology creates new possibilties for human life necessarily ring hollow.

One of the fundamental tasks of feminist analysis is to identify and refute questionable assumptions that sustain male dominance. Arguments concerning biological determinism are riddled with sexist biases no more tolerable in the works of feminist theorists than they are in the works of traditionalists or sociobiologists. Lacking empirical evidence, devoid of theoretical justification, and riddled with unsavory political implications, explanations of women's oppression grounded in human biology must be rejected as altogether unwarranted.

Force

If women's oppression is not natural, rooted in inherent biological differences between men and women, then how is the subordination of half the species to be explained? A second explanatory strain with a long history in feminist discourse identifies physical force as the chief cause of women's subordination.

In 1792, Mary Wollstonecraft argued in A Vindication of the Rights of Woman that men claim women's character, behavior, and social role are "natural," when in fact all are products of human artifice, generated by the imposition of severe discipline. Insisting that "the sexual distinction which men have so warmly insisted upon is arbitrary,"[47] Wollstonecraft suggests that men used physical force to subjugate women and then devised sophisticated rationalizations to make such subordination appear natural. "Man, from the remotest antiquity, found it convenient to exert his strength to subjugate his companion, and his invention to shew that she ought to have her neck bent under the yoke."[48] In subduing women by force, men used the same tactics that had been successfullly applied to conquer and enslave other tribes, nations, and peoples. In complying with commands imposed by force, women were no different from any other oppressed population. A prudent concern for survival mandated submission to superior force.

According to Wollstonecraft, recognition that the "brutal force that has hitherto governed the world"[49] is the cause of women's oppression is important, both for the sake of historical accuracy and to signal the anachronistic nature of women's subordination, for the modern world had renounced the use of force as barbaric: "Bodily strength from being the distinction of heroes is now sunk into such unmerited contempt that men, as well as women, seem to think it unnecessary."[50] Thus, Wollstonecraft's analysis of women's oppression carries prescriptive force: those who prize modernity would repudiate male dominance as a relic of a corrupt and brutal tradition, devoid of moral legitimacy.

In her essay, "The Enfranchisement of Women," Harriet Taylor Mill advances similar claims concerning the origin of women's oppression. To account for the customary subjection of women, "no other explanation is needed than physical force."[51] John Stuart Mill echoes this view in *The Subjection of Women*. "From the very earliest twilight of human society, every woman (owing to the value attached to her by men, combined with her inferiority in muscular strength) was found in a state of bondage to some man."[52] Both Harriet Taylor Mill and John Stuart Mill suggest that as political systems grew more sophisticated, law converted the odious use of force into legal right:

> That those who were physically weaker should have been made legally inferior, is quite conformable to the mode in which the world has been governed. Until very lately, the rule of physical strength was the general law of human affairs. Throughout history, the nations, races and classes, which found themselves the strongest, either in muscles, in riches, or in military discipline, have conquered and held in subjection the rest.[53]

Like Wollstonecraft, both Harriet Taylor Mill and John Stuart Mill also suggest that as an institution established by force, women's subordination was incompatible with a democratic world "in which the law of the sword is at last discountenanced as unworthy."[54] In this view, "the social subordination of women thus stands out as an isolated fact in modern social institutions; a solitary breach of what has become their fundamental law; a single relic of an old world of thought and practice exploded in everything else."[55]

To suggest that women's subordination was caused by men's use of physical force does not in itself explain why men would choose to use violence against women. Harriet Taylor Mill identifies two possible motivations for the oppression of women, the exploitation of women's labor, and the exploitation of women's sexuality: "In the beginning, and among tribes that are still in a primitive condition, women were and are the slaves of men for purposes of toil. All the hard bodily labor devolves on them. . . . In a state somewhat more advanced, women were and are the slaves of men for purposes of sensuality."[56] Contemporary feminists who share the belief that women's oppression is rooted in force have added men's desire to control reproduction to the list of motivating factors.[57] Thus, Janet Richards has noted that "the non-bearers of children wanted to control the bearers of children" in order to "define a breeding territory from which other men were excluded," thereby guaranteeing "both their having offspring and their being able to identify them as their own."[58]

In addition to supplementing the list of possible reasons for men's decision to oppress women, recent feminist accounts have offered quite a different image of the kind of force involved in women's subordination. Where Wollstonecraft and the Mills seem to believe that the muscular advantage of any particular male was sufficient to explain his ability to impose his will on any particular woman, contemporary feminists suggest that such individualist premises cannot adequately explain the systematic subjugation of women. Although advantages of size and upper body strength might account for sporadic instances of rape or physical violence, it cannot explain how half the species could be held in permanent subjugation. A slight advantage in arm, chest, and shoulder muscles might explain temporary mastery of one male over one female, but it cannot explain women's oppression without invoking questionable assumptions about women and about primitive societies.

In cases of individual aggression, the aggressor must eventually grow weary and fall asleep, affording his victim an opportunity to escape. If sleep functions as the great equalizer, restoring freedom to the temporary captive,[59] there is no reason to assume that a victim who has a keen interest in self-preservation and avoidance of pain would remain with her aggressor. Moreover, if one acknowledges that most humans live in communities, it is also conceivable that victims of sporadic violence would be aided by other men and women in their efforts to escape an aggressor. Thus, something more must be added if male musculature is to account for male domination. To move from tales of individual assault to systematic gender oppression, one must bridge crucial narrative gaps either with assumptions of women's passivity, dependence, and masochism or with assumptions of a callous and indifferent community that ignores the cries of victims of violence.

To avoid the pitfall of individualist premises, some contemporary feminists have offered accounts of women's subordination that emphasize the use of technological innovations by men acting collectively to promote male hegemony. An image of men cooperating in the deployment of technological advantages to achieve mastery over women supplants the image of the individual male overpowering the individual female. Several feminists have suggested that with the mastery of fire and the development of metallurgy, men invented weapons for hunting, which they then used against women:

> Men were able to conquer women with the weapons they developed for hunting when it became clear that women were leading a more stable, peaceful and desirable existence. We do not know exactly how this conquest took place, but it is clear that the original imperialism was male over female: the male claiming the female body and her service as his territory (or property).[60]

In these accounts of men organizing as a group for the specific purpose of dominance, rape figures prominently both as a method of subjugation and as a motive for oppression: "Physical terror and coercion, which were an essential ingredient in the process of turning free persons into slaves, took, for women, the form of rape."[61] As a strategy of domination, rape satisfied men's sexual appetites while simultaneously stripping women of autonomy: "Rape is the kind of terrorism which severely limits the freedom of women and makes women dependent on men."[62] When men banded together to institutionalize male dominance, rape became the preferred method of social control. Using gang rape randomly to intimidate all women and strategically to punish independent women, men devised a "male protection racket."[63] By structuring women's options in terms of exclusive sexual services for one male or unlimited gang rapes, individual women were driven to seek a male protector. Marriage was embraced by women as infinitely preferable to unending sexual abuse by multiple males. With time, the institutions established by collective male force were enshrined in custom and bolstered by laws that restricted women to marriage and reproductive labor by "denying them the right to remunerative productive labor, access to ownership and control of the means of production and the right to determine their sexual and reproductive lives."[64] With more time, that which was established by force and consolidated by law became shrouded in the comforting image of a convention that conforms to the dictates of nature.

The claim that the fundamental cause of women's oppression is brute force has a certain intuitive appeal. It seems compatible with a number of uncontroversial observations. On average, men have approximately 25–33 percent more strength in the upper body (arms, chest, shoulders) than women.[65] In contemporary society, some men, either singly or in groups, use this physical advantage to harass and physically assault women. Moreover, history records numerous instances of determinate groups of men banding together to press their advantage against weaker or less well-equipped populations.[66] The "facts" of physical size and advantage, rape and conquest seem to fit together into a coherent, albeit speculative, account of women's subordination. Notions of a sustained struggle for power within a primitive egalitarian society culminating in the "world historical defeat of the female sex" seem plausible.[67]

Despite its intuitive plausibility, this speculative account of women's subordination has serious theoretical and empirical defects. It is not surprising that genetic explanations filtered through the lens of contemporary experience satisfy contemporary expectations concerning what "must have happened" in the past. At the methodological level, such accounts of origins consist in nothing more than universalizing the present. It is indeed comforting when the forms of behavior and social relations characteristic of one's own epoch appear to surface in antiquity. Unfortunately, however, there is little evidence that the past was as consonant with the present as these speculations suggest.

That it is possible to weave intuitions about strength, coercion, and conquest into a coherent narrative does not prove that historical developments conformed to this plot structure. There is no a priori reason that a slight preponderance of muscle power must translate directly into coercion, manipulation, or dominance. To insist that Nature dictates that the strong do what they will and the weak suffer what they must[68] is to confuse a number of legitimating myths with the actual development of human societies. Whether one appeals to the doctrine of "might makes right" or "survival of the fittest" to support the conversion of physical advantage into dominance, strategies of justification are being conflated with historical necessity.

Closer examination of the claim that men collectively used brute force to subjugate women reveals a number of troublesome assumptions. Packed into this schematic account are a number of contentious presuppositions: men as universally larger, stronger, superior; women as victims, unable to defend themselves against superior force; men as "natural" rapists; women as unknowledgeable about and incompetent with weapons. The tacit presuppositions that lend plausibility to unexamined intuitions lose all credibility when confronted directly. Differences in the average sizes of men and women in developed nations, where prenatal care, diet, and preventive medicine have drastically improved health and heightened longevity, may be a very poor indicator of the comparative sizes of males and females among the early hominids or among primitive hunting and gathering societies. Significant sex differences in size and strength in contemporary populations may generate a culturally specific conception of men's "natural superiority" that is altogether at odds with the physiological characteristics and subsistence activities of our ancient ancestors. What counts as strength and physical advantage depends upon cultural context. It is impossible to arrive at a judgment of superior performance without a clear stipulation of the nature of the contest and the rules of the game.[69] If survival in primitive societies is the nature of the game, then there is simply no evidence that men held a universal advantage. Thus, accounts of women's oppression that begin with an assumption of men's "natural" physical advantage are suspect, for they assume precisely what needs to be proved.

As explanations of the motivation for women's oppression, extrapolations from contemporary life are also problematic. The behavior and character of rapists in contemporary society may be idiosyncratic, pathological, or a reflection of prevailing cultural values that demean women. But rapists remain a troubled, and imperfectly understood, minority of men. From a feminist perspective, the critical question to be explained is why some men rape. The answer to that question requires a precise determination of the ways in which rapists differ from other men. For this reason, suggesting that the rapist holds the explanatory key to women's oppression involves insuperable methodological problems: to the extent that the rapist is different from other men, the rapist's motivation can provide no information about the intentions and actions of most contemporary men, much less about all men throughout human history. Whether the average personality profile of the rapist reveals an excessive need for power, uncontrolled hostility toward women, an xyy genetic structure, or fluctuating testosterone levels, this profile cannot explain the actions of the majority of men who have contributed to the oppression of women: what causes a man to rape is precisely that which separates him from the rest of his sex.

The notion that women's oppression is rooted in force also presupposes an overly simplistic relation between intention, action, and achievement of objectives. In its most direct form, the argument suggests that men realized there were advantages to be gained from the oppression of women. They realized too that they could use their bodies, collective organization, and available weapons to overpower women. They devised a plan toward that end, implemented the plan, and succeeded. Intention flowed into action that realized the intention. What must one suppose about women for such an uninterrupted progression from the idea of domination to the institutionalization of domination to have occurred? Images of women as perennial victims, unable to organize in their own self-defense, unable to mount a credible resistance are clearly necessary for the story of a quick and irreversible victory to gain ascendency. But where do these images come from? They are not given in nature. Moreover, they are quite incompatible with historical and anthropological accounts of actual women who have contributed systematically to all dimensions of social life, including heavy physical labor and warfare.

Nineteenth century feminist attempts to unmask custom, to demonstrate that respected traditions were rooted in brutal violence were designed to shock the conscience and to trigger a strategic response. Capitalizing upon notions of an irreversible progress in history that pitted reason against force, civilization against barbarism, arguments that depicted women's role in society as a remnant of brute force carried a clear prescription. Reason, rectitude, modernity, and justice require the repudiation of such outmoded practices. Twentieth century feminist efforts to draw parallels between the heinous act of rape and the historical condition of women partake of the same logic. Once the full force of its brutality is apparent, civilized beings will forswear domination in all its various manifestations. Infused with a belief in the power of ideas to instigate social change, this rhetoric appeals to the values of modernity as a justification for a major break with the past. What is too frequently overlooked, however, is that the values of modernity also constitute the past conceived in these discourses. What appears as past is merely the underside of the present. As a rhetorical strategy, the shift from images of benevolent nature and benign custom to images of brutal subjugation might succeed in stimulating critical reflection upon contemporary gender relations, but it fails as historical explanation. The projection of ill-conceived stereotypes upon an amorphous state of nature cannot adequately explain the oppression of women.

The Sexual Division of Labor

Marxist-feminists and socialist-feminists have criticized biological determinism and physical force explanations of women's oppression for being reductionist, circular, and ahistorical.[70] As an alternative, they have advanced a materialist account of women's oppression that emphasizes the relation between women's social status and their roles in the processes of production and reproduction. Historical materialists suggest that the relations of power in a particular society are intimately tied to the specific conditions under which people produce the means of life, reproduce life, and in the process, create new needs. To understand the imbalance of power between men and women then, it is imperative to investigate the relations of production and reproduction in specific historical epochs. The key to women's oppression lies in the sexual division of labor in determinate social formations.[71]

In *The Origin of Family, Private Property and the State*, Friedrich Engels develops the first systematic materialist account of women's oppression. Drawing upon the work of nineteenth century anthropologists Johann Bachofen (*Das Mutterrecht*) and Lewis Morgan (*Ancient Society*), Engels argues that ancient societies provide a clear refutation of claims concerning women's "natural" inferiority, since the earliest societies were matriarchies. Within these classless societies characterized by communal ownership, women were independent, highly respected, and sexually free. Women's power in such societies had multiple bases. The maternal gens (clans) were the basic units of society, fostering both matrilocality and matriliny. Women's ability to create life was revered and men's role in the reproductive process was largely unknown; hence, motherhood constituted an important base of social power and status. But most importantly, women provided the necessities of life. Through food collecting, horticulture, subsistence agriculture, the production of clothing, shelter, cooking utensils, and the development of herbal medicine, women's productive activity ensured the survival of the group. The centrality of women's labor to the existence and subsistence of the species formed the foundation for women's social authority and power.

According to Engels, the overthrow of mother right coincided with the introduction of large scale agriculture and stock herding. With the shift to heavy agriculture, men's musculature could be used to their systematic advantage for the first time. Men developed heavy machinery and took over the heavy labor, laying the foundation for major transformations in social relations. Once men assumed responsibility for the production of subsistence, they became dissatisfied with communal ownership and matrilineal inheritance and determined to supplant them with private property, patrilineal descent, and inheritance.

Mother right, therefore, had to be overthrown, and overthrown it was. This was by no means so difficult as it looks to us today. For this revolution—one of the most decisive ever experienced by human history—could take place without disturbing a single one of the living members of the gens. All could remain as they were. A simple decree sufficed that in the future the offspring of the male members should remain within the gens, but that of the female should be excluded by being transferred to the gens of their father. The reckoning of descent in the female line and the matriarchal law of inheritance were thereby overthrown, and the male line of descent and the paternal law of inheritance were substituted for them.[72]

Engels suggests that women's subordination originated in the introduction of private property and men's consequent concern to ensure that their own children inherited the fruits of their hard labor. This relatively benevolent motive produced dire consequences for women: "The overthrow of mother right was the world historical defeat of the female sex. The man took command in the home also; the woman was degraded and reduced to servitude; she became the slave to his lust and a mere instrument for the production of his children."[73] Private property generated the law of patriarchal descent and inheritance, which in turn gave rise to male supremacy: the division of the world into public and private spheres, the arrogation of the public realm by men and the relegation of women to the home, as well as male control of women's sexuality and reproduction.

There are significant omissions and defects in Engels' account. It is not altogether clear why paternal concern for the financial well-being of children should produce the virulent hostility toward, the physical restriction, and the systematic devaluation of women Engels describes. Moreover, Engels was the victim of bad sources. Both the primitive matriarchies posited by Bachofen and the historical progression from savagery through barbarism to civilization recounted by Morgan have been challenged by twentieth century anthropologists for a number of reasons.[74] The evidence for matriarchy rests upon archaeological artifacts of mother goddesses and anthropological accounts of matrilineal and matrilocal societies. Twentieth century anthropologists have noted that:

> Even the existence of mother goddesses, no matter how well documented in the archaeological record, does not automatically prove the existence of an entire social organization based on women's power or fertility, or even higher social status for women. It is highly problematic to argue directly from a belief system, or the artistic representations of one, to social organization when the evidence is so scanty and so open to alternate interpretations.[75]

In addition, neither matriliny nor matrilocality can be taken as proof of matriarchy, for "in most matrilineal societies, it is a male relative, usually the woman's brother or uncle, who controls economic and family decisions."[76] Contrary to the views of Bachofen, Morgan, and Engels, contemporary anthropologists suggest that there have been no matriarchies: "There is not a single society known where women-as-a-group have decision-making power over men or where they define the rules of sexual conduct or control marriage exchanges."[77] In direct contrast to Engels' claims, neither women's role in matrilineal kinship structures nor their centrality to the production of subsistence and the reproduction of the species were sufficient to generate matriarchal power.

Central to Engels' account of matriarchy is a rudimentary conception of justice, a belief that the rewards in society are distributed according to the degree and significance of one's contribution to the society. Yet this tacit assumption of fairness in the allocation of social status is not at all consonant with the analysis of exploitation and class antagonism as the engine of history described by Marx and Engels at length.[78] Rather than embodying the principles of class struggle, Engels' depiction of primitive communal societies suggests an historical precedent for the distributive principle central to socialism. Engels' analysis of matriarchy is neither a scientific description of ancient social organization nor an accurate depiction of the actual moment in history when father right supplanted mother right. It is a teleological construction of the mission of history, a narrative that designates history's objective to be the restoration of justice in human affairs. Women's status in matriarchy serves as parable for the proletariat.

That society once was organized according to principles of fundamental fairness suggests clearly that a just society is within the realm of human possibility. That a markedly bourgeois concern with property and inheritance corrupted the golden age both reveals the nature of the culprit and prescribes the appropriate remedy, the abolition of private property. Feminists have frequently criticized Engels for endorsing a solution to the "Woman Question" that is woefully inadequate. The abolition of private property and the reentry of women into the productive labor force are not sufficient to eliminate all forms of gender oppression. The deficiency of this prescription follows directly from the simplicity of the parable from which it is derived. The vision of a just society in which social status is simply a reflection of social contribution necessarily omits power, self-interest, family connections, a desire for pre-eminence, envy, and an array of human vices that structure hierarchies in existing societies. The perfectionist assumptions that deny such forces any role in a just society also render this conception of a just social order unable to deal with the malignant dimensions of human life when they surface in the real world. The problem arises from the critical disjuncture between parable and real people. What feminists who rightly criticize Engels fail to note, however, is that this disjuncture characterizes more than Engels' defective prescription for women's equality. It permeates his "history" as well. In scripting a past with determinate lessons for a revolutionary future, Engels invented the world historical defeat of the female sex, he did not discover it in the mists of prehistory. Rather than capturing the truth about the changing relations between men and women in history, Engels' account attributes far more power to women than they had. If women did not possess the power in ancient society that Engels ascribes to them, then they could not have been "defeated" in precisely the way Engels describes. The women who appear in Engels' text are fictional creatures necessitated by the logic of his narrative. Neither their rise nor their fall can be taken as historical events, for they are simply an artifact of Engels' methodological presuppositions.

In his portrayal of the sexual division of labor under patriarchy—one in which women reproduce and men produce—Engels posits a degree of uniformity in sex roles more compatible with a biologistic account of women's oppression than with an explanation that takes history and the diversity of cultures seriously. Using anthropological and historical data more systematically, Claude Levi-Strauss advances an alternate explanation of the sexual division of labor that has influenced a number of recent feminist efforts to explain women's oppression.[79] Levi-Strauss notes that every culture divides tasks on the basis of sex, but which tasks are assigned to which sex varies markedly.[80] In some cultures, women perform all agricultural work, engage in heavy manual labor, conduct market relations, hunt, and make war. In other cultures, these tasks are performed by men. There are even some cultures in which men provide the primary child care. The endless variety in the sexual division of labor dispells any notion that the assignment of tasks conforms to some biological imperative. The key to the sexual division of labor lies in culture, not nature.

According to Levi-Strauss, "the sexual division of labor is nothing else than a device to institute a reciprocal state of dependency between the sexes."[81] It transforms two potentially self-sufficient and independent people into an interdependent couple. The sexual division of labor is constituted within social systems "to insure the union of men and women by making the smallest viable economic unit contain at least one man and one woman."[82] Sexual differentiation in social role creates the kind of people who will be drawn together by mutual need.

In this view, the sexual division of labor serves the interests of social systems by heightening interdependence and creating the conditions in which kinship can flourish, thereby fostering stability and continuity. But this device designed to promote reciprocal dependence does not affect men and women in precisely the same way. On the contrary, Levi-Strauss suggests that it consolidates male advantage. Despite the range of variation in cultural assignment of sex-specific tasks and in kinship systems themselves, Levi-Strauss identifies one transcultural constant that attests to a fundamental sexual asymmetry underlying human cultures. In all known societies, men exchange women in marriage, women do not exchange men.[83]

Levi-Strauss suggests that the incest taboo is the rudimentary cultural construct that regulates these exchanges. As the instantiation of "the supreme rule of the gift,"[84] the incest taboo mandates not only that a marriage exchange (exogamy) must take place, but also which women must be exchanged. As such, it establishes reciprocal relations among men: "The total relationship of exchange which constitutes marriage is not established between a man and a woman, but between two groups of men, and the woman figures only as one of the objects in the exchange, not as one of the partners."[85] Institutionalized in the incest taboo, the exchange of women structures a network of social relations conducive to peaceful coexistence and cooperation among men in different groups. According to this interpretation, women's subordination has far less to do with their ability to reproduce or perform an array of social and economic tasks, than with their status as objects men exchange in order to establish special relationships of trust, solidarity, and mutual aid with other men.

Drawing upon Levi-Strauss' analysis, Juliet Mitchell has noted that

> the legally controlled exchange of women is the primary factor that distinguishes mankind from all other primates, from a cultural standpoint. That is to say that though there are crucial biological differences—upright posture, position of the thumb, etc.—the systematic exchange of women is definitional of human society. This act of exogamy transforms 'natural' families into a cultural kinship system.[86]

Similarly, Linda Nicholson has suggested that the devaluation, as opposed to simple role differentiation, of women is closely related to men's exchange of women.[87] And Gayle Rubin has pointed out that if Levi-Strauss is correct, then women's oppression is coterminous with culture itself: "Since Levi-Strauss argues that the incest taboo and the results of its application constitute the origin of culture, it can be deduced that the world historical defeat of women occurred with the origin of culture and is a prerequisite of culture."[88]

Levi-Strauss' analysis has much to commend it: it is remarkably sensitive to cultural diversity; it offers an account of women's oppression that is cognizant of the role of human agency in the constitution of social practices; it is keenly attuned to the importance of the symbolic in human affairs and the means by which human behavior gains its meaning in the context of rich cultural conventions. Moreover, its depiction of the complex mechanisms involved in structuring conventional relations stands in marked opposition to all attempts at biological reductionism. Yet, despite these advantages, Levi-Strauss' influential account suffers from a number of empirical and theoretical defects.

Gayle Rubin has noted that there are good reasons to doubt the descriptive accuracy of Levi-Strauss' claims. "It is debatable that the 'exchange of women' adequately describes all of the empirical evidence of kinship systems."[89] Indeed, Rubin notes that Levi-Strauss ignores the practices of hunting and gathering cultures not conforming to his model. Given the selective applicability of the concept, Rubin argues that the "exchange of women is neither a definition of culture nor a system in and of itself . . . [it] is a profound perception of a system in which women do not have full rights to themselves. The exchange of women becomes an obfuscation if it is seen as a cultural necessity."[90] Thus, rather than describing gender relations in all societies, the exchange of women characterizes only those societies that are male dominant. It is an open question, then, whether the exchange of women is the cause or the effect of women's oppression.

The problems with the attempt to link women's oppression to the incest taboo and to the most elementary rules of social organization go well beyond the issue of empirical accuracy. Levi-Strauss offers a structuralist account of social life that raises important questions about human agency and the genesis of cultural practices. At the most basic level, Levi-Strauss suggests that gender differentiation, the division of labor by sex, and the exchange of women serve the system's "interests" by promoting interdependence, cooperation, and stability. But what precisely does this mean? If the claim is that; 1. men recognized that social systems require cooperation, trust, and stability in order to survive; 2. men realized that the incest taboo, the sexual division of labor, and the exchange of women would promote these ends; and 3. men acted collectively to institutionalize these practices then this account suffers from the same troublesome assumptions about intention, action, and outcomes characteristic of physical force explanations of women's oppression. Such a reading assumes excessive prescience and absolute control over cultural practices on the part of men and excessive passivity and unmitigated victimization on the part of women.

As a systems theorist, it is not likely that Levi-Strauss would accept such a voluntarist interpretation of his claim. As is the case with systems theorists as notable as Adam Smith, G. W. F. Hegel, and Karl Marx, Levi-Strauss would probably rely on a mechanism more akin to the "cunning of reason" or the "invisible hand" to explain the emergence of these practices.[91] In this view, no intentionality need be attributed to individuals either singly or collectively. Individuals pursue their own private interests and mechanisms operating at the systems level transform that behavior into benign outcomes that meet systemic needs. The very structures of social organization convert individual action into system-maintaining practices. Thus, the needs of the system are met as an unintended consequence of individual behavior.

While this mode of analysis manages to escape the overly simplistic conception of intention, action, and outcomes characteristic of voluntarist accounts, it has its own drawbacks. As a mode of functionalist argument, it cannot be relied upon to explain the origin of particular practices. That the incest taboo and the sexual division of labor serve system interests in cooperation and stability does not imply that this is why they were created. Their putative function at the systemic level can provide no insights into the genesis of these practices. Nor can they prove that the incest taboo mandates the exchange of women or that interdependence requires gender differentiation and the division of labor by sex. As causal claims about the origin of women's oppression, Levi-Strauss' functionalist speculations lack any explanatory force.

Closer examination of such functionalist speculations raises additional doubts. Levi-Strauss suggests that fundamental differences in the behavior and social role of men and women are socially created to induce a reciprocal state of dependency. What must be assumed for this claim to make sense? Only if one conceives human beings as isolated, self-sufficient, and largely indifferent to others is it necessary to invent social practices devised to force people into communal association. If one begins with a conception of humans as social, in need of other humans for friendship and affection, as well as for reproduction, nurturance, and physical subsistence, then one need not posit marked gender differentiation and the sexual division of labor as essential to social cooperation. Underlying Levi-Strauss' speculative account of the functions of the sexual division of labor is a problematic conception of human nature, an image of hermit-like adults who must be tricked into modes of association, an image of people who appear on the earth full-grown, without experiencing the dependency of infancy and childhood or the desire for physical and emotional bonds to other humans.

Rather than providing a coherent account of the origin of women's oppression, Levi-Strauss' depiction of women as objects of exchange advances a sophisticated legitimation of a sexual division of labor that privileges men. By claiming that some form of division of labor by sex is essential for social harmony and stability, Levi-Strauss vindicates sex segregation in social practices. By suggesting that gender differentiation and sex specialization in social roles are functional, Levi-Strauss conveys the impression that there is empirical evidence demonstrating the superiority of this mode of social organization for promoting the systems "interests." But no such evidence exists. The impression is an artifact of a functionalist methodology, which begins with the observation that the sexual division of labor appears to be ubiquitous. The existence of the phenomenon is then taken as evidence that the sexual division of labor must be "functional." The claim that the practice serves the system's interests in reciprocal dependency is then inferred from its apparent ubiquity. Such reasoning is circular and fallacious.

Functionalist language can legitimate social practices only if the claims advanced are not subjected to rigorous scrutiny. When the functionalist arguments advanced by Levi-Strauss are examined in detail, a host of problems emerge. The apparent ubiquity of the exchange of women depends upon a selective sample of human cultures that excludes societies that deviate from the model. The agency of humans in creating social practices is eclipsed by a concern with the putative interests of the system, advanced as the unintended consequence of human action. The alleged systemic functions of the incest taboo and the sexual division of labor "explain" the origin of women's subordinate status only if function is invalidly conflated with genetic cause. The very notion that the system's interests in reciprocal dependency necessitates the sexual division of labor rests upon questionable assumptions about human nature. And, finally, in the absence of experimentation with sexual equality in social roles, there is no more reason to believe that sex-segregated social roles are more functional than they are dysfunctional in social systems. The functionalist legitimation of the sexual division of labor turns on a sequence of invalid inferences.

Whether feminists rely on Engels or on Levi-Strauss, arguments concerning the sexual division of labor fail to explain the origin of women's oppression. Neither the introduction of private property nor the traffic in women can bear the explanatory weight that feminists have assigned to them.

Moreover, the uncritical adoption of such claims about the world historical defeat of the female sex commit feminists to speculative histories that may serve causes other than women's equality. Whether the beneficiary of the argument is the revolutionary proletarian movement or prevailing social systems whose inegalitarian practices are legitimated by functionalist rhetoric, women gain little from the discourse.

Psychological Explanations

In recognition that something more is needed to explain women's oppression than appeals to human biology, brute force, or the sexual division of labor, many feminists have turned to psychology for an explanation of male dominance. As the science of human motivation and behavior, psychology offers a wealth of insights into individual action and interpersonal relations. Thus, it seems to afford a promising foundation for an account of the subordination of women. Within feminist analyses, men's need for aggrandizement, their preoccupation with immortality, womb envy, and the psychological scars resulting from the oedipal conflict have been introduced to explain men's need to oppress women and the action that follows from that need.

To supplement his account of the use of force in the subjugation of women, John Stuart Mill adds a psychological reason to explain men's oppressive action. As a motivating factor, he cited the incomparable self-satisfaction that a man derives from growing up into manhood "in the belief that without any merit or exertion of his own, though he may be the most frivolous and empty or the most ignorant and stolid of mankind, by the mere fact of being born a male, he is by right the superior of all and every one of an entire half of the human race."[92] Similarly, Virginia Woolf suggests that ego aggrandizement constitutes the primary reason why men oppress women. Branded as inferior, women become "looking glasses possessing the magic and delicious power of reflecting the figure of man at twice its natural size."[93]

An irregularity in temporal sequence undermines the explanatory force of claims that a desire for aggrandizement causes men to oppress women. Ego aggrandizement is introduced to explain why men choose to oppress women. Yet, for men to experience such ego aggrandizement, women must already be oppressed. The psychological benefits accrue only after women have been subordinated. How could men know in advance what the fruits of oppression would be? How could they know that a conviction of superiority, a joyous affirmation of male supremacy, would follow from the heinous act of oppression, rather than guilt, remorse, shame? To introduce a psychological benefit that can be known only *a posteriori* as a cause of action is problematic: either it must posit a degree of male prescience uncharacteristic of mere mortals, covertly invoking male superiority, or it devolves into an unsatisfying conspiracy theory.

To avoid the problem of trading on unknowable future benefits as the explanation of male motivations for oppression, other feminists have relied upon male deficiencies to explain oppressive behavior. Drawing upon the works of Plato, Aristotle, and Arendt, Azizah Al-Hibri suggests that men's experience of being in the world generates a concern with immortality that is uniquely male.[94] To support this view, Al-Hibri suggests that the conception of the natural world developed in classical Greek texts is organized according to the principle of eternal recurrence. Nature's seasonal course represents a cycle of birth, growth, maturation, and death, followed by regeneration and repetition of the cycle. When men confront this natural cycle, they find themselves in a position altogether unlike beast or god. For men's lives follow a unilinear path from birth to death, without the inherent immortality characteristic of the gods or the species recurrence of mere beasts. Moreover, men see women as more tied to the natural cycle of eternal recurrence than they are themselves:

> Females can bleed suddenly and heavily without dying. (Perhaps this is the earliest reason for associating women with magic, since few men could have survived such bleeding.) . . . The bleeding can stop as suddenly as it starts. Furthermore, the woman's body can change shape and then produce a miniature human being which is subsequently nourished by the female body and grows to start another full life. Meanwhile the male body does not change, it does not reproduce, it has no nourishment for children even after they are brought into the world by females.[95]

A sense of isolation from the natural world creates an enduring feeling of inferiority and frustration in men:

> At the dawn of history the male had ample reason to experience the female Other as a substantial ego threat. In contradistinction to the male, the female exhibited a greater permanence. Not only did she constantly recover from her bouts with bleeding, but more significantly, she constantly reproduced herself—she had the key to immortality and he did not. The male then had cause to experience himself as inferior and mortal, as excluded and cut-off from the cycle of ever-regenerating life.[96]

Men's unrelenting sense of inferiority had dire consequences for women, for it was manifested in jealousy of and hostility toward women. To compensate for their sense of alienation and frustration, men decided to "appropriate" women, seizing control of sexual practices and of reproduction. In addition, men determined to make themselves indispensable. By taking control of production, men gained a sense of power and importance:

> The male was no longer helpless; he was no longer stuck with his human condition. . . . This technological endeavor was particularly suited to the feelings of inadequacy or hostility in the male. It supplied both the possibility of liberation from his perceived inferiority to the female, and also the possibility of a better, more effective foundation for her domination.[97]

Thus, Al-Hibri concludes that "both male technology and patriarchy are based on the male's feeling of inadequacy and mortality vis-a-vis the female, and his desire to transcend his human condition by forcing himself into the cycle of life from which he perceived himself to be cut off through no fault of his own."[98]

Without invoking a metaphysical concern with immortality, Eva Kittay suggests that psychoanalytic theory affords an alternate account of male domination linked to a fundamental "womb envy."[99] Claiming that both anthropological evidence and clinical evidence support the existence of such a phenomenon, she defines womb envy as an essentially negative and destructive emotion, an anger that men feel because women possess a capacity to give birth, coupled with an envious impulse to take away or spoil women's unique capacity. According to Kittay, womb envy assumes particularly virulent forms because it originates as a "narcissistic wound" during the child's formation of gender identity:

> Sometime after the age of four, the young boy must relinquish his aspirations to imitate and perhaps compete with his mother in her childbearing capacities. The realization that his body does not contain such possibilities would be affectively equivalent to the sense that these capacities were now irretrievably lost. Because he expected to be able to bear children and perhaps nurture them from his own substance—feats to which he attached immense importance, for they were the basis of his "belonging to" his mother—the relinquished expectations constitute a *loss*, indeed a narcissistic wound (and grounds for a lifelong sense of inferiority) at the very least comparable to the girl's vis-a-vis her "absent penis." With the lost capacities must come as well a sense of lost power, or better, belief in a serious limitation to one's power and hence a loss of self-esteem.[100]

In this view, the historical legacy of men's womb envy is the systematic depreciation and concomitant exploitation of women, the institutionalization of practices contemptuous of, condescending to, and abusive towards women.[101] Thus, womb envy is a "significant element" in men's personality development that has "explanatory force with regard to both individual actions and cultural institutions."[102]

The psychological account of women's oppression that has been most influential in feminist circles is that which links male behavior to specific defensive needs for separation and individuation that result from women's mothering.[103] Developed by Nancy Chodorow and Dorothy Dinnerstein, this view conceives male dominance as a consequence of the social organization of parenting.[104] Child-rearing practices dominated by women produce individuals with masculine and feminine personalities that guarantee sexual inequality, not simply role differentiation. Thus, women-only child care is said to have consequences for the internalization of gender-specific personality characteristics, for the reproduction of sex-segregrated social roles, and for the production and maintenance of male dominance.

Both Chodorow and Dinnerstein link the development of the masculine and the feminine psyche to infantile experiences of the "Omnipotent Mother." According to Chodorow, the omnipotent mother causes a narcissistic wound in the child; this necessitates the child's repudiation of the mother, producing life-long consequences for the gendered personality of the child. Because girls are of the same sex as their mothers, the process of separation is less traumatic and less complete. Indeed, suggesting that the identification between mothers and daughters approximates a fusion of identity, Chodorow claims that girls experience themselves as less differentiated from and more continuous with others. They have more flexible ego boundaries, are more related to the external object world, and remain preoccupied with the retention and extention of relationships throughout life.[105] Boys, on the other hand, must develop an identity by defining themselves in opposition to the mother, producing more emphatic individuation and more defensive framing of ego boundaries. In father-absent households, boys lack a positive model of masculinity, therefore they fall back upon a contemptuous negation of the feminine as the essence of maleness. Contempt serves to free the boy from the omnipotent mother but it does so at an exacting cost: the repudiation of all that is feminine in himself, and the systematic devaluation and objectification of women.[106]

According to Chodorow, the defensive male ego, excessively concerned with separation and individuation, constitutes the ground of women's oppression.

Mothering also has cultural ramifications fundamental to our sex/gender system. . . . The division of labor in child rearing results in an objectification of women—a treating of women as others, or objects, rather than subjects or selves—that extends to our culture as a whole. Infantile development of the self is experienced in opposition to the mother, as primary care-taker, who becomes the other. Because boys are of opposite gender from their mothers, they especially feel a need to differentiate and yet find differentation problematic. The boy comes to define his self more in opposition than through a sense of his wholeness or continuity. He becomes the self and experiences his mother as the other. The process also extends to his trying to dominate the other in order to assure his sense of self. Such domination begins with the mother as object, extends to women and is then generalized to include the experience of all others as objects rather than subjects. This stance, in which people are treated and experienced as things, becomes basic to Western culture. Thus, the "fetishism of commodities," the excessive rationalism of technological thought, the rigid self-other distinctions of capitalism or of bureaucratic mass societies all have genetic and psychological roots in the structure of parenting and of male development.[107]

In short, mothers produce men who sustain the culture of male domination and capitalism.[108]

Dorothy Dinnerstein also suggests that "the deepest root of our acquiescence to the maiming and mutual imprisonment of men and women lies in the monolithic fact of human childhood."[109] According to this psychoanalytic account, the omnipotent mother provokes an infantile rage in the child. Stemming from total dependence and neediness, this infantile rage results in the repression of such terrifying emotion and a concomitant devaluation of women and refusal to accept women in positions of social or political power. Thus, exclusive mothering by women

guarantees certain forms of antagonism—rampant in men, and largely shared by women as well—against women. These antagonisms include fury at the sheer existence of her autonomous subjectivity . . . a deeply ingrained conviction that she is intellectually and spiritually defective. . . . Finally, they include a sense of primitive outrage at meeting her in any position of worldly authority.[110]

Social practices that demean women and exclude them from positions of power and prestige are, in this view, nothing more than a predictable manifestation of repressed infantile rage.

Whether ego aggrandizement, preoccupations with immortality, womb envy, or the narcissistic wounds derived from women's mothering are taken as focal point, psychoanalytic accounts of women's oppression begin with a fragile, defensive male ego. Male dominance is explained in terms of the compensatory actions taken by men to offset their perceived (or real) deficiencies. A peculiar inversion characterizes the starting point of these psychological explanations: a weak, frustrated, and inferior male is introduced to explain a history of male power; and an omnipotent and terrifying mother is proposed to account for women's comparative powerlessness. At the heart of these psychoanalytic explanations lies an inverted image of gender hierarchy, not of gender equality. The premise of women's superiority provides the motive that explains men's unrelenting quest for mastery.

When filtered through the lens of psychology, the assumption of female superiority might be seen as a pleasing fantasy of the oppressed, as an attempt to unmask men's pretensions to superiority, as a defensive reaction formation by women, or as an unwitting effort to create sympathy for the oppressors. But as a foundation for an historical explanation of women's oppression, the assumption of women's superiority is markedly inadequate. Women's capacity to bear children and their social role in rearing children can no more support inferences of female superiority or omnipotence than can male musculature ground claims concerning men's natural superiority.

If the presumption of women's superiority is jettisoned, then men's compensatory motive for oppressing women becomes problematic. Psychoanalytic accounts typically trace the roots of the perception of women's omnipotence to experiences of infancy and early childhood. But, in doing so, they rely not on infants' or children's accounts of their relations to their mothers, but on "psychoanalysts' reconstructions of patients' reconstructions of how their mothers treated them in a pre-Oedipal phase."[111] Claims concerning the perception of the omnipotent mother, then, could be wrong for multiple reasons. Infants' experience of dependence could be altogether different from adults' speculations (inured in complex concerns about autonomy) about what it must have been like to have been wholly dependent upon another person. The psychoanalytic theories that guide therapists' in converting adult reconstructions of infancy into claims about infantile rage, narcissistic wounds, or Oedipal conflicts could be fundamentally mistaken. The pathological experiences of those who seek therapy may be an unreliable or misleading guide for normal experiences.

Attempts to develop psychological explanations of women's oppression begin on weak ground. They posit a conception of women's power at odds with historical evidence, dependent upon contestable claims concerning an invariant childhood experience, and characterized by contentious postulates of psychosexual dramas drawn from Greek myths. Even if one is willing to suspend disbelief and accept this framework for understanding men's motivation for oppressing women, can men's compensatory desires explain the subjugation of women?

Iris Young has pointed out that there is a critical disjuncture between an explanation of men's desire for power and an explanation of the power men wield in the world. While psychological claims concerning men's unconscious dread of women, resulting from male insecurity at being fundamentally different from women, might explain men's desire for power, they cannot explain male dominance: "Unless a psychological propensity to wield power itself makes men powerful, [psychological] accounts do not touch on the question of the sources of male power."[112]

Young has demonstrated that psychological explanations of women's oppression fail for a variety of reasons. Psychological explanations anachronistically project contentious twentieth century views of the unconscious upon the past, ignoring historical and cultural specificity and subtly denying that the past may have differed significantly from contemporary life. Psychological explanations tend towards an untenable idealism, suggesting that social institutions are determined by the relations among ideas, that is, ideas about Self and Other determine male personalities which in turn determine social institutions. Moreover, the notion that men's psychic needs determine the nature of social institutions accords men unwarranted credit for the creation of all social and political institutions, ignoring women's contributions to civilization and culture. Psychological explanations also rest upon an incorrect social ontology, assuming that social institutions are isomorphic with individual personalities and motives. As such, psychological explanations are incapable of explaining the dimensions of social life that transcend individual intention and action, whether they involve inherited traditions, technological constraints, institutional roles, structural forces, unintended consequences, emergent properties, or interaction effects.

Psychological accounts of women's subordination advance ambiguous images of women. At one level, the fragile, defensive male ego as universal explanans seems to support an image of women as victims, excluded from power and restricted to the narrow sphere of domesticity. But, at another level, men's insecurity and defensiveness emerge only in relation to an image of an omnipotent mother or threatening female. Thus, the explanation leads back to women themselves, who inadvertently cause their own oppression. Within these psychoanalytic accounts, opposites embrace: women as omnipotent victims are both the cause and the consequence of gender oppression. There is no need for feminists to embrace this contradictory image. The ahistorical nature of psychological explanations, the contentious assumptions that inform psychoanalytic theory, the problematic evidentiary base of psychoanalytic interpretations, the idealist tendencies of psychological depictions of social dynamics, and the patent inadequacy of psychological conceptions of the nature of social life offer ample grounds for the rejection of psychological explanations of women's oppression. In the absence of historical evidence of the inverted power relations embodied in the insecure male-omnipotent female dyad, feminists have nothing to gain and a great deal to lose by accrediting its dubious explanatory force.

Past As Prologue

If the etiological claims advanced by feminists concerning women's oppression suffer from damaging empirical and theoretical defects, why do they figure so prominently in feminist discourse? Alison Jaggar and Paula Rothenberg have suggested that feminists resort to speculative histories in order to heighten the intelligibility of contemporary social phenomena and to facilitate social transformation: "To uncover the root causes of women's oppression . . . is to discover not only which biological facts or which social institutions operate to limit women's choice but also which facts or institutions must be changed in order to effect a significant and permanent increase in women's capacity to choose."[113] While Jaggar and Rothenberg link feminist explanations of oppression to present and future concerns, David Kirp, Mark Yudof, and Marlene Franks suggest that accounts of oppression absolve women from responsibility for the past: "The paradigm of sexual oppression, whether focused on the system of production or the system of reproduction, serves a vital purpose in feminist analysis: it explains women's present condition in a way that absolves women from any responsibility for having entered into this condition."[114] There is a good deal at stake in feminist accounts of oppression that is not readily captured by either of these analyses. Central to the quest for the origins of gender oppression are assumptions about the philosophy of history, the nature of justice, and the relation between myth and social transformation.

A philosophy of history typically encompasses both a theory of historical agency (e.g., theist or humanist) and a conception of the "shape" or course of history (e.g., linear progressive, linear degenerative, or cyclical).[115] When feminists confront traditional philosophies of history, they find masculinist theories of agency. Whether the primary agent in history is conceived in terms of God or humans, it is ordinarily conceptualized as male.

In addition, discussions of the path of history contain a number of cautionary tales. Cyclical views insist that history repeats itself. The lesson of eternal recurrence is pessimistic from a feminist perspective, for it suggests that men, who have always ruled, will continue to rule.

Accounts of matriarchy and patriarchy drawn from nineteenth and twentieth century treatises also include a clear prescriptive agenda. Bachofen's theory of matriarchy sought to demonstrate that patriarchy was "the culmination of civilization, the inevitable result of man's long and difficult struggle with nature and unbridled passion."[116] Moreover, the structure of Bachofen's historical progression from the initial dominance of women through their inevitable conquest by inherently superior males offers multiple legitimations of male dominance. Equating the conquest of women with the process by which humans transcend the material, Bachofen characterizes patriarchy as a higher stage of moral and political development.[117] In addition, by suggesting that women created the first form of domination, Bachofen casts men as rudimentary revolutionaries who fight against abuses in power. As deposed tyrants, women deserve what they get.[118] Similarly, in *Moses and Monotheism*, Freud portrays the transition from a matriarchal order to a patriarchal order as "a victory of intellectuality over sensuality—that is, an advance of civilization, since maternity is proved by the evidence of the senses while paternity is a hypothesis, based on an inference and a premise."[119]

Feminist explanations of women's oppression should be understood, in part, as reactions against philosophies of history that vindicate male supremacy under the guise of accurate historical description. In this context, feminist accounts simply reproduce the tactics of a venerable tradition, while altering the lessons to be drawn from such speculative history. The moral supremacy of matriarchy in feminist discourse is a perfect match for the moral supremacy of patriarchy in malestream discourse. Conceived as an attempt to fight fire with fire, feminist recourse to speculative history has a certain logic. However comprehensible this logic might be, it cannot rescue feminist explanations of women's oppression from the serious flaws identified in this chapter. That feminist accounts merely reproduce the mistakes of a defective genre of history neither excuses the error nor advances the feminist case. Feminists gain far more from impugning the false teleologies underlying dominant discourses and repudiating the approach, than from reproducing failed visions.

Conceptions of justice also influence feminist efforts to reclaim the past. Starting from the assumption that men and women are equal, feminists have good reason to question gender asymmetry in distributions of power, status, and respect. When egalitarian premises are the point of departure, glaring inequalities require explanation. But concern with a very specific kind of justice pushes many feminists beyond explanation to the attibution of blame. Invoking notions of retributive and compensatory justice, feminists suggest that responsibility for contemporary practices must be laid somewhere if rectification is to be possible.

The conception of justice operative in these accounts has a long and noble tradition. It can be traced to Greek mythology's personification of justice in Dike, the daughter of Zeus, who reports to her father the wrongdoings of men in order that rectification be made. Or it can be tied to Aristotle's detailed account of compensatory justice as a reparatory transaction between one person and another. Whether one roots this conception of justice in mythology or philosophy, it is an individualistic and personalized notion, whose goal is to impose a penalty upon any party who inflicts an injury and to confer a corresponding benefit upon the injured individual in order to restore the kind of equality that existed prior to the injury. Within the framework of compensatory justice, identifying those responsible for the world historical defeat of women acquires new meaning. Etiological investigations are necessary if the culprits are to be brought to justice and the victims duly compensated.

The quest for justice is an important element in all feminist analysis. But all conceptions of justice are not equally amenable to feminist ends. Retributive and compensatory models fall far short of feminist objectives. For both establish expectations for retribution grounded in individualist assumptions that undermine cross-generational claims of justice for groups. That women have suffered discrimination at determinate points in history can be proven; but identifying the particular men responsible for that situation is often far more difficult. The model of compensation underlying this conception of justice requires identification of specific parties in specific instances. Absent such identification, no rectification is possible. Thus, the retributive conception of justice cannot support feminist claims for compensation to contemporary women for a legacy of historical injustices. Nor can it endorse strategies of rectification aimed at impersonal forces or institutions.

The conception of compensatory justice presents feminists with a classic double bind. It presses them to search for the historical agents of women's oppression in order set the stage for retribution. But when blame cannot be traced to specific individuals or when the individuals responsible are long since dead, then the retributive principle places rectification beyond human reach.

The analysis of the various explanations of women's oppression advanced in this chapter indicates that the compensatory conception of justice is inadequate for feminist ends. The forces that have contributed to women's subordination are multiple, varying with time and culture. Monocausal explanations fail to come to grips with a complex social process that involves biology, psychology, culture, and tradition, as well as individual agency, group interactions, technological sophistication, and institutional context. To do justice to contemporary women, feminists must eschew compensatory models with all their limitations. In their place, feminists must develop a conception of social or distributive justice with sufficient sophistication to deal with intergenerational equity and the distinctive problems of sexual, racial, and class inequality. Anything less will leave justice beyond reach.

To the extent that solutions to women's inequality require innovative conceptions of social justice attuned to the multiple dimensions of oppression, the key to feminist inquiry does not lie in the past. What is needed is not restoration of the *status quo ante* but the creation of new alternatives. Several feminist scholars have noted that feminist theories of oppression function as a heuristic device, "to free our minds and souls, to play with possibilities, to consider alternatives."[120] In this view, feminists reconstitute the past in order to envision a different future:

> Though the matriarchy debate revolves around the past, its real value lies in the future: not as a model for future society, for ultimately it doesn't resolve the problems of hierarchy, sex oppression, or class relations, and not in its mythic evocation of past glories, but in its rejection of power in the hands of men, regardless of the form of social organization. It pushes women (and men) to imagine a society that is not patriarchal, one in which women might for first time have power over their lives.[121]

Feminist conceptions of matriarchy constitute an enabling myth devised to free women's imaginations from patriarchal blinders and thereby inspire transformative politics. Central to this view are a number of contentious assumptions about the dynamics of social transformation. Chief among these is the optimistic notion that myths have motivational force, that political transformation can be instigated by changing the way people conceive of themselves and their past. The assumptions concerning models of politicization and the dynamics of social transformation that inform feminist rhetoric will be taken up in the next chapter. But before moving on to that discussion, one final point about the emancipatory potential of the matriarchal myth is in order.

Although myths make no claim to historical validity, their power derives from their ability to reveal startling insights about the human condition. They capture the imagination because their revelations ring true. If this is so, then what force can mythic depictions of matriarchy exact when the empirical evidence invoked to support the myth has been publicly discredited, when the philosophy of history that informs the myth is fundamentally flawed, and when the conception of justice that feeds the fabrication permits only the identification of wrongs that cannot be righted?

Chapter Four

Feminist Rhetoric: Models of Politicization

The feminist project aims at social transformation. Toward that end, feminists launch assaults on multiple fronts. They strive to make women, as well as their accomplishments and contributions to society, visible. They seek to dispel distortions about the nature of women contained not only in historical, philosophical, and scientific texts but also in popular stereotypes. They deign to criticize masculinist assumptions embedded in culture that sustain the glorification of all things male and the denigration of all things female. They work to illuminate critical junctures where the texts of male authority come up against the limits of their own explanatory force. They attempt to demonstrate the systematic and pervasive nature of women's oppression. They aspire to emancipate human life from the mindcuffs of phallogocentrism, striving to create new conventions amenable to egalitarian social practices and to reciprocal intellectual and interpersonal conversations.[1]

In advancing this project, feminists have long recognized the centrality of the politics of language to their multifaceted undertakings. Despite important differences concerning conceptions of equality and justice and marked divergence in their choice of issues and strategies,[2] feminists have agreed that the realization of their goals requires an assault on language in language. In the belief that understandings of individual possibility, human potential, and social relations are enormously influenced by tacit assumptions incorporated in language, feminists have consciously attempted to reveal mystifications and legitimations embedded in dominant discourses.

Convinced that social transformation depends as much upon the development of an alternative vision as upon the critique of the existing order, feminists have advanced emancipatory rhetorics specifically designed to politicize and to enlist the allegiance of large numbers of people in the transformation of their daily lives.[3] As discursive constructions, feminist rhetorics call worlds into being, inscribe new orders of possibility, validate frames of reference, accredit forms of explanation, and reconstitute histories serviceable for present and future projects. As linguistic productions, feminist rhetorics explicitly search for liberating metaphors and empowering images sufficient to instigate critical reflection and political action.

But what models of politicization underlie feminist imagery? How is this feminist project influenced by tacit assumptions concerning the dynamics of social transformation? This chapter undertakes an analysis of feminist rhetoric in order to identify rhetorical strategies that transcend theoretical differences, which separate liberal, radical, socialist, and psychoanalytic approaches within feminism.[4] It begins with a discussion of four distinct rhetorical strategies—the rhetoric of oppression, the rhetoric of difference, the rhetoric of reason, and the rhetoric of vision—that surface regularly in feminist discourse. It then examines the assumptions about individual motivation and the dynamics of social transformation that sustain these feminist rhetorics. In addition, this chapter considers tensions between explicit objectives and tacit presuppositions within these rhetorical strategies that may undercut their persuasive power. The chief purpose of this exploration of feminist rhetorics is to illuminate obstacles to the realization of feminist goals as well as strategies for recuperating feminism's emancipatory intent.

The Rhetoric of Oppression

In attempting to depict the systematic oppression of women, one recurrent tactic within feminism has been to supplant civilization's benign self-descriptions with an image of an implacable patriarchy, a grotesque reality in which the brutal force of male dominance is inescapable and unabated. Devoid of significant change over time and place, the imperatives of patriarchy—conquest, domination, hierarchy, necrophilia—are characterized as monolithic.[5] Within this world, women exist as a slave class to provide sexual gratification for men and to reproduce the species.[6] As a permanent underclass, women have experienced the forced repression of certain of their capacities (intellect, speech, action) and the overdevelopment of others (sentiment, sexuality, reproduction).[7] In the decisions concerning repression and cultivation of these abilities, it has been men's interests and desires that have dictated outcomes. An autonomous women's voice has played no role in these determinations. Yet, in order to create a facade of consent, woman's desire itself has become the locus of artful manipulation. To secure women's collusion in their own subordination, patriarchy has devised a sophisticated ideology to mystify women's minds and to constrain their hopes and expectations. Variously coded as philosophy, science, religion, and law, this ideological edifice has so distorted woman's perspective that it is impossible to think in terms other than those of the oppressor. Thus, it is said that "Male voices, perspectives, interests, ideas and modes dominate all thinking. For all intents and purposes 'official' intellection and male intellection become coextensive. In the realm of thought, the male is universalized."[8]

The rhetoric of oppression vacillates between a conception of language as a prison and a conception of language as a weapon. Whether imprisoned within the confines of phallogocentrism or battered into insensibility, woman's psyche is so overpowered by masculinist bias that it is incapable of achieving a "non-contingent" perspective: "The value system that has been thrust upon us [women] by the various cultural institutions of patriarchy has amounted to a kind of gang rape of minds."[9] Without the resources of an autonomous imagination, woman is reduced to suffering and silence, so destroyed by her own use and abuse that she is incapable of reclaiming her life through narrative, of transcending her plight through contributions to culture. The past depicted in this trope is dominated by the image of antiquity's headless, female statuary. Patriarchy produces the decapitated woman: without mind to think, without eyes to see, without ears to hear, without voice to speak—she exists as mutilated body.

The rhetoric of oppression enters the realm of speech as a choral groan. Circumscribed by the parameters of patriarchal thought, it can only amass descriptions of truncated relations between men and women. Perfecting the technique of "inventory and indictment,"[10] the ubiquitous victims generate a barrage of facts that can only be read as a record of atrocities. Thus, it is common to find in the rhetoric of oppression the juxtaposition of romantic love sonnets against journalistic accounts of rape, domestic violence, snuff pornography, child prostitution, genital mutilation, suttee, sterilization abuse, medical experimentation, female infanticide, foot binding, bride burning, sexual objectification, and sexual harassment.[11] With flat affect, the icy accounts record the malaise of the woman who lacks the power to name her affliction.

Tacitly invoking notions of mimesis as a model of politicization, the rhetoric of oppression recognizes that it has been the direct experience of male brutality—of rape, battery, devastating divorce, recurrent discrimination—that has radicalized many women. Thus, the multiplication of painful images, violent metaphors, and depictions of subjugating processes within the rhetoric of oppression is designed to convey the horror of these experiences vicariously, to create radical consciousness without the personal encounter of violence. The intensity and hyperbole dominating this trope seek to obliterate the comforts of denial by providing a pitiless description that forces its own acceptance. To heighten this effect, the rhetoric of oppression resurrects attestation as the principle path to knowledge. Giving voice to the victims serves to intensify the horror of the atrocity and to heighten the pathos of particular presentations. Moreover, accrediting the victim's testimony subtly subverts prevailing tendencies to validate only deductive logic or male corroboration as appropriate criteria of proof. Operating within a medium of first-hand accounts of systematic abuses, the rhetoric of oppression anticipates anger as its unconditional response. In moving from a silent past to an angry present, the rhetoric of oppression projects the progressive unfolding of a revolutionary future.

In invoking the "magic of the extreme" to fight on its behalf,[12] the rhetoric of oppression aspires to preclude indifference as a possible response to its imagery. However, the dour depiction of women's past and the vivid descriptions of the microtechnics of power produce willed repulsion as well as ardent attraction. In constituting a world in which the only relation of women to power is that of victimization, the impassioned speech of the oppressed may cause some women to recoil at the brutality of its vision,[13] and it may enervate rather than empower supportive readers. Positing an "irresistibility of the phallus dreamt of by men in fantasies of omnipotence,"[14] the rhetoric of oppression may paralyze the sympathetic reader. The unyielding emphasis upon the abominable male and his unrelenting depredations may undermine the possibility of imagining women as agents in history who could change their destiny. Repetition of claims about the remorseless, all encompassing, monolithic nature of patriarchal language and ideology negate the very possibility of resistance. As an oppositional rhetoric, the discourses of the oppressed may afford flashes of recognition for those overwhelmed by a sense of helplessness, but they are unsuited to marshaling forces for social change. Moreover, they may serve as a double-edged sword at the disposal of unsympathetic readers, for they fail to identify points of historical resistance by women, moments when women have acted singly and collectively to attack patriarchal power, just as they fail to recognize the multiple and diverse contributions of women to civilization and culture. Proponents of traditional gender relations may take such absences as proof that women are indeed "inferior" (Why else would they have submitted to such abysmal brutality?) and argue that the evidence of the oppressed themselves attests to their need for protection. In addition, the litany of abuses incorporated in the rhetoric of oppression may—through its imperviousness to the nuances, ambiguities, and complexities characteristic of human relationships—create such a caricature of the relations between men and women that skeptics will reject it out of hand.

The Rhetoric of Difference

The rhetoric of difference[15] has a long history in feminist circles. Claims concerning the moral superiority of women surfaced regularly in nineteenth century suffrage campaigns and women's social reform movements as part of an argument for the social utility of the incorporation of women into the public realm.[16] In the 1980s, assertions concerning women's difference have surfaced in political rhetoric under the rubric of the "gender gap," in academic rhetoric in relation to potential benefits of affirmative action and in theoretical claims concerning a distinct women's knowledge.[17] The precise cause of women's difference has been the subject of rich speculation: women's biology, morphology, psychology, sexuality, sexed-embodiedness as well as the singularity of women's experiences of childbirth, childcare, homemaking and gender oppression have all been cited as grounds for women's unique perspective on the world and distinctive code of values. Despite debate concerning its origin, however, there is a great deal of agreement concerning the nature of women's difference. Truthfulness, loyalty, altruism, nurturance, cooperation, maternalism, and pacifism are the chief virtues ascribed to women.[18] A finely honed intuition and a particular attunement to human psychology that enable women to read others' emotions are said to differentiate women's intellect from that of men and to contribute to the development of a more ethical cognitive style in women.[19] In addition, the blend of emotion and intuition characteristic of women's difference is said to have consequences for women's aspirations, producing a preference for affiliative relationships over individual achievement.[20] Thus, the rhetoric of difference offers an explanatory account of women's past and present that emphasizes life choices based upon women's preferences, thereby salvaging the liberty, agency, and dignity of women.

Within the Anglo-American tradition, the rhetoric of difference treats as suspect demands for liberation premised solely upon the incorporation of women into the public realm. Fascination with and emulation of male modes of action are depicted as "expressions of contempt for the female body, for pregnancy, childbirth, and childrearing."[21] The rhetoric of difference takes as one of its principle tasks the revaluation of women's role in the nurturance of life and in the cultivation of individual growth and development. By emphasizing the positive aspects of interpersonal relations within the family and the crucial role of love, concern, and nurturance for the development of individual identity, discourses on difference retrieve generations of women's work from opprobrium. Moreover, they highlight the importance of efforts to preserve some aspects of life from the intrusive forces of capitalist market relations and from the encroachments of the bourgeois state.

The commitment to difference that grows out of a belief in women's specific moral endowments and the value of women's traditional activities typically is accompanied by a wariness of the notion of "equality." Fear of assimilation to alien principles and dread of being reduced to a level of tawdry "sameness" generate suspicions about the uncritical pursuit of equality.[22] Within the rhetoric of difference, women are forewarned that in unreflectively attempting to imitate men, they may well destroy the best in themselves. To avoid this end, the rhetoric of difference demands that women's sexuality and procreative power be accorded a central place in feminist discourse. It demands that feminism recognize not only that sex differences are essential to individual identity but that they are constitutive of divergent ways of life. Feminist discourse must accord primacy to sexuality for it is this realm that holds the secret of woman's being and hence holds out the possibility of true knowledge of the self.

In turning away from assimilationist models of human possibility, the Anglo-American rhetoric of difference has drawn heavily upon French discourses on *différence* for imagery and for tactics of social transformation.[23] Building upon the Lacanian notion of an intrinsically phallogocentric Symbolic Order and the arguments of Luce Irigaray that women are not merely "invisible" in the texts of patriarchal thought but radically "absent"—repressed as a function of the male horror of castration—the rhetoric of difference advances a view that ties language inextricably to sexuality. Within this interpretive scheme, the Symbolic Order—the locus of the individual's acquisition of language and the origin of all culture and social life—is characterized as unidimensional, structured in accordance with *"l'hom(m)osexualité,"* the male desire for the same. Because it is language that structures sexuality around the male term within systems of consciousness, the problematic of language and the problematic of sexuality become coterminous for women. To liberate women from phallogocentrism necessarily requires the recovery of *différence:* the sexed embodiedness of women repressed by the phallic order must be reclaimed by the creation of a place for the feminine in language.

Irigaray's *"le parler femme"* (womanspeak)[24] and Cixous' *"écriture feminine"* (womanwriting)[25] constitute efforts to articulate the body by liberating the unknown, the obscure, the heretofore unsaid from the unconscious and from representational epistemologies that privilege evidence derived from "the gaze." Thinking in "analogy with sexed embodiedness" affords a new vocabulary steeped in metaphors of contiguity. Touch, taste, and smell offer new evidentiary bases for knowledge free from the contamination of representational economies. Language use becomes a therapeutic act that can simultaneously rescue the repressed sexuality of women, lay the foundation for the reconstitution of personal identity, and create the possibility of an altogether new womanculture. The rhetoric of difference proffers an invitation to women to participate in a multidimensional practice of self-exploration and self-valorization. Writing and speaking the body empowers women "to resist and explode all firmly established forms, figures, ideas and concepts"[26] and supplant them with *jouissance,* a libidinal economy structured by sexual pleasure.

The rhetoric of difference recognizes that the exclusion of women from the public stage has produced mixed results. While the deprivation of opportunities has ensured that much about women remains to be discovered, it has also enabled women to specialize in the profoundly important activities of nurturance and the cultivation of life. As a strategy of politicization, the rhetoric of difference seeks to capitalize upon women's strengths. In validating women's unique contributions to civilization, it offers a strategy for recuperating the past as a source of pride and as an object of allegiance. Moreover, it conceives a future in which women's traditional contributions are preserved and accorded the recognition that misogyny has so long denied them. Taken in consort, the Anglo-American and French discourses on difference offer a positive valuation of women's traditional activities, a homage to the mysterious and sacred nature of women's sexuality and procreative power, and a promise of wholeness through the recovery of the repressed. Projected onto the public sphere, the rhetoric of difference promises that women's values can produce a politics of peace and a politics of care, free from the corrupting imperatives of patriarchy and from the assimilationist agenda of feminist tokenism.

Although such a telos may serve to unite women from traditional backgrounds with women of more radical vision in collective action for the realization of the feminist project and, hence, appears an impeccable rhetorical strategy, there is much in the discourse on difference that may undercut its initial appeal. Discussions of women's difference, whether at the level of the elevated moral worth of femininity or the repressed jubilance of jouissance, tend to romanticize womanhood, failing to deal adequately with the distinction between the undesirable effects of oppression and autonomous women's values and choices. Ignoring crucial differences among women created by age, race, class, culture, ethnicity, nationality, history, marital status, maternal status, and sexual preference, the rhetoric of difference has a tendency to devolve into a "mass market romance in which other structuring relations of society fade and disappear, leaving the naked drama of sexual difference."[27] Moreover, to posit woman's difference as a function of biology, morphology, psychology, sexuality, or specific life experiences raises the specter of essentialism. Any such projection of "male" and "female" or "masculine" and "feminine" as unquestioned essences is dangerous for feminism, for any essential difference identified can provide a foundation for an argument to keep "woman" in her "natural" place, a ploy all too familiar within the patriarchal repertoire.[28]

In addition to perpetuating categories that have been used to sustain the subordination of women, the emphasis within the rhetoric of difference upon sexuality as the core of individual identity falsifies and distorts individual possibility. Although it provides a useful corrective to those who would argue that sexuality is irrelevant to the development of individual identity, the discourse on difference errs in the opposite extreme by asserting that sexuality holds the secret of being. Such a unidimensional conception of personal identity fails to do justice to the multiple forces within a particular family and within a particular society that interact with "nature" and "psyche" to shape a specific individual's sense of self. Feminist discussions of difference also have failed to recognize the extent to which discourses on sexuality and repression may themselves serve as agents of discipline, creating channels through which power may penetrate and control individuals right down to their most private pleasures.[29]

The conception of language as therapy also raises a number of thorny issues. Drawn from the model of psychoanalytic practice, the notion of therapy typically presupposes an intense, long-term interaction between client and therapist tht enables the client to use the insights gleaned from the process to heal him/herself. Within the feminist discourse on difference, the act of articulating the body, whether in speech or in writing, collapses into itself the roles of therapist and client. While it is not difficult to imagine trained psychoanalysts and academics—like Cixous, Fouqué, Irigaray and Kristeva—practicing this art of self healing, is it as plausible to believe that such a technique can afford liberation to the "average" woman, to all women? In privileging the acts of speech and writing as the key to liberation, does not the rhetoric of difference reproduce the biases characteristic of the intellectual elite and thereby restrict its appeal to a very narrow segment of the population?

The rhetoric of difference grasps the importance of viewing women as a distinct group in order to counteract the patriarchal strategy of subsuming women under the generic category, "man," thereby rendering them invisible and silent.[30] But it too often confuses this legitimate political strategy with metaphysical arguments about "Woman," losing sight of the extent to which the differences depicted are themselves socially and politically constituted. Reified in essentialist terminology, the rhetoric of difference may mask the social construction of gender and thereby understate the scope of possible social change. In so doing, the rhetoric of difference may also impose a burden of guilt upon those women who wish to pursue nontraditional activities. In addition, in overemphasizing the differences between men and women and ignoring their similarities, the rhetoric of difference may make it near impossible to attract a coalition of men and women to work collectively for a world in which one's sex is irrelevant to the determination of one's life prospects.

The Rhetoric of Reason

The classic texts of Western philosophy, history, literature, religion, and science are riddled with misinformation about women. The rhetoric of reason takes as its task the demonstration of the inadequacies of all existing systems of thought when they address the "woman question." It seeks to illuminate absences in the texts, to identify what has been omitted from these "authoritative" accounts produced by men, to dispel myths and distortions incorporated into the texts, and to indicate contradictions that arise when the central tenets of these theories are applied to women. Premised upon the boundless faith in reason characteristic of the Enlightenment and the unquestioning confidence in the authority of science typical of modernity, the rhetoric of reason wields the weapons of intellect against the bastions of ignorance.

The adoption of the rhetoric of reason as a feminist strategy can be traced to Christine de Pizan's fifteenth-century treatise, *The Book of the City of the Ladies*,[31] which asks: "how it happened that so many different men—and learned men among them—have been and are so inclined to express both in speaking and in their treatises and writings so many wicked insults about women and their behavior?"[32] Christine provides a complex explanation of these "slanders against women" that relies upon both psychological and intellectual factors, but the structure of her text implies the real problem to be one of ignorance. The text provides a systematic refutation of erroneous views: for every charge levelled against women, Reason and Rectitude construct impeccable rebuttals by drawing upon evidence from myth, history, and contemporary experience. Supplying counterexample after counterexample, Christine undermines the plausibility of all manner of misogynist beliefs: that women are deceitful, licentious, indiscreet, stupid, weak, cowardly, evil, incapable of high understanding, incapable of invention, corrupted by education, disinterested in politics and world affairs, fickle, inconstant, greedy, vain, flattered by unwanted sexual attentions, and secretly desirous of being raped. Christine destroys these falsehoods with such deftness and rigor that those who prize reason must consider her repudiations definitive.

For nearly six-hundred years, numerous feminists have reiterated that "it is only through insisting that the evidence should be looked at carefully that women are able to attack the prejudices of men."[33] They have labored long and hard to apply tools of logic and induction to the circumstances of women's lives. They have raised an epistemological challenge to men's claim to "know" women's "nature" and to "know" what is in women's best interests. They have argued forcefully that women should be considered "human" rather than a species apart. They have demonstrated that the values of freedom, equality, independence, knowledge, opportunity, self-determination so highly prized by men hold the same attraction for women. They have proven that the obstacles to women's full participation in social, political, economic, and intellectual life are humanly created and imposed and hence amenable to human alteration. They have argued on the grounds of justice, progress, individualism, and social utility that society be structured in accordance with the "principle of perfect equality, admitting no power or privilege on the one side, nor disability on the other."[34] The rhetoric of reason has attempted to elevate the discourse on women from the realm of irrebuttable presumption to the corrigible realm of systematic investigation.[35]

Many contemporary feminists in academic and public life apply the rhetoric of reason to their own disciplines, identifying and publicizing sexist bias both within the prevailing paradigms and within specific studies. Inspired by a particular conception of "objectivity," they seek to achieve true "value-neutrality" in the profession by purging all traces of male bias from the literature.[36] Within the discipline of political science,[37] efforts to produce a revised, nonsexist version of the canon have generated numerous studies challenging the received view of women as less interested and less active in politics than men; they have challenged views that women's political behavior is directly related to their domestic role and hence is restricted to interest in a narrow range of issues involving health care, education, children, and family policy; they have challenged explanations of the underrepresentation of women in elective and appointive office that emphasize women's self-selection out of the political realm; they have challenged the belief that women make bad candidates and the belief that voters will not elect women; they have challenged the notion that women are "temperamentally" unsuited to politics and the notion that women necessarily perform differently in public office.[38] Through rigorous investigations, they have developed a body of evidence concerning women's political behavior that shatters unwarranted stereotypes about women, which have dogged the discipline.

The rhetoric of reason operates within the trope of the scholarly treatise, generating dispassionate argument and measured comparisons and demonstrating that the tools of academic analysis can be successfully deployed against misogyny. In adhering to the standards of excellence of traditional intellectual enterprises, feminist scholars become living proof of the open horizon of women's potential once artificial constraints have been eliminated. Moreover, the excellence of their work repudiates claims concerning women's "innate inferiority." Functioning as a contemporary morality play, the rhetoric of reason tacitly incorporates a model of politicization that presupposes the inspirational power of the "exemplar" or role-model. However, like all morality plays, the moral of the story reinforces prevailing values. In focusing upon extending women's aspirations and providing models for emulation as transformative strategies, the rhetoric of reason may narrowly circumscribe the scope of social change. In validating the opportunities available within the prevailing social order, the rhetoric of reason exudes an image of the future markedly similar to the existing state of affairs. The myth of equality of opportunity is resurrected and harnessed to the promise of a truly nondiscriminatory meritocracy. Consciously eschewing recourse to exaggeration and polemic, the rhetoric of reason projects an agenda for social transformation which operates in the realm of understatement.

In deploying the techniques of rational analysis in the service of nonsexist investigations of gender, the rhetoric of reason appeals to the belief that reason will triumph, that those who are committed to the norms of science and logic will be persuaded by rational argument. Yet, despite Christine de Pizan's brilliant refutations of the "slanders against women," misogynist myths about women pervade twentieth-century discourses. Despite six-hundred years of cogent arguments concerning women's status as human, it is still common to encounter analyses that treat women as "a species apart." Despite an abundance of data which demonstrates that women do not conform to the stereotype presented in the literature of mainstream political science, this stereotype continues to dominate undergraduate textbooks.[39] These "facts" illuminate a serious problem with the rhetoric of reason. Premised upon an assumption that the cause of misogyny and the attendant oppression of women is ignorance, the rhetoric of reason is informed by a naive faith that the "truth can set us free." It envisions reason as a maieutic art, capable of purging error and thereby freeing the mind to grasp an ineluctable truth: "It is as if there were a set of objective facts that everybody could see if they just tried hard enough."[40]

The conviction that truth is manifest and can be discerned by all with the application of effort suggests the presence of a metaphysical realism and an ideal of transparency at odds with the insights of modern and postmodern philosophy. The rhetoric of reason's faith in the liberating virtues of knowledge also suggests tacit assumptions about moral action remarkably akin to Socratic Intellectualism, which optimistically posits that to know the good is to do the good. Within the logic of the rhetoric of reason, men and women need only see through their erroneous conceptions and cast off their fallacious conclusions; then liberation will be at hand. It is all a matter of evidence succeeded by a conscious act of will.

The pervasive presence of misogyny in the modern world despite the centuries-old tradition of corrective feminist argument suggests that the subordination of women is sustained by much more than ignorance. The tenacity of slanderous myths about women suggests they have more in common with prejudice, with beliefs rooted in custom impervious to evidence than with rational conclusions based on inductive or deductive logic. The feminist rhetoric of reason has failed to come to grips with the possible roles played by the passions, irrationality, and the unconscious in the determination of belief. The possibility that patriarchal prejudice operating through language and custom may mold individual attitudes at a preconscious level and produce "unreason resistant to claims of political justice and formal logic"[41] has not been countenanced by the rhetoric of reason.

By striving to make explicit the sexism that permeates the canons of "value-neutral," "objective" malestream thought, the rhetoric of reason has rendered visible the political underside of diverse methods and approaches and advanced an alternative account of human relations. Yet, it has not taken its own insights seriously enough, preferring to attribute sexist bias to improper application of reasonable and neutral methods rather than to acknowledge the inescapable ideological dimension of thought itself.[42] The preference for the conscious and the rational may undermine the rhetoric of reason's efforts to deal systematically with the problem of women's oppression.

The Rhetoric of Vision

To recognize the ideological force of language is to recognize that language imposes upon individual thought conceptual schemes which are taken as objective categories.[43] The particular conceptual schemes privileged by a prevailing ideology structure individual beliefs about what is "natural," "normal," "real," "possible," "rational," "reasonable," and "desirable," thereby influencing the individual's choices and action. Yet, despite this structuring power, the ideological force of language is not monolithic: "Language must not be understood as a closed system . . . a living tongue appears to be animated by a mysterious movement, as if the collective agreement sustaining it were in a state of constant renewal".[44] Within the interstices of language, there exists sufficient ambiguity to allow reflection upon as well as revision and mutation of dominant discourses. Informed by such understandings of language, the rhetoric of vision suggests that the ideological force of language ensures that liberation is inseparable from subversion and that the very porousness of language renders subversion possible. The task of the rhetoric of vision then involves simultaneous acts of discovery and invention: the discovery of gaps within the existing system of language that provide space for the invention of alternative articulations designed to capture what has escaped or defied encodation.

The rhetoric of vision synthesizes certain insights characteristic of the rhetoric of oppression, the rhetoric of difference, and the rhetoric of reason.

Like the rhetoric of oppression, it recognizes that language can be a potent ideological weapon. Like the rhetoric of difference, it seeks to revalue women's contributions to civilization and culture. And like the rhetoric of reason, it is keenly aware that women have a great deal more in common with men than the distorted accounts in malestream discourses acknowledge. But the model of politicization informing the rhetoric of vision is far more self-conscious than those incorporated into the other rhetorical strategies. In targeting the imagination as the primary site of ideological struggle, the rhetoric of vision consciously engages in the literary production of reality. For the rhetoric of vision, recoding the dominant cultural symbols constitutes the key to future social transformation.

Christine de Pizan recognized that to decenter patriarchal thought would take a good deal more than rational argument. She understood that one of the most destructive aspects of the "authoritative texts" on women was their capacity to make women doubt their own senses and experience. Because women accepted society's accreditation of male "superiority," they internalized the male "experts' " account of the nature of women. As a result, they were burdened for life with a virulent strain of self-hatred and misogyny. As a strategy to transform the "attitudes of women who despise themselves and their own minds and who, as though they were born in the mountains totally ignorant of virtue and honor, turn disconsolate and say that they are good and useful only for embracing men and carrying and feeding children,"[45] Christine chose to construct a "City of the Ladies." Drawing upon the rich resources of imagination and narrative, she created a haven for women, comprising tales of women of courage, integrity, authority, power, tales of women who had done everything: ruled empires, conquered enemies, contemplated the cosmos, loved men, borne children, invented language, agriculture, poetry, community. In developing the biographies of her "women worthies," Christine historicized myth, attributing concrete historical existence to mythical characters such as Dido, Minerva, Medea, the Amazons, and Griselda among others. Moreover, she mythologized history, carefully moving from concrete historical events through narrative to allegory. Her goal in this conscious manipulation of fact and fiction was to create a refuge for women, a space insulated from male calumnies, a space in which women could recover their senses and see what could not be seen through misogynous lenses.

In recent years, one of the most powerful voices in the rhetoric of vision has been that of Monique Wittig.[46] In order to confound the dichotomizing principle of gender, Wittig works to subvert the processes of reification and naturalization that sustain patriarchal discourses. She deals in the medium of myth and countermyth in order to illuminate the extent to which ideology's power to distort is matched only by its power to legitimize its own creations:

> in our case ideology goes far since our bodies as well as our minds are the product of this manipulation. We have been compelled in our bodies and our minds to correspond, feature by feature, with the idea of nature that has been established for us. Distorted to such an extent that our deformed body is what they call "natural," is what is supposed to exist as such before oppression. Distorted to such an extent that at the end oppression seems to be a consequence of this "nature" in ourselves (a nature which is only an idea).[47]

To subvert such naturalistic coding, Wittig launches an assault upon the systems of images and meanings that structure the contemporary imagination. She creates a world in fiction in which women warriors, *les guérillères*, do battle as much against linearity, continuity, and the seduction of organic wholeness as against the armies of men.[48]

Wittig further advances her assault on patriarchy by repudiating some of its fundamental terms. For example, she rejects the category "woman." An examination of etymology illuminates the extent to which the term "woman" (in English derived from the word "wife," in French "femme" means both woman and wife) blurs the distinction between the idea of an adult female human and a being socially defined in terms of a man. As language enters consciousness, the subtle force of the term "woman," acts to undermine the autonomy of women. For this reason, Wittig believes the term is better banished. To substitute for patriarchy's double-edged terms, Wittig has created a "dictionary" that omits the term "man" altogether and that defines "woman" as "Obsolete since the Glorious Age. Considered by many companion lovers as the most infamous designation. This word was once applied to beings fallen in an absolute state of servitude. Its meaning was 'one who belongs to another'."[49] Her preferred term for an adult female human is "lesbian," chosen to signify a being who constitutes herself without reference to a man, a being who constitutes herself free of the pain of sexual subordination.

In all of her work, Wittig strives to create a vision of a world freed from the distortions of male dominance. In *Lesbian Body*,[50] she attempts to recapture some of the central myths of western culture, revising the stories of Pandora, Orpheus and Eurydice, Isis and Osiris among others, to valorize women's existence, and to illuminate the contours of a world freed from patriarchal imperatives. Her project, like that of Christine de Pizan, opens up the imagination and demonstrates that language can be used for feminist ends.

The rhetoric of vision strives to create some space in our conceptual and perceptual worlds within which women can expand their subversive activities. In targeting the imagination as the site of the struggle to reconceptualize human possibility, the rhetoric of vision recognizes there is more to the problem of women's oppression than ignorance. In viewing language as a powerful force in the shaping of individual consciousness, it highlights the importance of recognizing the political nature of discourse and of placing the struggle for language high on the feminist agenda. However, in advancing its case, the rhetoric of vision constantly confronts the accredited views of the dominant discourse that militate against its subversive power. Steeped in myth, metaphor, and poetic language, the rhetoric of vision seems altogether alien to the disenchanted world of the contemporary age in which a pervasive scientism tends to banish the whole symbolic realm to the status of meaningless nonsense. It is not surprising, then, that the rhetoric of vision frequently is dismissed as mere fantasy. In such a disenchanted world, the rhetoric of vision exudes an aura of individual voluntarism. Its audience is small, self-selected, and tends to read and dream in isolation. The probable consequence of the expansion of vision for this tiny group is individual enlightenment, an enlightenment that may be a crucial first step towards but which remains a very long way from the total subversion of patriarchy.

Rhetorical Constructions and Systems of Signification

Up to this point, this chapter has focused upon distinct rhetorical strategies as independent linguistic constructions, each endeavoring to promote a social order in which a particular kind of person may prosper and flourish. But one could object that such an analysis privileges intentionality and fails to comprehend the manifold ways in which discourse determines its own agenda, encoding messages beyond the explicit intent of particular authors.

To engage this objection and explore the possibility that feminist rhetoric may be driven by its own tropes, it is valuable to examine the relationships among these rhetorical strategies, to treat them as a system of signification in which language may govern the play of particular signifiers. Hayden White's Tropics of Discourse lays out one approach that may illuminate internal relations among divergent feminist rhetorical strategies. White has suggested that the principal modalities of figuration—metaphor, metonymy, synecdoche, and irony—impose an archetypal plot upon discursive formations quite independent of the intentions of individual writers.[51]

This "theory of tropology" suggests there is a logic underlying particular figures of speech that leads discourse from one mode to another. Metaphor, the provision of meaning in terms of equivalence and identity, sustains a search for similitude through the development of unifying images, but the very attempt at the construction of identities draws attention to differences that elude unification. Recognition of difference is the principal mode of metonymy, which tends to deconstruct unities and ascribe meaning in terms of "parts" as definitive of the "whole." But the distinction between parts and whole raises questions concerning the relations binding the two, moving discourse to the mode of synecdoche. In grappling with the manifold ways in which totalities are constituted by multiple parts, synecdoche raises the possibility that every part may itself be conceived as a totality encompassing various microelements that differ internally. This recognition evokes irony with its thorough suspicion of the literal and its skepticism concerning all metaphorical identifications, reductions, and integrations. White's model suggests a pattern in which language produces sophistication as discourse progresses from a naive (metaphorical) to a self-critical (ironic) trope.

Extrapolating from White's analysis, one might argue that there is a language-driven progression in feminist rhetoric: the rhetoric of oppression gives rise to the rhetoric of reason, which in turn generates the rhetoric of difference, which is then superceded by the rhetoric of vision. To sustain such a reading, one might introduce the following considerations.

The rhetoric of oppression represents a preliminary recognition that women's condition is different from that of men. The difference is grasped primarily as one of deprivation, which raises the crucial issue of desert. Is women's inferior status a function of an inferior nature? Are women responsible for their own subordination? Has there been collusion in the perpetuation of patriarchy? The threat posed by such issues gives rise to a defensive assertion of innocence and its corollary insistence upon victimization. Although this strategy masks women's agency and resistance, it marshals anger as a catalyst for rudimentary organizing efforts.

Vague inklings of difference, now reconceived in terms of forced deprivation, triggers the emergence of the mode of metaphor and with it the rhetoric of reason's catalogue of resemblances between men and women. Displacing superficial and erroneous distinctions with detailed discussions of underlying similarities, the rhetoric of reason deploys the discourse on humanity for feminist ends. Liberty, equality, and the extension of basic rights to all in virtue of their common humanity become the rallying point for feminist mobilization, even though the emphasis upon similarity necessitates the suppression of gender-specific capacities, the denial of the body.

Sustained pursuit of the rhetoric of reason produces an acute awareness of its own limitations, as the mode of metaphor sows the seeds of its own destruction. As a method committed to capture all similarities, it is driven to an apprehension of that which refuses to fit its unifying images, to the recognition of recalcitrant difference. With the rise of metonymy, neglected difference wreaks its revenge. Taking women's unique characteristics as the primary datum of perception, the rhetoric of difference searches for the truth of women's existence in sexuality, in reproduction, in the experiences of mothers, of daughters, of nurturers. Particular aspects of femininity are generalized as models of knowledge, modes of interaction, ways of being. As metonymic consciousness gives way to synedochic consciousness, to a sense of unity grounded in the unique identity of women, the rhetoric of difference strives to organize women as a sex-class, conscious of its determinate interests, conscious of its implacable opposition to all that is male.

The figures of metonymy and synecdoche also invoke their own transcendence as the focus on parts in relation to totalities illuminates the possibility that any totality may itself be conceived as comprising many subparts. Thus, the rhetoric of difference's imagery and effort to organize women as a sex-class gives way to suspicion that the notion of a sex-class masks the diversity of women. Women are not a homogeneous group. On the contrary, women differ among themselves on the basis of age, race, religion, ethnicity, ideology, maternal status, sexual preference and so on, a point duly noted by the rhetoric of vision. Dispelling the illusory unity of gender, the irony featured in the rhetoric of vision embraces the ambiguity of denatured and decentered existence. Glorying in the freedom afforded by the destabilization of normalizing discourses, the rhetoric of vision consciously plays with fragmentation, with the reconstitution of imagery, with the emancipatory possibilities of poetry and myth.

When read as a system, the incompatible elements of these four feminist rhetorics disappear. Their contradictory reconstitutions of the past, their competing theories of politicization, and their contrary conceptions of the emancipated self are subordinated to a dialectical progression in which postmodern consciousness emerges as the *telos*. In this view, feminist rhetoric guided by language's "invisible hand" surmounts the limitations of particular figures and tropes to achieve the sophistication that only a self-critical irony can afford. Is this hypothesis concerning the internal dialectic of feminist rhetorics plausible? Are there good reasons to grant that such a dynamic is at work?

White's theory of tropology is attractive for it suggests that there is a clear progression among various feminist positions culminating in the development of a critical and self-critical feminist stance. In place of continuing conflict among feminists over strategies for political emancipation, this theory promises ultimate unity in approach and in attainment of an inevitable objective. Moreover, in suggesting that such unity will result from the internal operations of language, White's tropology predicts a determinate outcome regardless of the conscious choices of actual feminists in contemporary society. The beauty of the operation of language's "invisible hand" lies in its ability to produce a desirable outcome as the unintended consequence of the action of particular agents.

Both the beauty and the simplicity of this scheme raise grave suspicions about its ability to deliver what it promises. A critical and self-critical feminist stance may be crucial to the achievement of feminism's emancipatory objectives, but it is a bit too facile to believe that language will impel feminists unconsciously toward a mode of consciousness consonant with the tenets of postmodernism. White's theory of tropology fails to recognize crucial differences between linguistic processes and historical events—between word and world. If feminists are to achieve unity in approach to the numerous issues confronting contemporary women, this will require a great deal of political action including intense debate, successful persuasion, and conscious mobilization. It cannot result from the simple operation of the principal modalities of figuration.

Any taxonomy of feminist rhetorics that hierarchically organizes competing visions to make one particular trope emerge as the *telos* of the whole must be recognized as yet another rhetorical construction with an ideologizing agenda of its own.[52] That there is only one true feminist story, one inevitable outcome of the feminist struggle, whether structured by the laws of history or the logic of discourse, must be rejected as a fiction that diverts attention from central controversies within feminism. Moreover, to posit postmodernism as the inevitable outcome of the feminist struggle is to accredit an objective that many feminists find objectionable. The problems posed by postmodernism will be taken up in the next chapter, but it is important to note here that efforts to privilege postmodernism by appealing to the inherent logic of discourse are unacceptable. If postmodernists wish to win feminists' allegiance, they must press their case directly in systematic debate.

There are important issues of contention within the rhetorical strategies discussed in this chapter that cannot be treated adequately by efforts to harmonize them into a coherent system. Whether feminists attempt to constitute an identity and a political strategy for women on the basis of victimization and anger, on the basis of difference and traditional strengths, on the basis of common humanity and rational argument, or on the basis of imagination and myth has important implications not only for feminist practice and for the mobilization of a feminist political force but also for the ways in which dominant discourses may attempt to co-opt feminism. Images of victims, of sexualized bodies, of nurturing mothers, of disembodied intellects, or of mythic warriors may not pose as great a threat to patriarchal conceptions of gender nor provide as solid a foundation for politicization as feminists may wish.

In attempting to call a world into being for purposes of politicization, feminist rhetorics necessarily falsify and mythologize even as they reveal aspects of women's experiences. Yet, the tendency of many feminist images to reproduce stereotypes perfected within misogynist traditions may tend to deflect allegiance and thereby confound feminism's emancipatory project. Moreover, reliance upon voluntarist premises may render feminism powerless to eradicate institutional sexism. The assumption that the key to social transformation lies in changing individual consciousness may preclude an adequate feminist solution to modes of discrimination embedded in structural forces. Closer attention to models of politicization and to what is omitted, as well as to what is asserted and assumed in their rhetoric, may enable feminists to better convey their emancipatory ideal.

Chapter Five

Feminist Theory
and Claims of Truth

In confronting the classic canon, challenging the reification of difference, and analyzing social practices that advantage men, feminists advance views about the world that differ in important respects from accepted conceptions of the way things are. What is the status of feminist claims about the world? Do they capture the truth about social relations? Or do they merely provide another perspective on the world? In debates between traditionalists and feminists, are there reasons to accept the feminist case?[1]

In recent years, feminists have grown increasingly self-conscious about epistemological issues. A number of concerns have heightened awareness of the need for a secure epistemological foundation for feminist inquiry. Recurrent tendencies within the dominant disciplines to marginalize feminist scholarship as a subject of interest to "women only" inspire a quest for an epistemological foundation that can rescue feminist claims from trivialization by demonstrating their truth and importance.[2] The discovery of a pervasive androcentrism in the definition of intellectual problems as well as in specific theories, concepts, methods, and interpretations of research fuels efforts to distinguish between knowledge and prejudice.[3] Recognition that epistemological assumptions have political implications stimulates efforts to attain theoretical self-consciousness concerning the intellectual presuppositions of feminist analysis.[4] Dissatisfaction with paternalistic politics premised upon malestream conceptions of "women's nature" sustains feminist

130

epistemological challenges to men's claims to "know" women's nature or what constitutes "women's best interests."[5] Objections raised by Third World women and women of color to the political priorities of white, western feminists generate profound skepticism about the ability of any particular group of women to "know" what is in the interest of all women.[6] The identification of conflicts experienced by many women between the contradictory demands of "rationality" and "femininity" stimulates a search for theoretical connections between gender and specific ways of knowing.[7]

The various concerns that have stimulated feminist reflection upon problems of knowledge have also generated divergent arguments concerning the premises of a "feminist epistemology." Three models for a feminist theory of knowledge surface with great regularity: feminist empiricism, feminist standpoint theories, and feminist postmodernism.[8]

Feminist empiricism incorporates the tenets of philosophical realism (which posits the existence of the world independent of the human knower) and empiricist assumptions about the primacy of the senses as the source of all knowledge about the world. Feminist empiricists consider sexism and androcentrism to be identifiable biases of individual knowers that can be eliminated by stricter application of existing methodological norms of scientific and philosophical inquiry. In this view, the appropriate method for apprehending the truth about the world involves a process of systematic observation in which the subjectivity of the observer is controlled by rigid adherence to neutral procedures designed to produce identical measurements of the real properties of objects. The eradication of misogynist bias is compatible with, indeed is a necessary precondition for, the achievement of objective knowledge, for it promotes the acquisition of an unmediated truth about the world; it frees substantive knowledge about reality from the distorting lenses of particular observers.[9]

Drawing upon historical materialism's insight that social being determines consciousness, feminist standpoint theories reject the notion of an "unmediated truth," arguing that knowledge is always mediated by a host of factors related to an individual's particular position in a determinate sociopolitical formation at a specific point in history. Class, race, and gender necessarily structure the individual's understanding of reality and hence inform all knowledge claims. Although they repudiate the possibility of an unmediated truth, feminist standpoint epistemologies do not reject the notion of truth altogether. On the contrary, they argue that while certain social positions (the oppressor's) produce distorted ideological views of reality, other social positions (the oppressed's) can pierce ideological obfuscations and attain a correct and comprehensive understanding of the world.

Thus, feminist analysis grounded upon the privileged perspective that emerges from women's oppression constitutes the core of a "successor science" that can replace the truncated projects of masculinist science with a more systematic and sophisticated conception of social and political life.[10]

Taking the perspectivism intimated by standpoint epistemologies to its logical conclusion, "feminist postmodernism" rejects the very possibility of *a* truth about reality. Feminist postmodernists use the "situatedness" of each finite observer in a particular sociopolitical historical context to challenge the plausibility of claims that any perspective on the world could escape partiality. Extrapolating from the disparate conditions that shape individual identities, they raise grave suspicions about the very notion of a putative unitary consciousness of the species. In addition, the argument that "knowledge" is the result of invention, the imposition of form upon the world, rather than discovery of something pre-given undermines any belief that the Order of Being could be known even if it exists. As an alternative to the futile quest for an authoritative truth to ground feminist theory, feminist postmodernists advocate a profound skepticism regarding universal (or universalizing) claims about the existence, nature, and powers of reason.[11] Rather than succumb to the authoritarian impulses of the will to truth, they urge instead the development of a commitment to plurality, multivocity, and the play of difference.[12]

Even so brief a summary of the alternative epistemologies currently vying for feminist allegiance indicates that no single contender can address all of the concerns fueling feminists' turn to epistemology. The elements of feminist empiricism and feminist standpoint epistemologies that sustain feminist claims concerning a privileged perspective on the world are at odds with the insight—generated by the long struggle of women of color within the feminist movement—that there is no uniform "women's reality" to be known, no coherent perspective to be privileged. Yet, the feminist postmodernists' plea for tolerance of multiple perspectives is altogether at odds with feminists' desire to develop a successor science that can refute once and for all the distortions of androcentrism. So intractable is the pull of these competing demands that it has led one of the most astute feminist scholars to recommend that feminists simply recognize and embrace the tensions created by these alternative insights. As Sandra Harding puts it:

> Feminist analytical categories *should* be unstable at this moment in history. We need to learn how to see our goal for the present moment as a kind of illuminating "riffing" between and over the beats of the various patriarchal theories and our own transformations of them, rather than as a revision of the

rhythms of any particular one (Marxism, psychoanalysis, empiricism, hermeneutics, postmodernism . . .) to fit what we think at the moment we want to
say. The problem is that we do not know and we should not know just what
we want to say about a number of conceptual choices with which we are
presented—except that the choices themselves create no-win dilemmas for
our feminisms.[13]

Has feminism arrived at such an impasse that its best hope with respect
to epistemological issues is to embrace incompatible positions and embed a
contradiction at the heart of its theory of knowledge? There is an alternative approach to epistemological questions that can avoid this unhappy resolution. The purpose of this chapter is to explore certain troublesome shifts
in feminist arguments about knowledge that lead to the no-win dilemmas
outlined by Harding. By changing the focus of feminist epistemological investigations from questions about knowers to claims about the known, feminism can both preserve important insights of postmodernism and serve as
a corrective to a variety of inadequate conceptions of the world. By adopting a conception of cognition as a human practice, a critical feminist epistemology can identify, explain and refute persistent androcentric bias
within the dominant discourses without privileging a putative "woman's"
perspective and without appealing to problematic conceptions of "the
given."

Knowers

Both in academic institutions and in interpersonal interactions, feminists
often become acquainted with the claims of established knowledge from the
underside. The classic texts of Western history, philosophy, literature, religion, and science, riddled with misinformation about women, are handed
down as sacred truths. When individual women attempt to challenge the
adequacy of such misogynist accounts, they are frequently informed that
their innate inabilities preclude their comprehension of these classic insights. Hence, it is not surprising that brilliant feminists have agreed that
reason has served as a weapon for the oppression of women, that it has
functioned as "a kind of gang rape of women's minds,"[14] that "in masculine
hands, logic is often a form of violence, a sly kind of tyranny."[15]

In response to such widespread abusive intellectual practices, feminist
analysis often shifts very subtly from a recogniton of misinformation about
women to a suspicion concerning the dissemination of disinformation about
women. The fact that the Western intellectual tradition has been con-

ceived and produced by men is taken as evidence that this tradition exists to serve the misogynist interests of men. The existence of erroneous views is taken as proof of "sexual ideology, a set of false beliefs deployed against women by a conscious, well-organized male conspiracy."[16] The slide from misinformation to disinformation has a number of dire consequences for feminist approaches to epistemology. In focusing attention upon the source of knowledge, that is, men, rather than upon the validity of specific claims advanced by men, the terms of debate are shifted toward psychological and functionalist analyses and away from issues of justification. This in turn allows a number of contentious epistemological assumptions about the nature of knowledge, the process of knowing, standards of evidence, and criteria of assessment to be incorporated unreflectively into feminist arguments.

In feminist treatments of knowledge, one frequently encounters the curious claim that reason is gendered.[17] The claim takes a variety of different forms. It is said that rationality—a tough, rigorous, impersonal, competitive, unemotional, objectifying stance—"is inextricably intertwined with issues of men's gender identities" such as obsession with separation and individuation.[18] It is said that "distinctively (Western) masculine desires are satisfied by the preoccupation with method, rule, and law-governed behavior and activity."[19] It is said that the connections between masculinization, reification, and objectification are such that, should women attempt to enter the male realm of objectivity, they would have only one option: to deny their female nature and adopt the male mode of being.[20] It is said that all dichotomies—objective/subjective, rational/irrational, reason/emotion, culture/nature—are a product of the basic male/female hierarchy central to patriarchal thought and society.[21] It is said that reason is morphologically and functionally analogous to the male sex organ: linear, hard, penetrating but impenetrable.[22] And it is said that representational conceptions of knowledge privileging evidence based upon sight/observation/"the gaze" are derived from men's need to valorize their own visible genitals against the threat of castration posed by women's genitalia, which exist as "nothing to be seen."[23]

Underlying all these claims are speculative psychological notions about a fragile, defensive male ego that impels men to constantly "prove" their masculinity by mastering women, to affirm their own value by denigrating that which is "other."[24] Whether one wishes to defend these psychological claims or to attack them, it is important to note that what is at issue will be certain psychological theories, particular conceptions of psychosexual development, specific notions about the role of the body and of sexuality in the formation of individual identity, and speculations about the relationship between personal identity and sociability. While all of these questions are important and worthy of systematic investigation, they are not epistemological questions per se. The switch from consideration of claims about knowledge and about the truth of certain propositions about women contained in classical texts to concerns about the "will to power" embodied in the claims of "male reason" moves feminist inquiry to a set of highly complex psychological issues that in principle could be completely irrelevant to the resolution of the initial epistemological questions.

Feminist discussions of epistemology often devolve into modes of functionalist argument. Unlike psychological arguments that attempt to explain phallocentric claims in terms of the psychic needs of male knowers, functionalist arguments focus attention upon the putative "interests" served by particular beliefs, whether they be the interests of discrete individuals, groups, classes, institutions, structures, or systems.[25] Thus, it is said that "male reason" promotes the interests of men as a sex-class by securing women's collusion in their own oppression, transforming each woman from a "forced slave into a willing one."[26] It is said that sexist beliefs serve the interests of individual men, for each man reaps psychological, economic, and political advantages in a society organized according to patriarchal imperatives.[27] It is said that sexist ideology serves the interests of capitalism: it reproduces the relations of dominance and subordination required by capitalist production; it facilitates the reproduction of labor power on a daily as well as a generational basis; it creates a marginal female labor force willing to work for less than subsistence wages; and it creates divisions within the working class on the basis of gender that thwart the development of unified class consciousness and revolutionary action.[28] Finally, it is said that "male rationality," functioning in accordance with the "logic of identity," operates as a mechanism of social control. In the interests of unrelenting domination, "thought seeks to have everything under control, to eliminate all uncertainty, unpredictability, to eliminate otherness."[29] Authoritarian reason imposes conformity by policing thoughts, purging from the realm of the thinkable all that differs from its own narrow presuppositions.

Functionalist arguments are frequently offered as causal explanations for the existence of particular ideas on the assumption that the function served constitutes the *raison d'être* for the belief; for example, misogynist notions were/are invented precisely to serve as mechanisms of social control. Yet, this teleological assumption, which equates function with first and final cause, overlooks the possibility that the origin of an idea may be totally unrelated to specific uses made of the idea.[30] Functionalist explanations also tend to gloss over complex sociological, political, and historical issues that arise when one attempts to demonstrate that a particular idea or belief actually serves the latent or manifest functions attributed to it in a contemporary setting and that it served this function in a variety of different historical epochs. As feminists pursue the intractable problems associated with functionalist explanations, they are once again carried away from questions concerning the validity of particular claims about women. In the search for the putative purposes served by androcentric notions, arguments concerning the merits of these claims are abandoned.

Feminist analyses that focus on men as the source of knowledge and on the psychological needs and social purposes served by androcentric rationality as *the* central epistemological issues are premised on a number of highly problematic assumptions about the nature of reason and the process of knowing. Rather than acknowledging that reason, rationality, and knowledge are themselves essentially contested concepts that have been the subject of centuries of philosophical debate, there is a tendency to conflate all reasoning with one particular conception of rationality, with instrumental reason.[31] Associated with Enlightenment optimism about the possibility of using reason to gain technical mastery over nature, with rigorous methodological strictures for controlled observation and experimentation, with impartial application of rules to ensure replicability, with the rigidity of the fact/value dichotomy and means-ends analysis that leave crucial normative questions unconsidered, with processes of rationalization that threaten to imprison human life within increasingly dehumanized systems, and with the deployment of technology that threatens the annihilation of all life on the planet, instrumental reason makes a ready villain.[32] When this villain is in turn associated with uniquely male psychological propensities, it is all too easy to assume that one comprehends not only that men have gotten the world wrong but also why they have gotten it wrong. The supposition that error is the result of willful deception dovetails patly with uncritical notions about unrelenting male drives for dominance and mastery.

The notion that instrumental reason is essentially male also sustains the appealing suggestion that the deployment of a uniquely female knowledge—a knowledge that is intuitive, emotional, engaged and caring—could save humanity from the dangers of unconstrained masculinism.[33] To develop an account of this alternative knowledge, some feminists have turned to the body, to sexed embodiedness, to thinking in analogy with women's sexuality, to *eros*, and to women's psychosexual development.[34] Some have focused upon the rich resources of women's intuition.[35] Others draw upon insights from historical materialism, from theories of marginalization, and from the sociology of knowledge in an effort to generate an account of experiences common to all women that could provide a foundation for a women's standpoint or perspective.[36] The unification of manual, mental, and emotional capacities in women's traditional activities,[37] the sensuous, concrete, and relational character of women's labor in the production of use-values and in reproduction,[38] and the multiple oppressions experienced by women that generate collective struggles against the prevailing social order[39] have all been advanced as grounds for women's privileged epistemological perspective. In appealing to certain physical, emotional, psychological, and social experiences of women, all of these approaches attempt to solve two problems—the source of knowledge and the validity of knowledge claims—simultaneously by conflating the disparate issues of knower and known. They suggest that women's unique experience of reality enables them to pierce ideological distortions and grasp the truth about the world. Where men have gotten it wrong, women will get things right.

When stated so baldly, the claim that women will produce an accurate depiction of reality, either because they are women or because they are oppressed, appears to be highly implausible. Given the diversity and fallibility of all human knowers, there is no good reason to believe that women are any less prone to error, deception, or distortion than men. Appeals to the authority of the female "body" to substantiate such claims suffer from the same defects as appeals to the authority of the senses, which are central to the instrumental conception of reason that these feminists set out to repudiate. Both fail to grasp the manifold ways in which all human experiences, whether of the external world or of the internal world, are mediated by theoretical presuppositions embedded in language and culture.[40] Both adhere to a romantic conception of transparency that enables a "natural" self to speak a truth free of all ambiguity. Both adhere to the great illusion that there is one position in the world or one orientation toward the world that can eradicate all confusion, conflict, and contradiction.

These problems are not eliminated by moving from embodiedness to intuition. The distrust of the conceptual aspects of thought, which sustains claims that genuine knowledge requires immediate apprehension, presumes not only that an unmediated grasp of reality is possible, but also that it is authoritative. Moreover, appeals to intuition raise the specter of an authoritarian trump that precludes the possibility of rational debate. Claims based on intuition manifest an unquestioning acceptance of their own veracity. When one assertion informed by the immediate apprehension of reality confronts another diametrically opposed claim also informed by the immediate apprehension of reality, there is no rational way to adjudicate such a dispute. Of course, one might appeal to a notion of adjudication on "intuitive" grounds, but this is the beginning of a vicious regress. Thus, intuition provides a foundation for claims about the world that is at once authoritarian, admitting of no further discussion, and relativist, since no individual can refute another's "immediate" apprehension of reality. Operating at a level of assertion that admits of no further elaboration or explication, those who abandon themselves to intuition conceive and give birth to dreams, not to truth.[41]

The theoretical monism that informs claims of truth rooted in the "body" and in intuition also haunts the arguments of feminist standpoint epistemologies. Although proponents of feminist standpoint theories are careful to note that conceptions of knowledge are historically variable and contentious, certain aspects of their arguments tend to undercut the force of that acknowledgement. To claim there is a distinct women's "perspective" that is "privileged" precisely because it possesses heightened insights into the nature of reality, a superior access to truth is to suggest there is some uniform experience common to all women that generates this univocal vision. Yet, if social, cultural, and historical differences are taken seriously, the notion of such a common experience becomes suspect. In the absence of such a homogeneous women's experience, standpoint epistemologies must either develop complicated explanations of why some women see the truth while others do not, a strategy that threatens to undermine the very notion of a "women's standpoint," or collapse into a trivial and potentially contradictory pluralism that conceives of truth as simply the sum of all women's partial and incompatible views.[42] It might be suggested that this problem could be avoided by substituting the notion of a "feminist" perspective for that of a "women's perspective." Such a move could then account for the fact that some women grasp the truth while others do not by appealing to the specific experiences that make one a feminist. This move would also create the possibility that some men, those who are feminists, could also grasp the truth, thereby freeing this claim from the specter of biologism. But this strategy encounters other problems by assuming there is some unique set of experiences that create a feminist. The rich and diverse histories of feminism in different nations and the rivalry among competing feminist visions within contemporary American society (for example, liberal feminism vs. radical feminism vs. marxist feminism vs. socialist feminism vs. psychoanalytic feminism) raise serious challenges to the plausibility of claims concerning a uniform mode of feminism or an invariant path to feminist consciousness.

Starting from a subjectivist approach to epistemology that focuses on issues pertaining to the faculties and sentiments of knowers as the source of knowledge, feminist inquiry arrives at an impasse. Presuppositions concerning a romantic notion of a "natural" subject/self capable of grasping intuitively the totality of being and a homogeneous "Woman's" experience that generates a privileged view of reality fail to do justice to the fallibility of human knowers, to the multiplicity and diversity of women's experiences, and to the powerful ways in which race, class, ethnicity, culture, and language structure individuals' understandings of the world. Claims concerning diverse and incompatible intuitions about the essential nature of social reality premised upon immediate apprehensions of that reality overlook the theoretical underpinnings of all perception and experience, and consequently devolve either into authoritarian assertion or uncritical relativism. Moreover, the pervasive tolerance for and indulgence in "gender symbolism"[43] within feminist discussions of epistemology reproduce patriarchal stereotypes of men and women, flirting with essentialism, distorting the diverse dimensions of human knowing, and falsifying the historical record of women's manifold uses of reason in daily life.

Knowing

If the complex epistemological problems that confront feminist theory cannot be resolved by appeals to the authority of the body, intuition, or a universal Woman's experience, neither can they be solved by reference to a neutral scientific or philosophical method. Feminist empiricism, in its reliance upon scientific techniques designed to control for subjectivity in the process of observation, and feminist standpoint theories that rely upon historical/dialectical materialism as a method for achieving an objective grasp of reality depend upon problematic conceptions of perception, experience, knowledge and the self. An alternative account of human cognition can illuminate the defects of these conceptions.

Critiques of foundationalism[44] have emphasized that the belief in a permanent, ahistorical, Archimedean point that can provide a certain ground for knowledge claims is incompatible with an understanding of cognition as a human practice.[45] They have suggested that the belief that particular techniques of rational analysis can escape finitude and fallibility and grasp the totality of being misconstrues both the nature of subjective intellection and the nature of the objective world. Attacks on foundationalism, therefore, raise questions concerning specific forms of knowing, particular conceptions of subjectivity, and various theories of the external world. Insights drawn from antifoundationalism can delineate the contours of a critical feminist epistemology that avoids the limitations of feminist empiricism and feminist standpoint theories.

Standard critiques of foundationalism question the adequacy of deductive and inductive logic as the ground of objective knowledge. To challenge rationalists' confidence in the power of logical deduction as a method for securing the truth about the empirical world, critics typically point out that the truth of syllogistic reasoning is altogether dependent upon the established truth of the syllogism's major and minor premises. Yet, when one moves from relations of ideas governed by logical necessity to a world of contingency, the "established truth" of major and minor premises is precisely what is at issue. Thus, rather than providing an impeccable foundation for truth claims, deduction confronts the intractable problems of infinite regress, the vicious circle, or the arbitrary suspension of the principle of sufficient reason through appeals to intuition or self-evidence.[46]

Attacks on empiricist exuberance have been equally shattering. It has been repeatedly pointed out that inductive generalizations, however scrupulous and systematic, founder on a host of problems: observation generates correlations that cannot prove causation; conclusions derived from incomplete evidence sustain probability claims but do not produce incontestable truth.[47] Moreover, where rationalism tends to overestimate the power of theoretical speculation, empiricism errs in the opposite extreme by underestimating the role of theory in shaping perception and structuring comprehension.[48] Thus, the "objectivity" of the empiricist project turns upon the deployment of an untenable dichotomy between "facts" and "values"—a dichotomy that misconstrues the nature of perception, fails to comprehend the theoretical constitution of facticity, and uncritically disseminates the "myth of the given."[49]

As an alternative to conceptions of knowledge that depend upon the existence of an unmediated reality that can be grasped directly by observation or intellection, antifoundationalists suggest a conception of cognition as a human practice.[50] In this view, "knowing" presupposes involvement in a social process replete with rules of compliance, norms of assessment, and standards of excellence that are humanly created. Although humans aspire to unmediated knowledge of the world, the nature of perception precludes such direct access. The only possible access is through theory-laden conventions that organize and structure observation by according meanings to observed events, bestowing relevance and significance upon phenomena, indicating strategies for problem solving, and identifying methods by which to test the validity of proposed solutions. Knowledge, then, is a convention rooted in the practical judgments of a community of fallible inquirers who struggle to resolve theory-dependent problems under specific historical conditions.

Acquisition of knowledge occurs in the context of socialization and enculturation to determinate traditions that provide the conceptual frameworks through which the world is viewed. As sedimentations of conventional attempts to comprehend the world correctly, cognitive practices afford the individual not only a set of accredited techniques for grasping the truth of existence, but also a "natural attitude", an attitude of "suspended doubt" with respect to a wide range of issues based upon the conviction that one understands how the world works. In establishing what will be taken as normal, natural, real, reasonable, expected, and sane, theoretical presuppositions camouflage their contributions to cognition and mask their operation upon the understanding. Because the theoretical presuppositions that structure cognition operate at the tacit level, it is difficult to isolate and illuminate the full range of presuppositions informing cognitive practices. Moreover, any attempt to elucidate presuppositions must operate within a "hermeneutic circle." Any attempt to examine or to challenge certain assumptions or expectations must occur within the frame of reference established by mutually reinforcing presuppositions. That certain presuppositions must remain fixed if others are to be subjected to systematic critique does not imply that individuals are "prisoners" trapped within the cognitive framework acquired through socialization.[51] Critical reflection upon and abandonment of certain theoretical presuppositions is possible within the hermeneutic circle; but the goal of transparency, of the unmediated grasp of things as they are, is not; for no investigation, no matter how critical, can escape the fundamental conditions of human cognition.

Thus, the conception of cognition as a human practice challenges the possibility of unmediated knowledge of the world, as well as notions such as "brute facts," the "immediately given," "theory-free research," "neutral observation language," and "self-evident truths," which suggest that possibility. Because cognition is always theoretically mediated, the world captured in human knowledge and designated "empirical" is itself theoretically constituted. Divergent cognitive practices rooted in conventions such as common sense, religion, science, philosophy, and the arts construe the empirical realm differently, identifying and emphasizing various dimensions, accrediting different forms of evidence, different criteria of meaning, different standards of explanation, different tokens of truthfulness. Such an understanding of the theoretical constitution of the empirical realm in the context of specific cognitive practices requires a reformulation of the notion of "facts." A "fact" is a theoretically constituted proposition, supported by theoretically mediated evidence, and put forward as part of a theoretical formulation of reality. A "fact" is a contestable component of a theoretically constituted order of things.[52]

The recognition that all cognition is theory-laden has also generated a critique of many traditional assumptions about the subject/self that undergird rationalist, empiricist, and materialist conceptions of knowing. Conceptions of the "innocent eye," the "passive observer," and the mind as a "tabula rasa" have been severely challenged.[53] The notion of transparency—the belief that the individual knower can identify all his/her prejudices and purge them in order to greet an unobstructed reality—has been rendered suspect.[54] Conceptions of an atomistic self who experiences the world independent of all social influences, of the unalienated self who exists as a potentiality awaiting expression, and of a unified self who can grasp the totality of being have been thoroughly contested.[55] The very idea of the "subject" has been castigated for incorporating assumptions about the "logic of identity" that posit knowers as undifferentiated, anonymous, and general, possessing a vision independent of all identifiable perspectives.[56] Indeed, the conception of the knowing "subject" has been faulted for failing to grasp that, rather than being the source of truth, the subject is the product of particular regimes of truth.[57] In postmodernist discourses, the notion of a sovereign subject who possesses unparalleled powers of clairvoyance affording direct apprehension of internal and external reality has been supplanted by a conception of the self as an unstable constellation of unconscious desires, fears, phobias, and conflicting linguistic, social, and political forces.

In addition to challenging notions of an unmediated reality and a transparent subject/self, the conception of cognition as a human practice also takes issue with accounts of reason that privilege one particular mode of rationality while denigrating all others. Attempts to reduce the practice of knowing to monadic conceptions of reason fail to grasp the complexity of the interaction between traditional assumptions, social norms, theoretical conceptions, disciplinary strictures, linguistic possibilities, emotional dispositions, and creative impositions in every act of cognition. Approaches to cognition as a human practice emphasize the expansiveness of rationality and the irreducible plurality of its manifestations within diverse traditions. Perception, intuition, conceptualization, inference, representation, reflection, imagination, remembrance, conjecture, rationalization, argumentation, justification, contemplation, ratiocination, speculation, meditation, validation, deliberation—even a partial listing of the many dimensions of knowing suggests that it is a grave error to attempt to reduce this multiplicity to a unitary model. The resources of intellection are more profitably considered in their complexity, for what is involved in knowing is heavily dependent upon what questions are asked, what kind of knowledge is sought, and the context in which cognition is undertaken.[58]

The conception of cognition as a human practice has a great deal to offer feminist analysis, for it provides an explanation of androcentric bias within dominant discourses that is free of the defects of psychological and functionalist arguments. Rather than imputing contentious psychological drives to all males or positing speculative structural interests for all social formations, feminists can examine the specific processes by which knowledge has been constituted within determinate traditions and explore the effects of the exclusion of women from participation in those traditions. Feminists can investigate the adequacy of the standards of evidence, criteria of relevance, modes of analysis, and strategies of argumentation privileged by the dominant traditions. By focusing on the theoretical constitution of the empirical realm, feminists can illuminate the presuppositions that circumscribe what is believed to exist and identify the mechanisms by which facticity is accredited and rendered unproblematic. In raising different questions, challenging received views, refocusing research agendas, and searching for methods of investigation adequate to the problems of feminist scholarship, feminists can contribute to the development of a more sophisticated understanding of human cognition.

The conception of cognition as a human practice suggests that feminist critique is situated within established traditions of cognition even as it calls those traditions into question. Defects in traditional accounts of knowledge engender critical feminist reflection that relies upon a range of traditional philosophical techniques to criticize the limitations of received views. Thus, feminists must deal deftly with the traditions that serve both as targets of criticism and as sources of norms and analytic techniques essential to the critical project. The conception of cognition as a human practice also suggests that feminist analysis can itself be understood as a rich and varied tradition. To build feminist epistemology upon an understanding of cognition as a human practice, then, requires careful consideration of the diverse cognitive practices that already structure feminist inquiry. Rather than privileging one model of rational inquiry, feminists must consider multiple issues pertaining to the level of analysis, the degree of abstraction, the type of explanation, the standards of evidence, the criteria of evaluation, the tropes of discourse, and the strategies of argumentation that are appropriate to feminist investigations of concrete problems.

Awareness of the structuring power of tacit theoretical presuppositions requires detailed investigation of the political implications of determinate modes of inquiry. The politics of knowledge must remain a principle concern of feminist analysis, not only in the course of examining malestream thought, but also in determining the most fruitful avenues for feminist research. The analytic techniques developed in particular cognitive traditions may have unfortunate political implications when applied in different contexts. Cognitive practices appropriate for psychological analysis may not be appropriate for political and sociological analysis; hermeneutic techniques essential for an adequate interpretation of human action may be wholly inadequate to the task of structural analysis; statistical techniques crucial for the illumination of discrimination may be powerless to address problems relating to ideological oppression; semiotic analyses central to the development of feminist literary criticism may be insufficient to the task of feminist historical investigations; hormonal and endocrinological studies necessary for the creation of feminist health care may be altogether inapplicable as accounts of motivation or explanations of action. Causal, dialectical, genealogical, hermeneutic, psychological, semiotic, statistical, structural, and teleological explanations may all be important to specific aspects of feminist inquiry. But knowing which mode of analysis is appropriate in specific problem situations is an issue that feminist epistemology has not yet adequately addressed.

Feminist epistemology must be sufficiently sophisticated to account for the complexity and for the political dimensions of diverse cognitive practices. To equate feminist epistemology with any particular technique of rationality is to impose unwarranted constraints on feminist inquiry, impairing its ability to develop and deploy an arsenal of analytic techniques to combat the distortions permeating the dominant malestream discourses. Neither feminist empiricism nor feminist standpoint theories afford an adequate framework for addressing these difficult issues. Feminist empiricism is committed to untenable beliefs about the nature of knowledge and the process of knowing that render it unable to explain the persistence of sexist bias within established disciplines and unable to grasp the politics of knowledge. Feminist standpoint theories are far more attuned to the ideological dimensions of knowledge, yet they remain committed to an overly simplistic model of knowledge that tends to assume a "collective singular subject,"[59] to posit a false universality, to neglect the multiplicity of structuring processes that shape cognitive practices, and to underestimate the disjuncture between problems of oppression and questions of truth. The conception of cognition as a human practice provides a context for the development of a critical feminist epistemology that can transcend these limitations.[60]

Known

Understanding cognition as a human practice does not, in itself, resolve the question of what, if anything, can be known. Skeptics, relativists, deconstructivists, structuralists, hermeneuticists, and critical theorists might all concur about the social construction of cognition, yet come to different conclusions about the nature of truth claims. Within the context of feminist approaches to epistemology, many of the critiques of traditional conceptions of reason have been voiced by feminist postmodernists. Thus, it is important to consider whether feminist postmodernism constitutes an adequate epistemology for feminist theory. Such an assessment requires an examination of the theoretical and political implications of postmodernism as well as a discussion of the light that postmodernism sheds on the question of what can be known.

Discussions of the "situatedness" of knowers suggest that the claims of every knower reflect a particular perspective shaped by social, cultural, political, and personal factors and that the perspective of each knower contains blind spots, tacit presuppositions, and prejudgments of which the individual is unaware.[61] The partiality of individual perspectives in turn suggests that every claim about the world, "every account can be shown to have left something out of the description of its object and to have put something in which others regard as nonessential."[62] Recognition of the selectivity of cognitive accounts, in terms of conscious and unconscious omission and supplementation, has led some postmodern thinkers to characterize the world in literary terms, to emphasize the fictive elements of "fact," the narrative elements of all discourse—literary, scientific, historical, social, political—and the nebulousness of the distinction between text and reality. The move to "intertextuality" suggests the world be treated as text, as a play of signifiers with no determinate meaning, as a system of signs whose meaning is hidden and diffuse, as a discourse that resists decoding because of the infinite power of language to conceal and obfuscate.[63] Postmodernist discourses celebrate the human capacity to misunderstand, to universalize the particular and the idiosyncratic, to privilege the ethnocentric, and to conflate truth with those prejudices that advantage the knower. Postmodernist insights counsel the abandonment of the very notion of Truth as a hegemonic and, hence, destructive illusion.

Postmodernism has much to commend it. Its sensitivity to the hubris of scientific reason has illuminated the manifold ways in which scientism sustains authoritarian tendencies. Its merger of the horizons of philosophical and literary discourses has loosened the disciplinary strictures of both traditions and produced creative deconstructions of the tacit assumptions that sustain a variety of unreflective beliefs. Its attentiveness to discourse has heightened our understanding of the integral relations between power and knowledge and of the means by which particular power/knowledge constellations constitute us as subjects in a determinate order of things. Its refusal to validate univocal interpretations has generated a new appreciation of plurality and has stimulated creative thinking about ways to value nonreified differences.

But postmodernism also has a number of defects that militate against the uncritical adoption of all of its tenets into feminist epistemology. Indeed, crucial social and political insights of a critical feminist theory should serve as a corrective to some of the excesses of postmodernism.

The undesirable consequences of the slide into relativism that results from too facile a conflation of world and text are particularly evident when feminist concerns are taken as the starting point. Rape, domestic violence, sexual harassment (to mention just a few of the realities that circumscribe women's lives) are not fictions or figurations that admit of the free play of signification. The victim's account of these experiences is not simply an arbitrary imposition of a purely fictive meaning on an otherwise meaningless reality. A victim's knowledge of the event may not be exhaustive; indeed, the victim may be oblivious to the fact of premeditation, may not comprehend the motive for the assault, may not know the identity of the assailant. But it would be premature to conclude from the incompleteness of the victim's account that all other accounts (the assailant's, defense attorney's, character witnesses' for the defendant) are equally valid or that there are no objective grounds upon which to distinguish between truth and falsity in divergent interpretations. The important point here is not that it is easy to make these determinations or that they can always be made in particular cases, but that standards related to the range of human cognitive practices allow us to distinguish between partial views (the inescapable condition of human cognition) and false beliefs, superstitions, irrebuttable presumptions, willful distortions. Although it is often extraordinarily difficult to explicate the standards of evidence, the criteria of relevance, paradigms of explanation, and norms of truth that inform such distinctions, the fact that informed judgments can be made provides sufficient ground to avoid premature plunges into relativism, to insist instead that there are some things that can be known.

The world is more than a text. Theoretical interpretations of the world must operate within different parameters than those of literary criticism. Although both theories of life and theories of literature are necessarily dependent upon conceptual schemes that are themselves structured by language and, hence, contestable and contingent, theories of life must deal with more than the free play of signifiers. There is a modicum of permanence within the fluidity of the life-world: traditions, practices, relationships, institutions, and structures persist and can have profound consequences for individual life prospects, constraining opportunities for growth and development, resisting reconstitution, frustrating efforts at improvement or change. It is a serious mistake to neglect the more enduring features of existing institutional structures and practices while indulging the fantasies of freedom afforded by intertextuality. Contentment with relativist perspectivism does not do justice to the need for systematicity in analyses of the structural dimensions of social and political life. Although much can be gained from the recognition that there are many sides to every story and many voices to provide alternative accounts, the escape from the monotony of monologue should not be at the expense of the very notion of truth. The need to debunk scientistic pretensions about the unproblematic nature of the objective world does not require the total repudiation of either external reality or the capacity for critical reflection and rational judgment.[64]

A critical feminist epistemology must avoid both the foundationalist tendency to reduce the multiplicity of reasons to a monolithic "Reason" and the postmodernist tendency to reject all reasons *tout court*. Keenly aware of the complexity of all knowledge claims, it must defend the adoption of a minimalist standard of rationality that requires that belief be apportioned to evidence and that no assertion be immune from critical assessment. Deploying this minimalist standard, feminist analysis can demonstrate the inadequacies of accounts of human nature derived from an evidentiary base of only half the species; it can refute unfounded claims about women's "nature" that are premised upon an atheoretical naturalism; it can identify androcentric bias in theories, methods, and concepts and show how this bias undermines explanatory force; it can demonstrate that the numerous obstacles to women's full participation in social, political, and economic life are humanly created and hence susceptible to alteration. In providing sophisticated and detailed analyses of concrete situations, feminists can dispel distortions and mystifications that abound in malestream thought.

Based on a consistent fallibilism consonant with life in a world of contingencies, feminists need not claim universal, ahistorical validity for their analyses. They need not assert that theirs is the only or the final word on complex questions. In the absence of claims of universal validity, feminist accounts derive their justificatory force from their capacity to illuminate existing social relations, to demonstrate the deficiencies of alternative interpretations, and to debunk opposing views. Precisely because feminists move beyond texts to confront the world, they can provide concrete reasons in specific contexts for the superiority of their accounts. Such claims to superiority are derived not from some privileged standpoint of the feminist knower nor from the putative merits of particular intuitions, but from the strength of rational argument, from the ability to demonstrate point by point the deficiencies of alternative explanations. At their best, feminist analyses engage both the critical intellect and the world; they surpass androcentric accounts because in their systematicity more is examined and less is assumed.

Postmodernism's retreat to the text has a political dimension not altogether consonant with its self-proclaimed radicalism. There is an unmistakable escapist tendency in the shift to intertextuality, in the move from fact to fiction. The abandonment of reason(s) is accompanied by a profound sense of resignation, a nihilist recognition that there is nothing to do because nothing can be done. At a moment when the preponderance of rational and moral argument sustains prescriptions for women's equality, it is a bit too cruel a conclusion and too reactionary a political agenda to accept that reason is impotent, that the goal is impossible. Should postmodernism's seductive text gain ascendancy, it will not be an accident that power remains in the hands of the white males who currently possess it. In a world of radical inequality, relativist resignation reinforces the status quo. For those affronted by the arrogance of power, there are political as well as intellectual reasons to prefer a critical feminist epistemology to a postmodernist one. In confrontations with power, knowledge and rational argumentation alone will not secure victory, but feminists can use them strategically to subvert myths of male superiority and to transform oppressive institutions and practices.

Chapter Six

Re/Vision: Feminist Theory Confronts the Polis

Feminist theory has been characterized as a "mode of negation within a fundamental dialectic."[1] Taking the classic texts of Western political philosophy as their point of departure, feminist theorists have taken issue with the epistemological and metaphysical assumptions that structure the dominant discourses; with claims to universality premised upon the exclusion of half the species; with the adequacy of conceptions of the good life that presuppose the "natural" subordination of women; with demarcations of public and private that deploy the power of the state to establish male hegemony within the household while simultaneously declaring the household beyond the reach of the state; and with the proliferation of conceptual mechanisms such as forces, factors, structures, institutions, customs, instincts, influences, and attitudes, which serve to mask human agency and thereby artificially constrict the sphere of the political.[2] Feminist theorists have also, however, moved well beyond the sphere of negativity: they have taken positive steps to reconceptualize the nature of women and thereby enhance our understanding of human nature; to explore the extent to which all facets of human existence are socially mediated and hence, political; to devise a conception of politics that is consonant with corrective

149

action in the realm of the humanly actionable; and to identify principles capable of sustaining a just political order.[3] As a corrective to the peculiar male myopia of traditional political philosophy, feminist theory has made a number of significant contributions.

The purpose of this chapter is not to reiterate the manifold accomplishments of feminist theory, but rather to explore certain noticeable omissions from feminist texts on political theory, to consider possible explanations for these lapses and to offer an account of these lacunae that illuminates continuities between contemporary feminist political theory and the classical tradition in political philosophy. A detailed examination of feminist assumptions about the nature of a just polity suggests that feminists have not escaped the legacy of the classic canon. Despite their oppositional stance toward traditional political theory, models of the good society that surface obliquely in feminist discourse bear a marked resemblance to those advanced by Plato and Aristotle. In considerations concerning political life, feminist re/vision entails a reversion to the classical conception of politics as an activity inextricably linked with the inculcation of virtue.[4]

Omissions and Explanations

As systematic reflection upon the nature and purposes of political life, political philosophy typically includes an account of human nature, an explanation of conflict, identification of criteria of legitimacy, a discussion of the institutions necessary for successful operation of the preferred political order, and specific prescriptions for appropriate means of transition from a corrupt system to a moral polity. Although feminist theorists have devoted a great deal of attention to the issues of human nature, the causes of conflict, and the criteria of legitimacy, there is little discussion in their works of specific dimensions of the good society, either in terms of a delineation of particular institutions and precise mechanics of government or in terms of specific political strategies for the achievement of the just society. Although a great deal of attention has been devoted to substantive policy issues such as reproductive rights, day-care provisions, wages for housework, violence against women, pay differentials, job segregation by sex, and nonsexist health care (all of which provides insight into the kind of results one would expect from a sexually egalitarian political order), little has been said about a design for political institutions most conducive to the achievement of such results.[5] Given the frequency with which feminists describe their project as involving the "total transformation of all social relations,"[6] the "complete restructuring of power, institutions, personal relations and socially constructed gender relations,"[7] this lack of specificity with respect to the nature of the system toward which feminism is striving and the best means to attain that end is puzzling.

The contemporary corpus of feminist works contains a number of possible explanations for these omissions. One conceivable explanation could be derived from a tendency within feminist analysis to repudiate "theory" *per se.* This tendency surfaces in a number of contexts. French feminists such as Marguerite Duras, Christiane Rochefort, Claudine Herrmann, and Luce Irigaray have rejected the "will to theory" in general as one of the most pernicious of male prerogatives.[8] Arguing that theory is erected upon metaphysical assumptions that are inextricably bound to domination, hierarchy, the logic of identity, and the repression of alterity, they suggest that theory is incompatible with the feminist project. Those committed to "difference" must extricate themselves altogether from the style as well as the substance of the dictatorial discourses of men. As noted in the last chapter, there has also been a tendency within the works of some Anglo-American feminists to reject certain forms of abstract rationality as "male" and to embrace intuition and emotion as women's preferred mode of knowing, a mode that does not aspire to the detached, systematic, or analytic forms of knowledge characteristic of theory.[9] A second strain within contemporary feminism rejects theory not because it is inherently "male" but because it tends to be "elitist" and "idealist." Arguing that "pure" theory is based upon a misunderstanding of the relation between theory and practice, certain feminists have suggested that indulgence in abstract theorizing would lead feminism toward an antidemocratic vanguardism incompatible with feminist commitments to equality, while simultaneously distracting feminists from the immediate problems confronting them in the contemporary world.[10]

A second possible explanation for the dearth of discussion of the political institutions that would structure a just political order could be derived from a certain ambivalence concerning the nature of the state characterizing socialist feminist analysis. A recurrent theme within socialist feminism emphasizes that recourse to the state for solutions to women's problems or for the promotion of women's interests increases both women's dependence upon the state and the state's ability to control women and the women's movement.[11] Operating with a conception of the state as an instrument of oppression, this strain of feminism introduces an anarchist moment into feminist discourses, suggesting that in a just world the state would indeed "wither away." This anarchist tendency is manifested in arguments concerning "the abolition of politics and the state in favor of individual responsibility and communal social organization,"[12] arguments that afford a principled reason for abstention from discussions that depict the political institutions of a good society.

Both epistemological and practical concerns fuel the third explanation for feminists' silence concerning the contours of the good polity and the means for its creation. Whether in its liberal or socialist formulation, this account emphasizes that feminist discourse is not the elaboration of a theory that already knows how the world will turn out. Arguing that detailed attention to the institutions and values of an ideal world leads feminists too easily to descriptions of "states of affairs which are, for all we know, impossible to achieve by working with the materials which are available," liberal feminist Janet Richards suggests that "our ideals should not commit us to any details about the kinds of social arrangements which will be found in the ideal society."[13] Because it is impossible in a world of contingency to know what the future will hold, it is best for feminists to eschew all utopian speculation. Only through such an allowance for ignorance concerning matters of fact can feminists provide sufficient latitude for future revision of their views on the basis of better information and thereby avoid the excesses of the social engineer.

Socialist feminists such as Alison Jaggar, Mary O'Brien, and Sandra Harding approach the epistemological problem from a slightly different angle. Drawing upon Marx's insight that social being determines consciousness, they suggest that contemporary feminists, inured in the oppressive relations of capitalist patriarchy, cannot fully comprehend the nature of beings raised in an egalitarian society or the choices concerning social organization that such beings might make.[14] In the words of Alison Jaggar:

> The construction of a systematic theoretical alternative to prevailing ways of interpreting the world is an achievement linked inseparably with a transformation of power relations. Only when women are free from domination will they have access to the resources necessary to construct a systematic and fully comprehensive view of the world from the standpoint of women.[15]

Thus, discussions of the kinds of political institutions appropriate for a sexually egalitarian society must await the creation of a world free from sexual dominance. Pre-emptive attempts by contemporary feminists to design such institutions would not only lack the requisite knowledge for sound judgments but also would show an authoritarian disregard for the democratic right to self-determination of future generations.

Hypotheses concerning repudiations of theory, anarchist anticipations, epistemological modesty, and respect for the right of self-determination may shed some light upon feminist reticence with respect to the issues of the good society and the strategies for its attainment. Yet, whether considered individually or taken in combination, it is not clear that such hypotheses afford an adequate explanation of the omissions in feminist political analyses. Arguments endorsing the repudiation of theory fail to grasp the theory-laden nature of all human perception and action. In advocating an "antitheoretical" stance, such approaches may simply condone blindness to their own theoretical presuppositions. Anarchist anticipations typically fail to acknowledge that even in the absence of a coercive state, some mechanisms of social organization and collective decisionmaking will be necessary if the good society is to cope with the exigencies of human existence. To refuse to consider such issues seems naively utopian. To insist that in the absence of coercion such relations would no longer be "political" suggests a rhetorical sleight of hand. While epistemological modesty, a commitment to future generations' rights to self-determination, and avoidance of utopian excesses are in themselves commendable, the invocation of these principles may mask important facets of feminist criticism.

Whether internal or external, immanent or transcendent, critique is informed by an alternative vision.[16] Whether the focus of feminist attack is existing social policies, political systems, or traditions of philosophical thought, feminist arguments tacitly invoke an image of an alternative social order. Despite deliberate attempts to avoid detailed depictions of the good society, the trenchant criticisms advanced by feminists against male dominance in general and against capitalist patriarchy in particular tacitly incorporate assumptions concerning the contours of a world worthy of feminist allegiance. Although this vision does not receive the benefit of full articulation, glimpses of a cluster of related assumptions about the just political order emerge obliquely in feminist discussions of equality, liberation, democracy, and consciousness raising. Indeed, an excavation of these hidden assumptions reveals a conception of human excellence and a vision of a moral polity with striking similarities to an older tradition in political philosophy, one that envisions politics as inextricably linked with justice and the human telos as intimately connected with virtue.

An Alternative Account: The Politics of Virtue

The classical tradition of political philosophy conceived politics to be an activity freed from the realm of necessity through which humans could order their lives in accordance with a shared conception of the good. Deploying a rhetoric that linked a conception of human excellence to that which is "natural" for humans, Plato and Aristotle argued that human conventions ought to be used to foster the achievement of human excellence. As the master convention, politics should contribute to the attainment of the human *telos*. Thus, within the classical discourse on politics, a conception of virtue, the "natural" human *telos*, played a central role in arguments concerning the structure of political life, the grounds for membership in the political community, the criteria for effective leadership, the relations among different kinds of human beings, and the substantive policies of the good regime.

Arguing that an authoritative and incontrovertible understanding of the human *telos* is possible, Plato envisioned the task of politics to be "soul shaping," the conversion of a misguided population to personal and social justice.[17] Because personal justice (the attainment of correct order in the soul) is a necessary precondition for the achievement of social justice (the correct order among different classes in society), a good ruler, that is, one who comprehends the true nature of personal and social justice, faces two distinct problems. The first involves the transformation of the population, the inculcation of virtue. Described in terms of conversion and purification, this first crucial phase of the political process is nonexclusionary. All individuals, regardless of variations in intellect, talent, or aspiration, must achieve an order in the soul in which appetites and spiritedness defer to the guidance of reason.[18] Through this transformative process, all individuals regardless of the sexual, intellectual, and occupational differences that separate them would gain something in common. The politics of conversion creates a commonality among all members of the political community. The possession of a just order in the soul is the culmination of the first phase of the political process, a process that creates the minimal equality among members of the political community that is an essential precondition for the operation of the second phase of Platonic politics, the maintenance of a just social order.

Once all members of a political community have achieved virtue—a disposition to be governed by reason and to manifest temperance with respect to personal desires and social relations—it is possible for a good ruler to organize individual differences to redound to the benefit of the whole society. Having a virtuous soul in common, people with markedly different natural endowments, personal desires, social interests, and occupational objectives can be accorded different roles within a system of cooperative specialization that enables them to pursue their individual interests and be rewarded according to their unique social contributions. A carefully regulated educational system ensures that each individual is accorded the place in the social order that conforms to his/her particular interests and capabilities, thereby securing the coincidence of individual happiness and social justice. A division of labor premised upon the recognition of individual differences allows diversity to flourish along with individual happiness. Thus, in Plato's ideal republic, equality (defined in terms of personal justice and manifested in terms of the virtue of temperance) sustains the development of an inclusive political order that extends membership to markedly different kinds of people organized into a hierarchically structured meritocracy designed to promote social efficiency and individual contentment. The political community can recognize and embrace differences among its members precisely because the possession of an invariant virtue enables differences to be harmonized into a coherent social whole.[19] Moreover, the minimal commonality created by the first phase of the political process affords a legitimation for the hierarchical organization of differences in the second phase of the political process. Just as appetites defer to the guidance of reason within the individual psyche, so too, those citizens whose characters reveal governance by the passions accept the legitimate authority of those whose lives are governed by reason. Within Plato's just polity, the minimal equality of citizens with respect to the possession of a just soul not only coexists comfortably with the political institutionalization of class inequality, it provides the justification for it.

Aristotle's emendation of Plato's ideal did not challenge the centrality of virtue in political life. Rather, it redefined the precise relationship between politics and human excellence. Arguing that hierarchy is a necessary characteristic of relations in the prepolitical sphere of the household, a realm characterized by irremediable differences of "natural" inferiority and superiority, Aristotle suggested that hierarchical relations should not be confused with political relationships.[20] In contrast to the dominance and subordination appropriate to the private realm, the unique character of politics involves relations among equals. In Aristotle's view, the participation of equals in collective decision making concerning the direction of public life constitutes the essence of politics and, hence, the defining characteristic of the best political regime.

Aristotle combined arguments about the importance of political decisions to the destiny of a people, the level of skill requisite to sound decision making, and the "natural" inequality among human beings in order to support the claim that there must be rigorous requirements for membership in the polis. Equality itself had to be defined in terms of the possession of an excellence of character possible only for a small segment of the population. Thus, Aristotle insisted that the possession of moral and intellectual virtue, along with property and leisure, constitute the necessary preconditions for participation in political life. To be accorded the status of citizen, one who could participate in an "interchange of ruling and being ruled," individuals must be equal in the maximal sense of "differing in nothing."[21] Operating with a conception of equality understood in terms of homogeneity with respect to sex, education, class, leisure-time, and a cluster of character attributes or virtues, Aristotle drastically altered the relationship between the good society and diversity. Whereas Plato embraced a conception of justice that binds people together regardless of the differences that characterize their lives in the private realm, Aristotle excludes difference from the realm of the polis. Those who lack the characteristics requisite for membership in the political community could be acknowledged to be "necessary conditions without being integral parts of the state's existence."[22] But only those who share an identity of physical, intellectual, and social traits could be conceived as citizens. Harmony in Aristotle's ideal political system would arise not from the coordination of individual differences, but from an identity of interests among decision makers who share a perception of just and unjust, who share a collective commitment to a particular set of values. Difference might serve to demarcate the political from the nonpolitical realms of life or to differentiate one political community from another, but, it had no place within the polis per se. Although equality is the hallmark of Aristotle's conception of political life, it is a notion of equality premised upon an exclusionary uniformity that banishes difference from the political community.

Although this debate drawn from classical antiquity may at first seem very far removed from the discourses of contemporary feminism, the following sections of this chapter will suggest that the assumptions concerning the just political order that surface in feminist texts operate within the parameters established by Plato and Aristotle. Plato's notion of a politically constructed commonality that can bind a heterogeneous population together in a hierarchically organized meritocracy is mirrored in liberal feminist rhetoric concerning negative liberty,[23] equal citizenship, and political participation. Aristotle's conflation of equality and uniformity as the precondition for political membership in an exclusionary polis reverberates in the dream of separatist solutions to the problems of women's oppression, as well as in visions of the perfect polity structured around a uniform, nonsexist code of values. Moreover, tacit assumptions concerning human excellence as a precondition for the achievement of liberation and justice create a situation in which Plato's conception of soul shaping, recast in the language of consciousness raising, continues to haunt the feminist imagination when it confronts the intractable problem of the means of transition to the just political order.

Liberal Feminism and the Political Construction of Commonality

It has frequently been noted that liberal feminism has focused almost exclusively on the extension of the franchise, the achievement of equal constitutional rights, and the elimination of discrimination under the law as its essential political agenda.[24] What has not been noted, however, is the manner in which this focus upon formal equality affords liberal feminism a mechanism for dealing with the related problems of commonality and difference within the context of unstated assumptions concerning the best political order.

Steeped in the assumptions of the liberal tradition, liberal feminists take as axiomatic the presumption of human equality.[25] It provides the foundation for their arguments that all individuals are entitled to liberty and to have some say in the determination of their destiny. Yet, it simultaneously creates serious problems of justification for any political order other than a radical democracy: if people are fundamentally equal and, as such, equally entitled to determine their own ends and to participate equally in decision making about public concerns, any political hierarchy that accords disproportionate power to some (the rule-makers) and imposes constraints upon the freedom of others (the subjects) seems arbitrary and unwarranted.[26] Although liberals have typically argued for representative democracy on pragmatic grounds,[27] they have also used the public/private split in conjunction with a conception of negative liberty, the ideal of "neutral" constitutional language, and pluralist notions concerning interest group activity to justify indirect democracy. Appropriated by liberal feminists, these justificatory strategies become the principal conceptual tools for dealing with the problems of sexual equality and difference.

The public/private split within liberal discourse creates a sphere of negative liberty, a private sphere over which the individual alone is sovereign, free from intrusion by the state. The promise of negative liberty in the realms of association, employment, education, commerce, living arrangements, religion, sexuality, reproduction, and interpersonal relationships ensures a tolerance for diversity. By constructing a private sphere insulated from intrusion by the government, liberal discourse condones indulgence of the multiplicity of desires and fosters the development of difference: different religions, different occupations, different ways of life, different languages, different goals sought and achieved, become the hallmark of liberal society.[28] But what becomes of equality amidst this proliferation of difference?

The liberal response turns upon the creation of the status of the "citizen," ensconced in the neutral language of constitutional law. To protect negative liberty while simultaneously maintaining its commitment to equality, the liberal state proclaims that all differences within the private sphere are, in principle, irrelevant in politics. With the constitutional recognition of the "equality of all citizens," the liberal polity immunizes itself against any recognition of the effects of difference. The system of public law concretizes this equal status by guaranteeing equal rights and immunities to all regardless of the differences in wealth, power, and prestige that characterize their existence in the private sphere. Citizenship recognizes the essential equality of all persons that underlies the differences of private life. Moreover, it affords markedly different individuals a formal public persona as a basis for meaningful equality in the political realm.

In a system of representative government serving a society known for its heterogeneity and multiplicity of interests, equal citizenship becomes synonymous with the right to participate for purposes of self-protection and to form groups to promote private interests. Each citizen is equally entitled to compete in the public forum to press claims, to advance interests, and to air perceived grievances. The guarantee of equal political rights offers the assurance to individuals and to groups that their views will receive due consideration in the policy-making process. Equal citizenship affords different persons an equal weapon for self-defense through the simple act of political participation. Moreover, because representative governments define fair laws in procedural rather than substantive terms, the right to participate is depicted as the most meaningful equality that the state can accord its citizens. Whether wealthy or poor, educated or not, Protestant, Catholic, Moslem, Jew, or atheist, banker, farmer, teacher, or homemaker, the individual as citizen can, in principle, influence the legislative process. The inequalities characteristic of the private sphere coexist with equal political rights in the political sphere.

The liberal creed assumes that the formal equality of citizens will not be contaminated by the inequality characteristic of the private realm. In donning the public persona of the citizen, the individual is expected to transcend the experiences of private life. Constraints imposed by the realities of socioeconomic status, class differentials, or collective identities based on sex, race, religion, or ethnicity are expected to be obliterated by the uplifting balm of equality before the law. Indeed, in the latest theoretical reformulation of the liberal creed, John Rawls claims that the experience of equal citizenship is sufficiently powerful to generate a sense of "being equal" in the self-image of each citizen. The political equality guaranteed by a just constitution culminates in the dissemination of equality of self-respect.[29]

For liberal feminists, the good society need not be described in detail for it is understood to be only a slightly modified version of the existing sociopolitical order. A sexually egalitarian society is not one that purges differences (inequalities) characteristic of the private sphere, for this sphere is perceived to fall outside the realm of legitimate political action. The conception of inequality that is amenable to political remedy is precisely women's exclusion from and lack of representation in the political arena. Attainment of equal political rights, the formation of women's interest groups, the mobilization of women as a political force, utilization of the "gender-gap" as a mechanism to ensure politicians' sensitivity to and accountability on women's issues constitute the limit of the liberal feminist quest for equality.[30] Preservation of the existing political order constitutes the minimalist ideal of liberal feminism; hence, women's participation in political life is the focal point of the liberal feminist strategy, and elimination of legal impediments to such participation constitutes the pragmatic political agenda. But liberal feminists, like their predecessors in the liberal tradition, believe that public participation will have a spill-over effect on the individual's identity. Ratification of the Equal Rights Amendment would be an important symbolic victory, for the constitution's recognition of women as equals would override the disparities of wealth, power, and privilege in the private sphere and bolster women's self-image. The possession of equal political rights would instill in women the conviction that they are indeed the equals of men in all important respects.

The liberal feminist vision of the good society solves the problem of equality by entrenching a disjuncture between public and private life in the center of its theory. The disjuncture is necessary for the assumption of natural human equality to coexist with marked social and economic inequalities. The assumption of natural equality itself rescues liberal feminism from the need to indulge in a Platonic politics of conversion. The state need not create a commonality among markedly different persons; since such equality occurs naturally, the state can restrict its intervention to the constitutional protection of that equality through the establishment of the formal rights and immunities of citizenship. The legal recognition of the formal equality of "citizenship" constitutes a minimalist conception of commonality consonant with radical differences in wealth, power, status, and life prospects in the private sphere. Like Plato's politics of the second phase, this minimalist notion of equality affords a legitimation for a hierarchically organized society. The doctrine of equal opportunity combined with a faith in education as the avenue of upward social mobility suggest that the grounds for hierarchy is merit. Moreover, the initial assumption of human equality sustains the belief that one's place in the meritocracy reflects only the morally meritorious differences of hard work and initiative. Thus, the assumption of equality reinforces the myth of personal responsibility for individual success or failure.[31]

Convinced that meaningful equality consists in the achievement of formal constitutional rights in the public sphere, the liberal feminist ideal of the good society embraces diversity in the private sphere, but it is a diversity that is hierarchically organized and politically neutralized. The virtue of this model of the just polity is that it allows diversity and particular forms of individual liberty to flourish within the private realm. Its chief deficiency is that it sanctions a form of difference completely consonant with the perpetuation of life-constraining inequality.

Equal Participation in the Nonsexist Polity

Radical feminists, Marxist feminists, and Socialist feminists have challenged the liberal prescription for equality, arguing that formal equality of rights in a patriarchal/bourgeois state is an inadequate mechanism for the achievement of meaningful equality for all women.[32] In addition to emphasizing the unfair class advantage accorded bourgeois women in such a system and to denouncing liberal meritocracy as a truncated conception of a just society, the radical critique of liberal feminism challenges the bifurcation of the public and private realms. Insisting that the law does not exist apart from the social and cultural milieu in which it originates, these critics argue that formal equality of citizens is corrupted by the sexism that pervades contemporary society and by the inequalities that characterize individual existence in the private sphere. Living in a society that officially affirms their "equal status" as citizens while ignoring their subordination in the private sphere can only heighten women's psychological oppression,[33] while reinforcing divisions of labor, responsibility, and power on the basis of sex.

Convinced that the "primary sources of women's oppression are outside, even beyond, judicial influence, that is to say, they rest within or arise from, prevailing material conditions, cultural values, customs, and social practices, such as differential socialization of male and female children within the family, schooling, forms of speech and language, media propagated stereotypes and numerous other innocuous social processes,"[34] radical feminists condemn the liberal prescriptions for women's equality as hopelessly ineffective. The problem that feminists must attack is the continuing existence of a "sexual caste system, ordained by religion and sustained by science,"[35] and internalized by individuals, shaping the very structure of the psyche.[36] Sexism is so thoroughly embedded in the contemporary world that no aspect of individual existence can escape its influence. Neither liberal pseudo-solutions nor individual attempts to "live the good non-sexist life at home"[37] will succeed in eliminating women's oppression. What is required is collective action to destroy the institutions of sexism. For the radical feminist, politics involves the eradication of the sexist ideology that is at the heart of the dominant culture, permeating both the public and the private realms. The political agenda must include collective action to transform both the public and private realms, for the two are inseparably linked.

Diagnosing the problem in terms of the corrupting influence of the patriarchal values that structure both individual consciousness and the institutions of liberal democratic society, the radical feminist prescription for the just polity suggests that the development of a new, nonsexist code of values is the essential precondition for the realization of democracy. The scope of the radical feminist political revolution is comprehensive, presupposing a systematic restructuring of all dimensions of social life. Changes in thinking,[38] in language,[39] in the very categories of the mind,[40] in work life,[41] in family relations and childrearing practices,[42] in sexuality,[43] in community structure[44] as well as political association are essential to the establishment of a new way of being.

At the level of political strategy, emphasis upon the creation of a truly egalitarian mindset supplants the discussion of rights and immunities in radical feminist texts. The maxim "the personal is political" shifts the focus away from the constitutional sphere and toward the private realm. Yet, sweeping changes in the private sphere are repeatedly justified as the conditions necessary for the creation of democracy in the public sphere. At the heart of this discussion of the dimensions of social transformation, there rests an Aristotelian assumption that decision making among equals requires that participants in a democratic polity "differ in nothing."

A good deal of debate within radical feminism can be interpreted as an attempt to delineate the precise requirements for membership in a sexually egalitarian participatory democracy. Recent calls for a new conception of justice premised upon "maternal thinking"—a commitment to mutuality and connection, to caring, nurturing, and concern for all living things—represents one model for a code of values that could serve as a litmus test for membership in an egalitarian polity.[45] Adherence to such values is said to promote not only sexual equality, but also pacifism, ecology, friendship, and supportive community relations.[46] While emphasis upon a particular code of values that could in principle be adopted by men and women alike constitutes one approach to the criteria for membership in the good society, other approaches suggest that more radical restrictions may by required. Several radical feminists have argued that a nonsexist value code must be supplemented by elimination of biological differences between men and women and the elimination of the sexual division of labor with respect to reproduction and childrearing if true egalitarian democracy is to be achieved.[47]

Calls for a uniform nonsexist value code and for changes in the relations of men and women to reproduction and childrearing both suggest that men and women could participate together in an egalitarian polity. Some feminists have been less sanguine about such prospects. Demands for separatist responses to the problem of sexism have taken a number of forms. Images of women banding together to create self-sufficient communities have a long history in feminist thought.[48] Yet, in recent years, there has been increasing consideration of the possibility that even the category "women" may be too inclusive for a successful participatory community. Thus, it has been suggested that bourgeois women or "pseudo-men"[49] and "male-identified" or heterosexual women may be too "different" to be included in an ideal political community.[50]

As the criterion for membership in a sexually egalitarian democracy shifts from adherence to a particular code of values to possession of certain physical characteristics or sexual orientations, the political ideal becomes increasingly exclusionary, tolerating a smaller range of difference within the sphere of political association. The conception of equality invoked in these discourses starkly resembles Aristotle's demand for uniformity as the precondition for participation in political decision making, a uniformity permeated by perfectionist expectations concerning individual virtue and community values. A consideration of the scope of democracy envisioned in the ideal community may reveal a rationale for the conflation of equality, homogeneity, and moral excellence.

Within the radical feminist framework, the ideal political order is a sexually egalitarian democratic society that is capable of liberating the human personality from the distortions and oppressive constraints characteristic of capitalist patriarchy. It is a polity in which people share a recognition of the fundamental equality of all members and consequently treat each other with dignity and respect: "Equality supposes simply that everyone has a right to the socially possible."[51] Specific decisions about the extent of the socially possible are to be made democratically: "full democracy requires that decisions regarding every area of life should be made by everyone affected by those decisions in a situation where each person is fully confident to participate freely in debate and is heard with equal respect."[52] In a political order that has repudiated the bifurcation of public and private realms, every area of life is a potential topic of political concern and collective decision making. In a system in which the people are sovereign, there are no areas of life altogether immune from political intervention. Thus, in the absence of determinate limits to the scope of political action, community members might well turn to perfectionist standards of morality to ensure that all are treated fairly in the political process and in community life.

In recognition of the expansive scope of politics within such an order, certain feminists have described the good society as a "reproductive democracy," one in which childbearing as well as childrearing become community concerns: "Democracy in procreation will come to pass only when every member of society is able to participate fully in decisions over how many children are born, who bears them, who cares for them and how they are reared."[53] If all members of the community are to be allowed to participate in intimate personal decisions such as those pertaining to conception, birth, and care of infants and children, then demands for a uniform set of values or even a virtuous mindset become increasingly comprehensible. Requiring all participants in the decision-making process to share certain values or characteristics might heighten the possibility that unanimous agreement upon such issues could be reached. Requiring virtue to be the primary determinant of political choice might ensure that unanimous decisions would also be just. Thus, exclusionary and perfectionist criteria for membership in the political community can be understood as mechanisms for the minimization of discord and for the facilitation of particular substantive decisions.[54] Discussions of reproductive democracy covertly rely upon a uniform, nonsexist value code to ensure that democratic decision making about all aspects of social and personal life will culminate in unanimous and just decisions on substantive questions.

In advocating a conception of equality that incorporates tacit assumptions about homogeneity and human excellence, the radical agenda for politics appears to repudiate all tolerance for difference, whether it be differences of opinion about the correct course of action in particular situations, reasoned differences about the applicability of various moral values to a specific debate, intellectual differences that defy the prevailing moral consensus, or behavioral differences that transgress community mores. The variety in values and the diversity of perspectives characteristic of a heterogeneous population appear to be banished by the exclusionary egalitarian polis that aspires to a "womb-like community where no voices speak in discord, where there is only harmony, agreement and love."[55]

The image of the just community incorporated in the texts of radical feminism recognizes the complex interdependence of public and private realms and the need for comprehensive remedies for the problem of sexual inequality; however, its reliance upon an exclusionary Aristotelian model of political life generates a proclivity toward uniformity that holds little promise for dealing with the issues confronting heterogeneous populations currently coexisting in vast bureaucratic states.[56] Moreover, emphasis upon the dissemination of a universal nonsexist value system as the key to the creation of an egalitarian democracy fosters prescriptions for the transition to the ideal polity with unsettling similarities to Plato's conception of soul shaping.

Consciousness Raising and the Politics of Conversion

Questions concerning the means of transition from an oppressive political regime to a just political order are perhaps the most intractable of the issues addressed by political theorists. Although there have been isolated discussions of armed resistance against male domination and of the potential efficacy of specific forms of violence and terrorism to promote the liberation of women,[57] the most frequently identified mechanism of social transformation in feminist works is consciousness raising. Within radical feminist discourse, traditional political action such as vote winning, power wielding or revolution making tends to be supplanted by advocacy of tactics designed to "change the social structure from the inside, by starting with the way people think about social structures and personal relationships."[58] Arguing that the "arena of sexual revolution is within human consciousness even more pre-eminently than within human institutions,"[59] radical feminists suggest that social revolution will grow out of raised consciousness. The dissemination of a new nonsexist code of values will create the conditions in which people may live their lives differently.[60] The transformation of the self achieved within the confines of the consciousness-raising group constitutes the key for subsequent transformation of daily life.

The model of consciousness raising is chosen by radical feminists precisely to avoid the image of the authoritarian imposition of correct principles upon a corrupt population. Consciousness raising assumes voluntary participation and noncoercive interpersonal exchanges. As a strategy for liberation, consciousness raising embodies nonhierarchical principles and the notion of self-criticism and self-reform. Yet, there are issues associated with consciousness raising that challenge its status as a liberating political strategy. Although the politicization of the psyche within radical feminist discourse stems from the realization that an individual's conceptual world is not politically neutral, it also legitimizes efforts to target individual consciousness for corrective political action, efforts that raise serious questions about the range of individual liberty and spontaneity that would be tolerated in the good society. Despite the explicit concern to avoid paternalist models of politics, consciousness raising involves a collective process that can indeed become a "coercive consensus,"[61] a soul-shaping exercise, not by one nor by the few but by the many. Beyond heightening individual awareness of the political dimensions of interpersonal relations, consciousness raising typically projects and endorses a particular communal perspective that can be "distorted into an anti-individualist mania."[62] Emphasis upon relations of equality and reciprocity within the consciousness-raising group can be wielded in such a way that "disagreement, difference or deviation are interpreted as a breech of sisterhood."[63] Even for a willing subject, consciousness raising constitutes a form of discipline, "a method of power whose operation is ensured . . . not by law but by normalization, not by punishment, but by control."[64] Like other forms of discipline, its goal is the constitution of an individual "who assumes responsibility for his(her) own constraint, an individual who becomes the principle for his(her) own subjection,"[65] precisely because the individual has internalized the norms of the prevailing group.

Consciousness raising, like Plato's politics of conversion, presupposes the inculcation of virtue. The ideal of heightened consciousness incorporates a stringent conception of human perfection: those who have completed the process are expected to have cultivated uncompromising commitments to women in particular and to social justice in general. The expansionist conception of politics that informs the model of consciousness raising seems to require that the individual's soul, will, mind, and heart be helped to embrace a particular conception of virtue. That this project is advanced in the language of liberation does not preclude the possibility that it bears coercive implications for concrete individuals involved in the transition to the good society.

Transcending the Legacy of the Classics

The concern with human excellence, the conception of politics as inextricably linked with justice, the politicization of the soul, and the exclusion of difference from the realm of the polis are all characteristic of the classical discourses on politics. When confronted directly, these concerns of the ancient world seem remarkably foreign to contemporary political philosophy, which has explicitly cast its allegiance with the "legitimacy paradigm" and repudiated the "virtue paradigm."[66] Skepticism about the possibility of knowledge of the human *telos*, commitments to individual liberty and to the institutionalization of procedural safeguards against unwarranted state intrusion in the domain of privacy, doubts about the value of a conception of a transcendent subject, and concern about the coercive implications of political attempts to inculcate virtue have combined to sustain a powerful challenge to the desirability of the classical political ideal. Yet, despite this direct assault, the terms of debate originated by Plato and Aristotle continue to surface obliquely in contemporary discussions of freedom and equality.[67]

These classic conceptions have also infiltrated feminist discourse. The visions of the ideal political community that are embedded in feminist analyses of equality, justice, and liberation draw heavily upon the terms of debate developed in classical texts. The liberal feminist conception of the citizen, like Plato's notion of the just order of the soul, offers a minimalist notion of commonality sufficient to legitimate a hierarchically organized political system. It is a notion of commonality highly prized by its proponents, but one which seems incapable of providing much solace to those within the underclasses. Radical feminist calls for total separatism as well as their visions of a perfect polity bound by a shared, nonsexist perception of right and wrong, of just and unjust, represent neo-Aristotelian efforts to produce a community of equals who participate in ruling and being ruled. Yet the Aristotelian legacy, the conflation of equality, uniformity, and virtue, results in the exclusion of all difference from the realm of the polis. Moreover, tacit assumptions concerning human excellence as the precondition for participation in democratic decision making generates a discussion of consciousness raising as the primary means of transition to the just political order, a discussion that leads feminism back to Plato's notion of soul shaping as a legitimate form of political activity.

That these ideals drawn from classical conceptions of political life are too narrow to deal adequately with the issues of individual autonomy, democratic decision making, and the wealth of differences that structure social and interpersonal relations in contemporary life becomes apparent as soon as the assumptions underlying these texts are made explicit. Perhaps the best prescription, then, for the development of conceptions of the good society—conceptions that accommodate difference (without reifying differences into metaphysical categories) while simultaneously ensuring that differences do not entail the perpetuation of oppression—is to encourage feminist theorists to take up explicitly the issue of the pragmatic reconstitution of political life.

Part Three

Toward a World Worthy of Feminist Allegiance

Chapter Seven

A Constitutional Proposal

What feminists want is a world in which women can live complete lives, a world that affords women opportunities for freedom, creativity, cultivation of the intellect, work, self-expression, political action, friendship, intimacy and love on the same terms as men. What feminists want is a world in which gender no longer functions as a capricious prisonhouse that imposes life-constraining sentences without regard to individual desire, capability, or culpability.

Feminists concur that existing political systems, whether traditional, liberal democratic, or socialist, are a far cry from the egalitarian world of their aspirations. Despite their diversity in structure, operation, and principle, contemporary polities have been largely ineffective in recruiting women to policy-making positions and in devising substantive policies that enhance sexual equality and provide fair and equitable treatment for women. The near universal agreement among feminists concerning the inadequacies of existing constitutional provisions, however, masks a great deal of disagreement about the remedial strategies necessary to overcome these problems.

Some feminists have advocated strategies that work within the prevailing order as the best means to achieve sexual equality.[1] In liberal democratic systems, these feminists emphasize efforts to extend existing constitutional provisions to women, to form women's interest groups and lobbies, to finance women candidates for political office, to mobilize women as a political force around key issues such as day-care or reproductive freedom, and to utilize the "gender-gap" as a mechanism to ensure politicians' sensitivity to and accountability on women's issues. Other feminists have identified specific principles that can provide a foundation for "gender-justice." According to this strategy, "the basic principles of sound gender policy are readily specified: individuals must have opportunities to choose, the capacity to make choices, information on which to base preferences and a climate of tolerance in which to explore alternatives."[2] Implementation of these principles by the courts, the legislature, the bureaucracy, and the economic sector will then produce a world in which "sex counts for naught in the public sphere of life."[3] Other feminists have detailed substantive policy proposals pertaining to marriage, pregnancy, reproductive freedom, divorce, housework, child-care, privacy, rape, violence against women, pay differentials, job-segregation by sex, sexual harassment, pensions, social security, and pornography in order to mark the contours of and guide the transition to a sexually egalitarian polity.[4]

In contrast to those feminists whose transformative tactics operate within liberal democratic systems, radical feminists, Marxist feminists, and socialist feminists have suggested that the preservation of patriarchal/bourgeois society is incompatible with meaningful equality for all women. Arguing that the eradication of sexism requires the total subversion of capitalist-patriarchy, these feminists focus their energies upon developing revolutionary consciousness, transforming sexist values, and restructuring the relations between men and women in interpersonal interactions, family life, childrearing practices, sexuality, the workplace, and in community and political associations.[5] Other feminists, convinced that subversion is impossible in consort with unregenerate men, have called for separatist solutions.[6] And still others have advocated armed resistance against male domination.[7]

Thus, despite a shared dissatisfaction with existing political systems and a profound understanding of the pernicious consequences that the perpetuation of these systems have for women, contemporary feminists form a fragmented opposition, divided in their understandings of both the causes of women's oppression and the strategies for political transformation. Dissension within the feminist movement on such questions has contributed to an impasse in feminist politics. The radical feminist critique of liberal feminist prescriptions for formal equality raises grave doubts about the worth of equal constitutional rights in a society pervaded by a sexist value system, while the liberal critique of the radical feminist alternative raises equally

sizable doubts about the possibility of creating a nonsexist polity characterized by individual virtue and a shared conception of substantive justice.
The gulf between these alternatives demarcates the contemporary feminist
dilemma: the creation of a perfect egalitarian community free of all hierarchy, exploitation, and dominance appears to be a utopian dream that
lies far beyond contemporary possibilities; yet neutral constitutional principles in the absence of community recognition of the equality of men
and women seem incapable of eradicating the pervasive practices that privilege men. Feminists are left with political strategies that demand either
too much or far too little. As a political force, feminism is immobilized
equally by the futility of utopian visions and by the frustration of liberal
tokenism.

Futility and frustration are not the inevitable fate of feminism. What
feminists need is a new approach to questions of justice, an approach that
avoids both perfectionist expectations and minimalist resignation to the
status quo. Feminists need a vision of a sexually egalitarian polity that lies
within reach and that carries sufficient intellectual and moral force to mobilize large numbers of people in an effort to instantiate its principles in
existing institutions. This chapter will attempt to meet that need. It identifies one mechanism for the reconstitution of political life that may appeal
to feminists despite the range of differences separating them. To set the
stage for an alternative vision of a sexually egalitarian polity, this chapter
will first consider a number of problematic assumptions about gender that
help entrench divisions within feminist ranks. It will then explore one constitutional provision that can be manifested in a variety of institutional
arrangements in order to promote a world worthy of feminist allegiance.
Finally, it will engage possible objections to this proposal and reply to those
objections.

Gender: Analogies and Dysanalogies

In attempting to articulate the nature of women's oppression, feminists
have often compared the condition of women with that of other oppressed
peoples. Thus, analogies drawn from oppression related to race, class, ethnicity, and religion have figured prominently in feminist analysis. Although
such analogies have played an important role in making women's oppression visible and in fostering understanding of the constraints that circumscribe women's existence, each comparison also introduces assumptions
that can be highly problematic for feminists, for each comparison suggests a

rationale for and mechanisms of subjugation, as well as prescriptions for liberation that may not be applicable to women's case.

No form of oppression has been more systematic and pervasive than that rooted in race. Drawing upon the history of racism to illuminate the nature of sexism, feminists have traced an array of manifestations that range from subtle denigrating attitudes, through egregious deprivations of rights to brutal enslavement.[8] Parallels drawn between race and sex, however, may suggest a biological basis for oppression fraught with perils for feminism.[9] As critics of radical feminism have pointed out, the spectre of biologism posits a false universalism in the analysis of gender that may devolve too easily into the ahistorical "dogma that all women face the same oppression in the same form."[10] Ignoring both the social construction of gender in markedly different societies and the different dynamics of sex oppression within the same culture related to variables such as class and ethnicity, such analyses may generate either biotechnological solutions or separatist solutions that neither secure the allegiance of a majority of women nor eradicate the sexism that permeates the dominant institutions of contemporary societies.[11] In addition, efforts to blur the distinctions between the historic treatment of women and slaves give rise to claims that the experiences of middle- and upper-class white women are roughly comparable to those of blacks in the underclasses, claims that both strain credulity and fail to do justice to unique torments of racism.

The experiences of particular racial and ethnic minorities (Blacks, Asians, Jews, Hispanics) at the hands of a dominant population have also provided feminists with a model of the means by which a group can be stereotyped, marginalized, and used as a scapegoat for a variety of social ills. By drawing upon accounts of the external process of victimization, internalized as a pervasive sense of inferiority or a virulent strain of self-hatred, feminists have gleaned insights into both the phenomenology and the psychology of sexual oppression. Yet, historical examples of the conquest, enslavement, and economic exploitation of minority groups may be markedly misleading as an explanation of the oppression of half the species, leading feminists to search futilely for an event that could be labeled the "world historical defeat of the female sex."[12]

To escape marginalization, minority groups have typically chosen one of two divergent paths—assimilation or the preservation of cultural specificity, neither of which holds much promise for contributing to the creation of a sexually egalitarian polity. The ideal of assimilation may encourage "gender-blind" policies that deny the specificity of women's reproductive capabilities and thereby preclude recognition of legitimate needs related to those capabilities.[13] Conversely, feminist strategies devised to preserve "traditional women's values" often valorize characteristics that are far more likely to be a consequence of centuries of oppression than to represent some "authentic" women's culture.

In contrast to metaphors of race and ethnicity that emphasize ties of blood, language, and culture, feminists have drawn upon the concept of class to illuminate a kind of common interest that is said to transcend nationality and even subjective awareness. Within this framework, the daily activities of women as daughters, wives, mothers, and nurturers constitute a fundamental commonality sufficient to sustain claims concerning the "objective interests" of women.[14] These objective interests in turn form the core of an international feminist agenda that can serve as a catalyst for the mobilization of women on a world-wide scale. While analogies rooted in class oppression have the great virtue of drawing attention to specific historical processes by which one class gains ascendency and to the social structures through which it institutionalizes its power, these comparisons too may divert attention from the specifics of sex oppression. In emphasizing the economic dimension of women's subordination, the notion of women as "sex-class" may exaggerate the commonalities of women's experiences in the realms of production and reproduction, neglecting the range of variation introduced by occupation, race, ethnicity, marital status, sexual preference, reproductive history, culture, and ideology. Moreover, the metaphor of women as a sex-class may sustain strategies for social transformation that render women invisible by incorporating them within the larger proletarian struggle.[15]

As a focus for political mobilization, the notion of women's objective interests has distinct disadvantages, for it invokes a conception of false consciousness that functions as a double-edged sword. It might be said, for example, that all women have an objective interest in the development of nonsexist health care; but when such a general claim is given specific content (usually by white, Western feminists) in order to provide a basis for political organization, it can also raise the specter of elitism, paternalism, and cultural imperialism. The idea of false consciousness can play a vital role in fostering critical reflection and self-transformation within the confines of small, voluntary consciousness-raising groups, but when used as a rhetorical strategy in the context of mass politics, it is far more likely to provoke righteous anger, resentment, and distrust.

Class analogies link the oppression of women to the larger struggle for social justice. Thus, they have been used intentionally to enable women, workers, and Third World peoples to comprehend the injustices suffered by each and to work together to eliminate exploitation and oppression. Such coalition building is essential if democratic means are to be used to promote just ends. But total submersion of gender justice within the rubric of social justice may have deleterious consequences. It may lead to the unwarranted expectation that one kind of revolution will eradicate all forms of oppression, an expectation that fails to take seriously the differences that distinguish oppression rooted in race from that rooted in class, sex, and ethnicity. A conception of social justice as a seamless web may also foster a brand of purism that is intolerant of partial solutions and that repudiates any incremental measures as implicated in the perpetuation of the status quo and, as such, "tainted." When imported into feminism, this brand of purism may lead to the rejection of proposals that would improve the condition of women, while falling far short of eliminating all social injustice.[16]

In the rise and fall of religious persecution, feminists have found not only an example of a heinous social practice that has been largely eradicated in contemporary liberal democracies and a model of tolerance that may inspire a mode of peaceful coexistence for the sexes, but also a helpful guide for the treatment of sexual difference before the law:

> Religion can provide an illuminating analogy for gender, because the central aspiration of the law in each instance may be stated in broadly similar language: to protect free exercise, whether of religion or of free choices; and to proscribe governmental imposition of conventions, establishments of religion or sex-role stereotypes.[17]

In working the analogy between religion and gender, feminists recommend neither the abolition of sexual difference nor the rigorous enforcement of norms of masculinity and femininity. On the contrary, they suggest a policy of governmental indifference: one's gender, like one's religion, should be relegated to the private sphere, a sphere that is shielded against intrusions by the state. To treat gender as a private matter, then, is to encourage individual freedom in terms of self-image, lifestyle, and behavior and to consolidate that freedom through the institutionalization of a legal policy of gender neutrality. Through the use of gender-neutral language, the law will take no notice of sex.

To free women from intrusive regulations and unwarranted prohibitions appears a progressive step, but closer attention to the implications of the religion/gender analogy should give feminists cause for concern. To relegate religion to the private realm is not to abolish religion, but to give it free play in a realm beyond the notice of the state.[18] When gender is relegated to the private sphere, tradition is far more likely to gain ascendency than is a mythic freedom of choice and self-definition. Like religion, gender is something that is tradition-bound and imparted to the young through a process of socialization, a process that renders suspicious claims concerning free choice. To grant traditional conceptions of gender free reign under the guise of individual choice is to neglect the extent to which gender is imposed upon the young, at a time when they can neither reject the imposition nor anticipate fully its lifelong consequences.

A policy of governmental indifference has consequences that are far from benign in the context of gender relations. Traditional definitions of the private realm have not protected men and women equally. On the contrary, insulating domestic relations from state scrutiny and intervention has served to increase the significance of power differentials within the family, providing a venue for violence against women without the possibility of redress in the courts. Governmental indifference cannot be tolerated in the context of continuing social practices that pose life-threatening dangers to women while simultaneously protecting assailants from prosecution.[19]

As a strategy for the attainment of gender justice, sex-neutral laws may also prove markedly unsatisfactory. At its most elemental level, justice requires that those who are alike be treated alike and that those who are different be accorded differential treatment.[20] Thus, a preliminary step in any attempt to formulate just laws is the identification of relevant similarities and significant differences. Rather than encouraging a case-by-case investigation of such relevant considerations, the ideal of sex-neutrality in the law pre-emptively forecloses the issue, insisting that in the eyes of the law sex is never relevant. But such an insistence can have patently unjust consequences. If the law has been used as a mechanism of discrimination, then those who have been victims of such discrimination are entitled to redress. In the case of women, laws have played a critical role in excluding them from the public realm, depriving them of the rights of citizenship, and subjecting them to unwarranted constraints with respect to ownership, occupations, and a wide range of activities. In casting contemporary laws in sex-neutral terms, the perpetuation of such overt discrimination is prohibited but no compensation is afforded to the victims of past discrimination. In treating men and women as equals, gender-blind laws can render invisible inequalities that have been created, sustained, and sanctioned by law.

In addition to erasing evidence of past discrimination and failing to compensate victims of formerly sanctioned sex inequalities, gender-neutral principles and laws may be incompatible with the attainment of a sexually egalitarian society for yet another reason. Gender-neutral language has been advocated by feminists as a means of effacing men's hold on the public imagination. The use of neutral or inclusive terms is designed to bring women into "people's mental landscapes."[21] But there is a good deal of evidence to suggest that "many language users when saying or writing common terms that might in principle refer to either sex, simply do not think of them as referring to women. The words are neutral on the surface, but masculine underneath."[22] If such linguistic habits encompass legal terminology, then rather than rectifying the absence of women introduced by exclusionary legislation and sustained by custom, the guise of neutrality may further perpetuate women's invisibility.

If governmental indifference and gender neutrality offer feminists less than they might hope for, the analogy of religion and gender has additional implications that are troubling. In dis-establishing religion and consigning it to the private sphere, governments accord religion the same status as any other private, voluntary association. Churches vie for individuals' allegiance as do other social, economic, and civic organizations. Individuals freely join groups that promote their interests and abandon organizations that cease to interest them. Thus, the analogy of religion and gender subtly introduces a pluralist conception of political life that derives a good deal of its legitimacy from unquestioned voluntarist assumptions. But the extension of such voluntarist notions to gender is both misleading and detrimental to feminist objectives. It is misleading because it makes no sense to say that women "choose" their gender or "join" the female gender to promote particular interests.[23] On the contrary, gender is inscribed in the personality through a variety of social rituals without consultation or consent of the gendered subject. To treat gender like membership in a voluntary organization is to attribute to men and women a level of freedom that they do not possess.[24] Moreover, it creates a situation in which women may be held to account for a freedom that is purely fictive.

Within the framework of pluralist assumptions, the political arena is open to all. Any individual is free to promote his/her own interests or to join together with others to press for their collective advantage. In a gender-blind pluralist world, if women fail to press for their own advantage, if they refrain from promoting their interests, if they are absent from politics, "it is by their own free choice."[25] With the legacy of past discrimination erased, with gender neutral laws on the books, and with the pluralist assumption that women are an interest group like any other, it is all too easy to conclude that women have no one to blame but themselves. In short, pluralist assumptions mask contemporary practices that privilege men and in so doing they render the forces that constrain women's choice invisible.

Feminists have gained great insight into the dimensions of women's oppression by drawing analogies with racial, ethnic, class, and religious oppression. But taking the analogies uncritically can preclude a full understanding of the specificity of gender oppression. Indeed, exclusive attention to the lessons to be drawn from the oppression of others may blind feminists to the extent to which gender symbolism itself has been used to legitimate the subjugation of racial, ethnic, and religious groups. Notions of "natural" or "divinely ordained" relations between the sexes have been displaced onto other oppressed groups in order to legitimate hierarchy and justify inequities.[26] The point here is not to suggest that sex oppression is the primary oppression, but rather to note that rationalizations of power often depend upon the deployment of analogies designed to undermine specificity and establish equivalences where none exist. If feminists are to subvert such machinations of power, they must develop a sensitivity to critical distinctions and a readiness to embrace relevant differences.

An adequate analysis of women's oppression, then, must include not only that which women share in common with other oppressed peoples, but also that which distinguishes sex oppression from other modes of oppression. Strategies for sex equality must take into account significant dysanalogies between gender, race, class, ethnicity, and religion. Women lack the defining characteristics of a race[27] and the uniform roles and interests of a class. They are not bound by ties of blood, language, culture, or belief. They are neither a minority group nor a voluntary association. They do not share a coherent worldview, possess a set of determinate interests, or experience an invariant reality.

As slightly more than half the world population, women are a majority of every race and of every ethnic group. Differing from one another by culture, language, religion, class, ideology, genetic structure, education, personality, personal history, aspiration, and capability, women have had all their individuating characteristics subordinated to an imputed ideal of femininity. Their individual identities have been effaced by norms of womanhood that operate within an extraordinarily narrow range of possibility. Defining the female as inferior, tradition and law have denied the vast range of characteristics that men and women share as members of the same species, imposing instead an artificial dichotomy on the sexes that glorifies the male and denigrates the female. Treating women as an undifferentiated mass, confining them to legal categories from which they cannot escape, denying their talent and their crucial contributions to culture and history have been staples of male hegemony. To subvert such dehumanizing practices, feminists must envision a world in which justice, equality, and liberty are neither gender-specific nor gendered concepts. They must structure political relations to ensure that neither institutions nor laws privilege half the species.

Reconstituting Political Life: Tinkering with the Institutions

The challenge that confronts feminists is the creation of meaningful sexual equality, the institutionalization of a conception of gender justice that liberates individuals from the straitjacket of gender and frees the talent of the whole species for innovative projects. In developing a proposal for the reconstitution of political life, feminists must transcend defective ideals of the classic canon. They must eschew the reification of difference, the authoritarian imposition of virtue, and the dream of an exclusionary polis, as well as liberal indifference to persistant harms in the private sphere, utopian expectations of a perfect citizenry, and nihilist resignation to the status quo. To avoid the failed visions of traditional political theorists, feminists need not repudiate the canon completely. On the contrary, the creative application of certain principles may lay the foundation for a feminist transformation of public life.

In designing political institutions to prevent the tyranny of an entrenched group, one strategy involves the empowerment of an official opposition. Incorporated in the doctrine of separation of powers, such empowerment suggests that government institutions be structured to incorporate different interests in such a way that no group can gain unfair advantage in the processes of policy making and policy implementation. In this view, a self-regulating equilibrium that prevents the aggrandizement of any particular individual or group can be established by capitalizing upon the self-interest of officeholders who have been accorded the constitutional means necessary to resist the encroachments of others. By thus wedding the interest of the individual to the constitutional rights of office, "ambition can be made to counteract ambition" so that the private interest of the individual becomes a sentinel over public rights.[28] By enabling individual officeholders to prevent abuses before they are institutionalized, citizens are protected from the depredations of tyrants, whether it be the tyranny of one, the tyranny of a minority or the tyranny of the majority. Could this principle be extrapolated to empower women to prevent sexist abuses?

Suppose it were acknowledged that sex has been a factor of political relevance in that the absence of women from positions of power has been the result of human action, whether witting or unwitting. Suppose it were recognized that exclusionary legislation restricting officeholding, the rights of citizenship, and the rights to self-determination in the private sphere to men were neither divinely ordained nor necessarily inspired by a benevolent grasp of the best interests of women.[29] Suppose too that it were understood that the adoption of gender-neutral laws and universal guarantees, without any systematic effort to redress past and present discrimination, would merely perpetuate male dominance. Under such circumstances would it not appear that justice requires that sex, the factor that has been relevant for purposes of exclusion and discrimination, ought also to be relevant for purposes of rectification?

Rather than aspiring to a gender-blind constitution that insists that sex is never relevant in the eyes of the law, it seems *prima facie* fair to accord women a power for self-defense "commensurate with the danger of attack."[30] This could be done by introducing a constitutional principle mandating that women hold 50 percent of all elective, appointive, and bureaucratic offices.

Sex Parity and Distributive Justice

A conception of distributive justice lends moral force to the sexual integration of political institutions. Unlike models of compensatory or retributive justice that confront the present through a lens focused upon the past, subtly suggesting that discrimination is a social atavism, distributive justice takes ongoing discrimination as its point of departure. The persistence of a wide range of practices that continue to privilege men constitutes the problem that sex parity in public office is designed to solve. As symbol and instantiation of tacit pro-male bias, political institutions continue to be a nearly exclusive preserve of men. Changing constitutional rules in order to redistribute political office on a sexually equitable basis would eliminate marked sex bias in the official institutions of state. It would thereby bring the frequently invoked ideal of human equality into conformance with existing constitutional practices. It would afford women a powerful weapon that could prevent any future efforts to institute sexual discrimination in public policy. In addition, a sexually equitable distribution of public offices would strike an immediate blow against tacit assumptions of male superiority.

A move to sexual parity in public office supplements established notions of political representation as an activity on behalf of and in the interests of others with a conception of descriptive representation.[31] Developing the idea that political institutions reflect what we are as a people and what we believe, descriptive representation suggests that public offices, like the legislature, "should be an exact portrait, in miniature, of the people at large, as it should think, feel, reason and act like them."[32] As a mechanism designed to heighten visibility of particular characteristics, descriptive representation is most appropriate and relevant in contexts where one purpose of representation is to supply information about the people or the nation.[33] Equal numbers of men and women in public office would serve as a constant reminder that women are half the population, that the capacities for leadership, initiative, and judgment essential to good government are not gender-specific, and that the nation takes seriously its commitment to gender equality. Sex equality in office would provide palpable evidence that women are just as capable as men of acting on behalf of others, of advancing the interests of their constituents, of engaging in processes of negotiation and compromise, and of formulating policies that meet the needs of the nation.

To endorse a constitutional prescription for equal numbers of men and women in public office is not to assume that women have a determinate set of interests, that they will restrict their attention to a narrow range of issues, that they will represent only women constituents, or that specific substantive policies will be the guaranteed outcome of their presence in political life. On the contrary, it is to assert that, like men, women differ from one another in a plethora of ways, including significant differences with respect to party affiliation, political conviction, ethical principles, class, occupation, race, and ethnicity, and, for precisely this reason, women can represent a diverse constituency just as men can. It is to assert that despite the numerous differences characterizing individual women, sex remains a relevant consideration in the composition of elective and appointive offices for contemporary as well as for historic reasons. As half the population, half the citizenry, and half the taxpayers, women deserve half the positions that determine how public life will be regulated and how public resources will be allocated.

An assertion of the equal competence of men and women with respect to the responsibilities of public office, accompanied by a recognition that there can be no guarantee that women in office would necessarily change the substance of policy, might produce a predictable objection. It might be said that the sex of the officeholder is therefore irrelevant for the genders of those "who enact statutes are, presumably, significant only if they bear some relation to legislative behavior—significant only if they affect the content or form of laws, or influence the procedure by which laws are enacted."[34] A number of factors should be considered in response to this objection.

Taking any nation as a case in point, it can be demonstrated that the gender of office holders has been historically significant. Whether one focuses upon legislation passed to ban women from office, to restrict their educational, professional, or employment opportunities, to impose different standards upon their conduct, to establish different levels of punishment for their transgressions, or to deny them citizenship rights, it can be shown that exclusively male law making has affected the content of legislation. Thus, it seems appropriate to provide women with a constitutional safeguard against any such future abuses, even if the substance of most pending legislation is not immediately affected by their presence.

Women in every country have serious substantive grievances against their governments. This fact accords moral legitimacy to any effort to enhance women's freedom and to increase women's opportunities for self-determination. Opening half of all positions of political and bureaucratic power to women would help to reduce the gender inequities that continue to plague contemporary societies. It does not follow, however, that the presence of women in 50 percent of the decision-making positions of a polity will guarantee specific substantive policy outcomes. Procedural mechanisms, like a constitutional mandate for sex parity in public office, can never guarantee substantive results.[35] Because individual women are as different from one another as they are from men, it would be a mistake to expect a univocal stance from women in office. Because the pressures upon legislators from constituents, lobbyists, political parties, colleagues, committee responsibilities, personal loyalties, and individual expertise and conscience all play a role in determining officials' policy stances, it would be absurd to expect women in office to form a unified and invariant voting bloc.

What could reasonably be expected is that women in office would be sensitive to forms of disadvantage that uniquely affect women and that they would take such problems seriously. Thus, sex parity in office would function as a procedural mechanism designed to ensure that the relevance of sex in any particular policy instance would remain an open question. Rather than foreclosing the issue by fiat, equal numbers of men and women in public office would encourage investigation of what constitutes a significant difference for purposes of specific legislation. To the extent that justice does require treating like cases alike and different cases differently, detailed investigations of the pertinence of gender to proposed policies would foster justice in the policy-making process. In cases where sex is irrelevant to the policy under review, women officials could be expected to act in a manner indistinguishable from their male counterparts; but in cases where sex is a relevant consideration, women officials could use their power to defend themselves and their gender, amending, stalling, or killing potentially abusive proposals. Regardless of the outcome of specific policy debates, sex parity in office could serve as a means by which to incorporate concern with justice into the policy-making process, while simultaneously affording half the population a viable means for self-defense against any efforts to demean, subordinate, or oppress them.

To the extent that women elected and appointed to public office (or hired, in the case of bureaucratic posts governed by civil service procedures) come from different backgrounds than their male counterparts, having performed different social and economic roles and having established different ties to community organizations, it could be expected that they might expand the terms of debate on specific policy questions. Drawing upon their unique experiences, individual women might offer different insights, introduce new considerations into policy deliberation, increase the range of options available in negotiated settlements, and enhance the range of political choices. But, in such instances, the degree of influence that women's contributions might have would depend upon the persuasive power and political skills of the individual involved. The airing of women's views could not ensure the enactment of substantive policy proposals. At most, the articulation of novel perspectives could guarantee more comprehensive and systematic reflection about the possible consequences of specific policies. It might then help prevent the unwitting enactment of discriminatory laws, especially of those laws that are fair on the face but discriminatory in fact.

A constitutional provision mandating sex parity in public office challenges deeply entrenched gender prejudices. Many will argue that the prescription is wrong-headed, for the sex of an office holder is irrelevant: men can represent women and "women's interests" perfectly well. But will these interlocutors be as willing to grant that women can represent men and "men's interests" adequately?[36] If sex really were irrelevant to office holding, then there should be little opposition to this constitutional proposal for it would not matter who represented persons, interests, institutions, or ideas. To the extent that the proposal for equal numbers of men and women in public office is depicted as extreme, absurd, or unnecessary, it suggests the persistence of lingering sexist bias. This bias permeates unquestioned assumptions that it is "natural" or "fair" for men to represent women, but that it would be "unnatural" or "unfair" for women to represent men. Only a tacit acceptance of male superiority can make the concentration of power in men's hands appear natural or fair.[37] By suggesting that sex equality in office is *prima facie* fair given the sex-ratio of the population, this constitutional prescription imposes the burden of proof upon those who maintain that male dominance in public office is preferable. Those opposed to sex equality in office must demonstrate that men are more capable of performing the tasks of governance than women. Such a demonstration will be difficult because it calls for empirical evidence pertaining to the comparative performance of large numbers of men and women in office—evidence that does not exist at the present time, precisely because no country has allowed women to assume an equal role in political life. In the absence of empirical evidence of superior male competence in political office, opponents of sex parity can defend male privilege by appealing to the myth of male superiority, a strategy marked by a degree of circularity that undermines its logical integrity. Alternatively, opponents of sex parity in office can appeal to tradition, suggesting that the social utility of male dominance is proven by the fact that it has worked so well in the past. Yet, the claim that male dominance has "worked well" must be considered in the context of a mode of social organization that squanders the talent of half the species. If social systems that educate and accord power to a small proportion of their populations can be said to "work well," then surely systems that educate and empower all its people would "work better." In the absence of opportunities to assess the comparative merits of male dominance versus sexual equality in public life, there is no good reason to assume that traditional practices are maximally beneficial. Moreover, even minimal concern for human dignity, for fairness in the treatment of human beings, and for the benefits that might accrue from a doubling of the talent available to society suggest that there are good reasons for trying to improve upon traditional practices.

The argument that sex is irrelevant to office holding because men can represent women and "women's interests" also misses the larger point of sex parity in office as a principle of distributive justice. Within the framework of distributive justice, the central issue is not merely whose interests or what interests are represented, but who does the representing. When 80–95 percent of public offices are held by men and women are not only ensconced in but identified with the private sphere, there is good reason to interpret women's condition not merely in terms of an absence from the public realm, but rather in terms of a privation of a social role.[38] Under such conditions, the continuing exclusion of women from public office imposes a badge of inferiority upon women. Sex segregation in political office perpetuates an image of women as less capable, less competent, and less fully human than men. The state's complicity in the continuing denigration of women is compounded by the fact that available evidence suggests that women's absence from political office is not a matter of individual preference, but rather a consequence of discrimination in the nominating and appointment processes.[39] If women's absence from public office actively fosters stereotypes that demean women by ratifying assumptions of women's inferiority, then constitutional guarantees of formal equality are subverted. Whether the formal equality of women is undermined intentionally or unintentionally, sex parity in public office constitutes an appropriate remedy. Equal numbers of men and women in public office eliminate once and for all women's privation of public roles and responsibilities.

The institutions of state are a particularly appropriate target for feminist efforts to achieve equality, for politics is the legitimate venue of collective action to promote justice, and political institutions are a necessary means to achieve collectively determined ends:

> In a variety of intellectual traditions the compelling importance and priority of the state is thought to reside in its unique responsibility to promote social justice and the public interest through conscious and purposive action. The authority of the state, its legitimate use of coercion, its war-making power, its accountability to citizens, the structure of its constitution, the loyalty and patriotism of its citizens, the protection of citizens' rights against it—all these prerogatives, concerns, practices, and limits take an overriding importance because the state is supposed to promote common purposes not by accident (as the market was thought to do), not habitually (as established tradition does at its best), but consciously through policies supported by binding law."[40]

If democracy means anything, it means that a majority of the sovereign people may choose to alter the rules governing the composition of offices with respect to the gender of office holders. Political institutions are by definition more responsive to the will of the majority than are private institutions. If feminists can convince a majority of voters of the moral legitimacy of sex parity in public office, then the reconstitution of political life lies within reach. The traditional association of the state with justice and the structuring power of the constitution with respect to state offices contribute to the feasibility of the sex parity proposal. What is required is not the total transformation of human nature, nor the inculcation of virtue, but the creation of a political will to achieve gender justice in political institutions.

Tactics for Mobilizing a Majority

The mobilization of a democratic majority in support of sex parity in public office will require grass roots activism, systematic efforts to illuminate existing practices that privilege men, sustained arguments to demonstrate the unfairness and the social costs of pro-male bias, and intensive attempts to illustrate that the persistent harms that women experience in contemporary societies are amenable to political solutions. To build a coalition in support of the reconstitution of political life, feminists must demonstrate the validity of the case for gender justice; they must convince people of the worthiness of their vision of sexual equality. In so doing, feminists must confront entrenched gender prejudices and strive to change men's and women's views about the natural capabilities and appropriate social roles of half the species.

A grassroots campaign to mobilize support for sex parity in public office involves an educational component that bears some similarities to consciousness raising. But as a collective political effort to convince a voting majority to press for constitutional change, feminist advocacy of sex parity in office must also differ from consciousness raising in important respects. Rather than focusing upon intensive, long-term relationships among women in small groups, feminists must seek a mass audience of men and women. Rather than focusing upon redress of individual women's grievances against particular men or specific organizations, feminist activists for constitutional change must emphasize the issue of distributive justice and societal remedies.[41] The goal of feminist educational efforts cannot be to disseminate a set of substantive beliefs about men and women, much less to accredit perfectionist notions that all social and environmental problems will be solved by the mere presence of women in office. Fallible humans will always fall far short of perfectionist ideals, and some men and women will always deviate from whatever substantive claims are advanced about "all men" and "all women." Predictable failings and welcome deviations from constraining gender generalizations should not be allowed to derail the feminist quest for equality.

In attempting to challenge the reification of difference that is accepted as normal and natural by a mass audience, feminists must seek to stimulate critical reflection about the intricate relations between public and private spheres, conventional expectations and individual aspirations, traditional norms and individual freedom. Feminists must seek to heighten awareness of the means by which tacit assumptions of male superiority can produce unintentional discrimination every bit as pernicious as the discrimination that proceeds from intentional action. They must strive to deepen popular understanding of the means by which the unquestioned acceptance of gender stereotypes creates an inhospitable or even hostile environment subtly excluding women from educational and occupational opportunities. In seeking a public audience, feminist activists must not stifle opposing views nor silence different perspectives. On the contrary, they must strive to engage alternative arguments in constructive debate. Feminist research has generated ample evidence to challenge myths of male superiority, to discredit traditional claims concerning women's natural proclivity for subordinate social roles, and to counter arguments that blame victims for the harms that befall them. Feminist activists can use this wealth of evidence to capture the terms of debate, to articulate a feminist stance on the issues, and to demonstrate the importance of public action to eliminate persisting sex inequities. By using the overwhelming evidence of continuing gender injustice to their advantage, feminists can prove that the issue of sex equality is not merely one of symbolic guarantees.[42] Persistent harms that uniquely affect women, circumscribe their life choices, and jeopardize their physical and mental well-being are the constitutive elements of contemporary sexism, and they are the reason that meaningful sexual equality remains a pressing item on the political agenda.

In the past two decades, feminist efforts at consciousness raising have had some success. The remarkable increase in numbers of rape crisis centers and shelters for battered women, in state efforts to purge blatant forms of sex discrimination from legal codes, in significant victories in the courts in cases involving sex discrimination in hiring, pay, and promotion, as well as sexual harassment, and certain laws pertaining to property ownership, pensions, insurance, marital rape, and pregnancy discrimination are a testament to the efficacy of feminist efforts. These achievements have required vast amounts of effort; yet, they do not begin to eradicate the systemic harms affecting women as a consequence of pro-male bias. The inadequacy of these individual advances is not related to lack of ardor or effort on the part of feminists. On the contrary, it stems from a critical disjuncture between method (consciousness raising) and objective (transformation of social institutions). Although "social institutions are constituted in part by the concepts, beliefs and aspirations of participants, changes in those beliefs and commitments cannot suffice to reconstitute an institutional complex."[43] To transform social institutions, feminists need institutional remedies. A constitutional proposal for sex parity in public office offers an institutional mechanism for dealing more systematically with consequences of continuing gender bias. It does not guarantee either that the women elected, appointed, or hired in public offices will be feminist or that feminist solutions to women's problems will be incorporated into legislation. In eliminating institutional sexism from the offices of state, however, it would create a situation in which women, for the first time, are 50 percent of the decisionmakers who investigate, reflect upon, and devise mechanisms to deal with pressing social problems.

Sex Parity and the Constitutive Role of the Political

Some feminists might fault the proposal for sex parity in public office for being another ineffective liberal feminist panacea. Acknowledging that as a procedural mechanism sex parity in office cannot guarantee substantive remedies to sex inequities, they might suggest that this constitutional proposal will merely advantage those women ("pseudo-men") who are already privileged in prevailing systems and who are therefore qualified to assume public offices, but that it will leave gender injustice in the private sphere untouched. This criticism fails to consider significant differences between the tenets of liberal feminism and a proposal for sex parity in office that could be implemented in any political system.[44]

Liberal feminists envision a restricted role for the state in remedying gender injustices because they accept a rigid bifurcation between public and private realms. In accordance with the liberal presumption that the private sphere is self-constituting, that is, that the family, the economy, and an array of voluntary associations are independent of politics and as such must be sheltered from unwarranted intrusions by the state, liberal feminists typically suggest that it is inappropriate for the state to meddle with the inequalities that structure private relations. Within this framework, women office holders would be as incapable of remedying private injustices that women experience as are male office holders, for the private sphere lies beyond of the legitimate reach of the state.

The liberal bifurcation of public and private realms is not the only, nor the most insightful, analysis of the relations between public and private.[45] In contrast to the liberal notion that the private pre-exists the political, and that the private sphere is altogether autonomous, an examination of the range of practices construed as public and those considered private in different cultures and in different historical epochs suggests that the very notion of the private is socially constructed and politically protected. Virginia Woolf has illuminated the complex interdependencies of these spheres: "The public and private worlds are inseparably connected; the tyrannies and civilities of the one are the tyrannies and civilities of the other."[46] What Woolf grasps is not merely that what is considered the private realm, how legitimate interests in privacy are conceived and protected, and whether the privacy of some is protected at the expense of others are inherently political questions. Woolf also captures the constitutive role of the political—the role of political ideas and institutions in structuring the individual's private imaginings, legitimizing personal judgments, delimiting expectations, and shaping personal identity. When the role of the political in creating and accrediting beliefs about the public and private is recognized, the limits upon policy makers in dealing with all forms of sexual inequities is not as clearcut as liberal premises would suggest. Should women be half of those participating in deliberation about the appropriate contours of the private realm, a range of perspectives on women's experiences of the private, privacy, and privation might be aired and taken seriously for the first time.

To acknowledge that the definition of the private realm and the protections afforded individuals against the state are political matters—matters created in order to achieve certain ends and subject to change should political objectives change—is not to repudiate all conceptions of individual rights. Nor is it to renounce limited state power and privacy as worthy ideals. It is simply to open an area for investigation and debate. It is to suggest that liberal rhetoric concerning the inviolability of individual rights should not be confused with the equal protection of all individuals in existing states. Whether women benefit as fully as men from the rights and immunities afforded citizens and subjects in contemporary political systems is a matter for empirical inquiry. The findings of such studies would be relevant to the deliberations of the men and women in office who seek to create policies to ensure the equal protection of the laws for all citizens.

Privacy understood as a "degree of inaccessibility of persons, of their mental states and of information about them to the senses and surveillance devices of others" including the state is as important to women as to men.[47] Whether one focuses upon privacy in relation to seclusion, solitude, anonymity, confidentiality, secrecy, intimacy, or reserve, women need and deserve privacy every bit as much as men do. A good deal of feminist research has documented that "women have had too much of the wrong kinds of privacy [privation] but are very much in need of beneficial privacies."[48] Sex parity in public office could not guarantee that individuals would be more systematically protected from the intrusions of vast bureaucratic states. But the presence of equal numbers of men and women in policy-making positions might significantly transform the assumptions that inform privacy debates. When evidence concerning rape, domestic violence, sexual harassment, sex discrimination, and other dimensions of women's experiences in the private sphere are introduced into such debates, the presence of women in positions of power might preclude facile presumptions of male innocence, refusals to accredit women's testimony, and victim-blaming rationalizations of male violence. By changing the gender of half the participants in privacy debates, sex parity in public office might trigger the recognition that positive action by the state is required if the privacy of men and women is to receive the same level of protection. Sex parity in public office might contribute to the creation of innovative solutions to gender-related injustices in the private realm.

Recognition of the constitutive role of political ideas and institutions in shaping prevailing values and in structuring individual identities illuminates another reason that sex parity in public office is conducive to meaningful equality for women. To suggest that prevailing political institutions circumscribe the individual's sense of self is to suggest much more than that the prohibitions established in law constrain individual action. Acknowledgement of the constitutive power of political practices involves not simply the individual's conscious compliance with legal codes, but also the individual's internalization of tacit beliefs, norms, and mores that sustain determinate ways of being. Incorporated within one's tacit preunderstandings, political values structure perception, judgment, attitudes, actions, and aspirations. Because they operate at a preconscious level, political norms can have profound effects without being recognized. In structuring what is to be taken as normal, natural, rational, and sane, tacit presuppositions camouflage themselves, achieving their greatest effect when least noticed. When considered in the context of tacit presuppositions that structure perceptions and expectations, the pervasive pro-male bias in contemporary cultures acquires new meaning. In a political system in which the vast majority of offices are held by men, the assumption of male superiority makes a great deal of sense. The naturalness of male power is encoded in the preunderstandings of individuals as an unquestioned lesson of existing institutions. If this is the case, then sex parity in public office could subtly effect tacit assumptions about the appropriate role of women in society. Women in power could empower individual imagination. Assumptions about what is normal and natural for women might be profoundly affected by the reconstitution of political life.

Some might object that any effort to use the institutions of state to influence individual attitudes is illegitimate, for it targets the psyche for political action and opens the door for totalitarian abuse. Thus, it might be said that a commitment to individual freedom and respect for individuals as they are requires the rejection of the proposal for sex parity in office as an ill-conceived strategy with ominous coercive implications. This objection fails for a number of reasons. It overlooks a critical distinction between direct political efforts at brainwashing or mind-control and a subtle alteration of individual attitudes that develops as an indirect consequence of the elimination of sexual inequality in political institutions. Moreover, in attempting to conflate a possible indirect consequence of sex parity in public office with thought-control, this objection fails to take seriously the constitutive influence of existing political institutions upon the perceptions, appraisals, and identities of contemporary citizens. Political institutions dominated by men also disseminate indirect lessons that are neither neutral nor value-free. Minimally, they corroborate the myth of male supremacy. To reject sex parity in public office as an unwarranted intrusion by the state upon the hallowed domain of freedom of thought is not to strike a blow for the autonomy of individual conscience, it is merely to insist that the state's tacit sanctioning of male supremacy will not be challenged.

Descriptive Representation, Oppression, and Pluralism

Sex parity in public office promises to remove from the official institutions of state all vestiges of women's exclusion. By demanding that women be accorded positions of elective, appointive, and bureaucratic power in rough proportion to their presence in the species,[49] the proposal for sex parity in office may provoke another objection. It might be said that in relying upon descriptive representation as a means to achieve a sexually egalitarian polity, this proposal devolves too quickly into a morass of pluralist claims that could easily mask the importance of gender justice. In this view, feminist demands for descriptive representation are misguided because they will quickly be eclipsed by a proliferation of pluralist arguments that every minority group be accorded political office in proportion to its presence in the population.[50] Furthermore, as a political strategy, the sex parity approach is mistaken for a number of reasons. It substitutes concern with putative group rights for legitimate concern with individual rights. In addition, in a "nation of minorities," where the "white majority itself is composed of various minority groups, most of which can lay claim to a history of prior discrimination at the hands of the state and private individuals,"[51] the call for descriptive representation lays the foundation for virtually unlimited demands for rectification. Most importantly from a feminist perspective, as more and more minority groups assert their "right" to demographic representation, the urgency of need for gender justice will be lost amidst the multiplication of minority grievances.

The belief that the moral arguments supporting sex parity in public office could be appropriated unproblematically by any group that perceives itself to be oppressed rests upon a number of contentious assumptions. Much of the objection gains its force in the context of the individualistic assumptions that circumscribe the conception of compensatory justice.[52] It has already been noted that the model of compensatory justice subtly suggests that the central issue for contemporary society is the rectification of past injustices. When advanced in conjunction with the image of the United States as a nation of minorities, this model suggests that there is no way to differentiate between injustices experienced by w..ite immigrants prior to assimilation and ongoing discrimination against women. It also implies that there is no way to distinguish between the legitimate claims for justice advanced by those who have personally experienced discrimination and the claims of contemporary white men, who have descended from immigrants who experienced injustice upon their arrival in this country. By conflating past and present, arguments for compensatory justice envision a world in which virtually everyone is a victim needing compensation. But the monumental task of compensating everyone for everything quickly convinces rational beings that nothing can be done. Thus, compensatory arguments for justice for all give rise to a pragmatic resignation to the status quo.

The claim that white males—descendents of ethnic immigrants—are themselves oppressed in the same way that their ancestors were and to the same degree that contemporary women are assumes that oppression is a matter of subjective perception rather than of objective reality. Only if one assumes that oppression exists in the mind of the oppressed, rather than in the external world, does it make sense to insist that there is no way to adjudicate legitimate from illegitimate claims of oppression. To the extent that oppression is acknowledged to be an objective condition, instantiated in a range of social practices that privilege some while disadvantaging others, claims concerning oppression are empirically verifiable. It is perfectly possible to investigate claims of oppression, to distinguish those that have merit from those that are fraudulent, and, indeed, to assess degrees of oppression.[53] Systematic inquiry can provide good reasons for accrediting those claims that have substance, and it can identify sound reasons for the rejection of claims that are spurious and self-serving.

In response to the pluralist objection then, it is important to insist that rather than simply assuming all are equally oppressed, claims concerning oppression must be investigated.[54] Moreover, since distributive justice rather than compensatory justice is central to the proposal for sex parity in office, the timeframe for such investigations must be circumscribed. In contrast to "an amorphous concept of injury that may be ageless in its reach into the past,"[55] legitimate claims must demonstrate that discrimination is ongoing. Requiring objective substantiation of claims of continuing oppression is likely to prevent a vast proliferation of claims, but it will not eliminate all such claims, for some groups in contemporary society do experience continuing discrimination.[56] Should those groups who can demonstrate ongoing discrimination also press for descriptive representation in public office? To deal fully with this question, it is important to consider the issue of justice for groups, the potential benefits of multicultural representation in public office, and the likely efficacy of descriptive representation as a solution to minority oppression.

One of the consequences of the reification of difference, whether it be racial, ethnic, or gender difference, is that the individuality of those to whom "difference" is ascribed is eclipsed. Individual characteristics, individual desires, individual possibilities are supplanted by the imputed traits of the group. Indeed, the group is constructed as a stereotype and all individuality is effaced as prejudice imposes categories of expectation, social role, and imputed interest upon group members. The reification of difference creates a situation in which people are treated as beings less human and less worthy of respect, not because of individual foibles, but solely because they are members of particular groups. When membership in a group is the ground of discrimination, then justice for groups who have experienced invidious discrimination is morally legitimate. That members of unjustly privileged groups prefer to attribute their advantages to individual initiative and effort does not alter the fundamental nature of group advantage. For this reason, the rhetoric of individual rights should not be allowed to obstruct legitimate remedies for injustices imposed upon determinate groups.

Descriptive representation could have symbolic advantages for members of oppressed minorities comparable to those likely to accrue to women from sex parity in public office. The presence of minority group members in office would help challenge prejudice by demonstrating the humanity and competence of members of the oppressed group. In addition, descriptive representation would indicate that a nation takes its commitment to human equality seriously; it would help transform the rhetoric of equal rights into meaningful equality. Moreover, the presence of members of oppressed groups in positions of power might help foster an appreciation of multiculturalism. It might generate not merely tolerance of but an active appreciation and respect for nonreified human differences. Finally, the presence of representatives of oppressed groups in elective, appointive, and bureaucratic offices would give an official voice to the oppressed. Additional perspectives could be aired, alternative experiences could be articulated, and the lessons learned by the oppressed could be introduced into the policymaking process. For all these reasons, a polity concerned with justice might wish to reconstitute itself in order to achieve descriptive representation for oppressed groups.

The benefits that might accrue from the inclusion of representatives of oppressed groups in public office should not be confused with efficacy in eliminating social injustice. As an effective mechanism for redressing group-based injustice, descriptive representation of oppressed minorities faces an obstacle that sex parity in public office does not confront. As 50 percent of all public officials, women would have the power to block any policy that treated women unfairly. Sex parity in office would afford women an effective weapon to wield against gender injustice perpetrated by the institutions of state. The individual interest of women in office could serve effectively as a sentinel over women's rights because any policy that advantaged men would by definition disadvantage women in office as well as women in the larger population. Thus, women in office would have the motive, opportunity, and power to defend their gender successfully. Oppressed minorities face markedly different problems in the policy-making process. As a minority of officeholders, representatives of oppressed groups would not have the numbers to thwart oppressive proposals. They might be able to mobilize a coalition against abusive proposals, but by definition they could not thwart abuse on their own. Thus sex parity in public office has a far greater chance of advancing women's equality than descriptive representation of oppressed minorities has of eliminating other forms of discrimination.

The problem of efficacy should not be taken as an argument against descriptive representation of oppressed groups. The reconstitution of political life to include multicultural representation might well be a step toward a more just polity and, hence, be worthy of support. Whether one wishes to support descriptive representation for oppressed groups or whether the problems raised by minority status suggest that alternative strategies to achieve social justice for minorities might be more effective, the case for sex parity in public office remains strong. Contrary to the pluralist objection, there is no reason to believe that descriptive representation would be prone to abuse. Moreover, legitimate claims of justice could be served by incorporating this procedural mechanism into the offices of state.

A Flexible, Morally Acceptable First Step

A constitutional provision mandating equal numbers of men and women in office is compatible with a variety of institutional arrangements. As a procedural means to promote sex equality, it could be employed effectively in any regime in which women are markedly underrepresented in positions of power. Thus, the proposal would be as pertinent to traditional and socialist polities as it is to liberal democracies. Within democratic systems, the implementation of this constitutional principle would require changes in election rules and party policies pertaining to the recruitment and nomination of candidates. Implementation might be simpler in systems that feature party slates of candidates in multimember electoral districts that operate on the basis of proportional representation; but sex parity in elective office could also be achieved in systems that have single-member districts and winner-take-all electoral contests, if parties nominated women for the appropriate number of "safe" seats.[57] The important point to note is that architects of election procedures have been ingenious in devising a wide range of practices to conform to constitutional mandates. There is no reason to believe that their ingenuity would be drastically curtailed by the introduction of a provision mandating sex parity in elective office. If the constitution requires sex parity in public office, party strategists will devise mechanisms to achieve that end.[58]

It might be objected that sex parity in office would be unfair to those male officeholders who would be displaced as the overrepresentation of men in office is eliminated. To respond to this objection, it is necessary to consider the factors that have contributed to the overrepresentation of men in public office. To the extent that men are overrepresented as a result of ongoing discrimination against women in hiring civil servants, in appointing state officials, and in the nominating stage of the electoral process, the beneficiaries of such injustice have no moral claim upon our sympathies. As a system of gender oppression, sexism not only disadvantages women; it also accords unwarranted privileges to men. Men who currently hold positions of power and prestige in contemporary social organizations have been the beneficiaries of a form of preferential treatment:

> they are members of a group of persons who have been privileged in hiring and promotion in accordance with normal practices of long-standing, persons who have been offered better educational preparation than others of the same basic talents, persons whose egos have been strengthened more than members of other groups.[59]

The men who staff the major institutions of state did not deserve systematic preference; they had no right to the advantages afforded by a sexist society. For this reason, no rights are violated when unfair advantages are eliminated. As a mechanism to promote justice for women who experience continuing injustice in contemporary society, sex parity in public office may require that some men lose unwarranted privilege; but it will not subject these individuals to invidious discrimination or to social injustice.

As a procedural mechanism that leaves the substance of government action to democratic decisionmaking, a constitutional requirement of sex equality in public office is not a panacea for all forms of gender injustice, much less for all forms of social injustice. As a constitutional mechanism designed to afford women a weapon for self-defense in the formulation and implementation of government policy, this proposal does not guarantee the eradication of pernicious inequalities related to race and class; it does not resolve important questions related to the alienating character of work in late-industrial societies or to the dehumanizing practices of technology-addicted cultures. Moreover, as a prescription for the reconstitution of political life, it does not automatically redress the inequities of the private sphere either in terms of the economic sector or of familial relations.[60] Nevertheless, it does promise significant benefits for women. It would instantly change the gender of public life, opening positions of leadership, power, and prestige to women. In so doing, it would afford women opportunities to shape future policy and to introduce creative proposals to deal with the specific problems that confront women in the home and in the workplace. It would directly attack entrenched notions of women's inferiority and provide avenues for women to demonstrate their talents throughout the public sector. It would structure political situations in such a way that in order to achieve their own objectives, men would have to interact with women in office on the basis of equality. In addition, a constitutional proposal for sex parity in public office would place gender justice on the political agenda, both as a topic for critical reflection and as a focal point for political mobilization. Although not an instantiation of perfect social justice, a constitutional mandate for sex parity in public office is a pragmatic and feasible step toward a world worthy of feminist allegiance. Targeting sexual equality in political life as an immediate objective and as a mechanism for creative solutions for continuing gender inequities, a movement for sex parity in public office constitutes a concrete political strategy that could unite men and women in a productive effort to move beyond oppression.

Notes

Introduction

1. Janet Richards has argued that feminists must be concerned with the elimination of a particular type of injustice—that related to gender. *The Skeptical Feminist* (London: Penguin, 1982), p. 18. For related arguments, see David Kirp, Mark Yudof and Marlene Franks, *Gender Justice* (Chicago: University of Chicago Press, 1986).

2. See for example, Nicholas Davidson, *The Failure of Feminism* (Buffalo: Prometheus Books, 1988).

Chapter 1: The Reification of Difference

1. Gayle Rubin, "The Traffic in Women: Notes on the Political Economy of Sex," in Rayner Reiter, ed., *Toward An Anthropology of Women* (New York: Monthly Review Press, 1975), pp. 179–180.

2. This chapter will focus on arguments specifically designed to differentiate men from women. For more systematic discussions of the treatment of women in the Western philosophical tradition, see Lorenne Clark and Lynda Lange, eds., *The Sexism of Social and Political Theory: Women and Reproduction from Plato to Nietzsche* (Toronto: University of Toronto Press, 1979); Susan Moller Okin, *Women in Western Political Thought* (Princeton: Princeton University Press, 1979); Martha Osborne, *Women in Western Thought* (New York: Random House, 1979); Jean Elshtain, *Public Man, Private Woman* (Princeton: Princeton University Press, 1981); Linda Nicholson, *Gender and History: The Limits of Social Theory in the Age of the Family* (New York: Columbia University Press, 1986).

3. Because Plato argued for the inclusion of women in all aspects of public life, he has from time to time been categorized as a feminist. For excellent arguments against such a classification, see Julia Annas, "Plato's *Republic* and Feminism," in Martha Lee Osborne, ed., *Women in Western Thought* (New York: Random House, 1979), pp. 24–33.

4. Plato, *The Republic*, V 455d2–3.

5. Plato, *Timaeus*, 42e.

6. Ibid., 42b3–c4; cf. 90e6–91a4.

7. Plato, *Laws*, 781b 2–4.

8. Ibid., 780d 9–781b.

9. Similar assumptions of women's inferiority coupled with a commitment to competition as the chief mechanism for hiring have provided the foundation for "efficiency" arguments that restrict certain jobs to men. In this view, interviewing women for such jobs wastes precious resources, since their inferiority makes it unlikely that a "qualified" woman could ever be found. An efficient manager conserves resources by restricting the candidate pool to those more likely to possess the needed qualifications. John Stuart Mill demonstrated the defects of such reasoning in *The Subjection of Women*, noting that the presumption of women's inferiority only served to squander talent—denying jobs to more qualified women and securing jobs for mediocre men. Mill argued that competition alone would ensure that the most qualified person is hired, hence women should always be allowed to compete.

10. Aristotle, *Metaphysics*, 1058a30.

11. Ibid., 729a11.

12. Ibid., 738b20.

13. Ibid., 728a17–21.

14. Aristotle, *Politics*, 1260a22–24.

15. Ibid., 1260a30, 1277b21, 1277b27, 1158b11–13.

16. Aristotle, *Oeconomica*, Book I, Chapter 3.

17. Aristotle, *Politics*, 1259b.

18. Tertullian, "On the Apparel of Women," cited in Katherine M. Rogers, *The Troublesome Helpmate: A History of Misogyny in Literature* (Seattle: University of Washington Press, 1966), p. 14.

19. I Corinthians 11:3–12.

20. Augustine, *De Genesi ad Lit.*, 9.5.

21. Augustine, *Confessiones*, 13.32; *De Opere Monach.*, 40.

22. Augustine, *De Contin.*, I.23.

23. Precisely because women posed such a danger to men, a number of Christian thinkers advanced advice concerning the best means tu avoid women's temptations. Consider St. John Chrysostom's "Exhortation to Theodore After His Fall," which suggests that full comprehension of the nature of women can protect men against the loss of virtue:

> If you consider what is stored up inside those beautiful eyes, and that straight nose, and the mouth and the cheeks, you will affirm the well-shaped body to be nothing else than a whited sepulchre; the parts within are full of so much uncleanness. Moreover, when you see a rag with any of these things on it, such as phlegm or spittle, you cannot bear to touch it even with the tips of your fingers, nay you cannot even endure looking at it; and yet, you are in a flutter of excitement about the storehouses and depositories of these things?

Cited in Katherine M. Rogers, *The Troublesome Helpmate: A History of Misogyny in Literature*, pp. 16–17.

24. Thomas Aquinas, *Summa Theologica*, 3 vols., English Dominican Province. ed., (New York: n.p., 1947), I 92 I ad 1 and I 99 2 ad 1.

25. Ibid., I 92 I.

26. For a fascinating analysis of this discussion, see Kari Elizabeth Borresen, *Subordination et Equivalence: Nature et role de la femme d'apres Augustin et Thomas d'Aquin* (Oslo: Universitets-forlaget, 1968), p. 136.

27. Christian doctrine does allow individual women an alternative to subordination to a husband. Women can escape the natural subordination and inferiority to which they are ordained by their sex by choosing virginity and the pursuit of religious perfection while on earth. Within the patristic tradition, the choice of virginity is characterized as woman's assumption of "male" nature, of the "truly human form"—rational, strong, courageous, steadfast, loyal, and spiritual. For a discussion of this alternative, see Eleanor Commo McLaughlin, "Equality of Souls, Inequality of Sexes: Women in Medieval Theology," and Rosemary Radford Ruether, "Misogynism and Virginal Feminism in the Fathers of the Church," both in Rosemary Radford Ruether, ed., *Religion and Sexism* (New York: Simon and Schuster, 1974), pp. 213–266 and 150–183.

28. John Locke, *Second Treatise on Government* in *Two Treatises of Government* (New York: Hafner Press, 1974) pp. 122–128.

29. Ibid., p. 146.

30. Locke, *First Treatise on Government* in *Two Treatises of Government* (New York: Hafner Press, 1974), p. 38.

31. Locke, *Second Treatise on Government*, p. 122.

32. Ibid., p. 161.

33. *Genesis* iii, 26; cited by Locke in *The First Treatise*, p. 35.

34. Locke, *The First Treatise*, p. 37.

35. Locke, *The Second Treatise*, p. 150.

36. Jean Jacques Rousseau, *A Discourse on the Origin of Inequality* in *The Social Contract and the Discourses* (New York: E.P. Dutton, 1950), pp. 199–221.

37. Jean Jacques Rousseau, *Emile*, trans. Barbara Foxley (New York: E.P. Dutton, 1955), p. 332.

38. Ibid., p. 322.

39. Ibid.

40. Ibid., p. 328.

41. Ibid., p. 333.

42. Ibid., pp. 333–334.

43. Ibid., p. 333.

44. Immanuel Kant, "Of the Difference of the Sublime and the Beautiful in the Counterrelation of Both Sexes," in *Observations on the Feeling of the Beautiful and Sublime*, trans. John T. Goldthwait (Berkeley: University of California Press, 1965), pp. 76–77.

45. Ibid., pp. 78–79.

46. Arthur Schopenhauer, "On Women" in *The Pessimist's Handbook*, trans. T. Bailey Saunders (Lincoln: University of Nebraska Press, 1964), p. 205.

47. Ibid., pp. 201–202.

48. Ibid., pp. 202–203.

49. Ibid., p. 199.

50. Ibid., p. 215.

51. Nietzsche, *Beyond Good and Evil*, section 239 (emphasis in the original) in *Basic Writings* (New York: Modern Library, 1968).

52. Ibid., section 232.

53. Ibid., section 238.

54. Ibid., section 232.

55. Ibid.

56. Ibid., section 239.

57. Ibid., section 238 (emphasis in the original).

58. For an insightful analysis of Nietzsche's notion of untruth as the condition of human life, see Alexander Nehamas, *Nietzsche: Life As Literature* (Cambridge: Harvard University Press, 1985), pp. 42–73.

59. For an excellent analysis of sexism in Sartre's complicated ontological views, see Margery Collins and Christine Pierce, "Holes and Slime: Sexism in Sartre's Psychoanalysis," in Carol Gould and Marx Wartofsky, eds., *Women and Philosophy: Toward a Theory of Liberation* (New York: G. P. Putnam and Sons, 1976).

60. Jean-Paul Sartre, *Being and Nothingness*, trans. Hazel Barnes (New York: Washington Square Press, 1966), p. 666.

61. Sandra Harding defines gender symbolism as the attribution of dualistic gender metaphors to distinctions having nothing to do with sex differences. *The Science Question in Feminism* (Ithaca: Cornell University Press, 1986), p. 17.

62. Sartre, *Being and Nothingness*, pp. 776–777.

63. Ibid., p. 782.

64. Ibid. Adler's complex is an inferiority complex experienced by women.

65. Arlene Saxonhouse offers such a reading of Plato's construction of gender, noting that "In order to create a unified city, society must destroy the female as female, as a threat to the unity of the species. She is integrated into the polis not as herself but as a weaker man." *Women in the History of Political Thought* (New York: Praeger, 1985), pp. 46–47. For an interesting discussion of the logic of identity in relation to feminist discourse, see Iris Young, "The Ideal of Community and the Politics of Difference," *Social Theory and Practice* 12(1):1–26.

66. Derrida's most extensive treatment of the hymenal fable occurs in *Dissemination* (Chicago: University of Chicago Press, 1981). He also invokes this metaphor in *The Archaeology of the Frivolous* (Pittsburgh: Duquesne University Press, 1980) and in *Positions* (Chicago: University of Chicago Press, 1981).

67. Derrida's notion of *différance* is typically translated as differing/deferring to emphasize a refusal of fixity and an acceptance of ambiguity, a recognition that ultimately all texts are self-differing and as such undecidable.

68. Derrida's precise language is: "There is no such thing as the essence of woman because woman averts, she is averted of herself." *Spurs/Eperons* (Chicago: University of Chicago Press, 1979), p. 50. One need not embrace essentialism to question the locus of power in such a claim. If women have been denied access to

the educational, social, and political resources necessary to the cultivation of the reflective capacities associated with self-definition, does it make sense to character- ize women's silence in this respect as a tactic of averting the self?

69. Derrida, *Spurs*, p. 51.

70. Ibid., pp. 61–62.

71. Gayatri Spivak has questioned the image of woman appearing in Derrida's hymenal fable, suggesting that in appropriating woman's voice, Derrida produces a male female-impersonator. "Displacement and the Discourse on Woman," in Mark Krupnick, ed., *Displacement* (Bloomington: Indiana University Press, 1983), p. 190.

72. This phrase is borrowed from Drucilla Cornell and Adam Thurschwell, "Feminism, Negativity, Intersubjectivity," *Praxis International* 5(4): 484–504.

73. It is frequently suggested that "man" in the classic texts of Western philos- ophy is already "generic," encompassing both men and women. But even the most cursory reading of traditional theorists' views on women quickly dispels that erro- neous notion.

74. As examples of this strategy, one might consider Mary Deitz's appropriation of Aristotle's conception of politics in "Citizenship with a Feminist Face: The Prob- lem with Maternal Thinking," *Political Theory* 13(1):19–37 or Katherine Parson's use of Nietzsche in "Nietzsche and Moral Change," *Feminist Studies* 2(1974):57–74.

75. Genevieve Lloyd, *The Man of Reason: 'Male' and 'Female' in Western Philos- ophy* (Minneapolis: University of Minnesota Press, 1984), p. 104.

76. Christine DiStefano, "Dilemmas of Difference: Feminism, Modernity and Postmodernism," unpublished manuscript, p. 4.

77. Ibid.

78. For an excellent discussion of the potential uses of gender as an analytic category, see Joan W. Scott, "Gender: A Useful Category for Historical Analysis," *American Historical Review* 91(5):1053–1075.

79. Ibid., p. 1070. Consider, for example, Locke's reliance upon arguments con- cerning the power of mothers over their children to undermine Filmer's claims about the absolute power of patriarchs and, derivatively, of kings.

80. Machiavelli's advice—that "is better to be impetuous than cautious, for for- tune is a woman, and it is necessary, if you wish to master her, to conquer her by force" [*The Prince* (New York: Modern Library, 1950), p. 94]—is perhaps the most notorious but by no means the only instance of this phenomenon.

81. Scott in "Gender: A Useful Category for Historical Analysis," (p. 1072) suggests a variety of examples drawn from the experiences of the Jacobins, Stalin, Hitler, and, most recently, the Ayatollah Khomeni.

82. Lloyd, The Man of Reason, p. 104.

Chapter 2: Social Consequences of Gender Misconceptions

1. Due to limitations of space and expertise, this chapter will focus primarily on the United States. For studies of the consequences of gender bias in other cultures, see Eugene Lupri, ed., *The Changing Position of Women in Family and Society: A Cross National Comparison* (Leiden: E. J. Brill, 1983); The National Women's Conference Committee, *Report of the World Conference to Review and Appraise the Achievements of the United Nations Decade for Women: Equality, Development and Peace* (New York: United Nations, 1985); Michele Zimbalist Rosaldo and Louise Lamphere, eds., *Women, Culture and Society* (Stanford: Stanford University Press, 1974); and Rayner Reiter, ed., *Toward An Anthropology of Women* (New York: Monthly Review Press, 1975).

2. This chapter should not be taken as an exhaustive treatment of practices that advantage men. In choosing to focus upon perceptual bias, underrepresentation, underutilization, job segregation by sex, pay differentials, sexual harassment, rape, and domestic violence as examples of practices that privilege men, I do not mean to imply that these are the only contemporary practices manifesting sex bias. Feminists have investigated comparable bias in the sexual objectification of women in advertising and entertainment, in prostitution, pornography, and surrogacy contracts, as well as in specific social policy areas such as health care, housing, welfare, and criminal justice. Rather than attempting to present an exhaustive treatment of such practices, I have focused on a few illustrative examples in order to show that gender bias exists in multiple forms in contemporary life, ranging from subtle to blatant. My point in choosing this range of examples is to demonstrate that sex discrimination is a continuing problem and neither a social atavism nor a figment of the feminist imagination, as critics of feminism typically assert.

3. P. Goldberg, "Are Women Prejudiced Against Women," *Transaction* 5(1968):28–30; and G. Pheterson, S. Kiesler, and P. Goldberg, "Evaluation of the Performance of Women as a Function of their Sex," *Journal of Personality and Social Psychology* 19(1971):110–114.

4. K. Deaux and T. Emswiller, "Explanations of Successful Performance on Sex-Linked Tasks," *Journal of Personality and Social Psychology* 29(1974):80–85.

5. J. Taynor and K. Deaux, "Equity and Perceived Sex Differences: Role Behavior as Defined by the Task, the Mode and the Action," *Journal of Personality and Social Psychology* 32(1975):381–390.

6. B. Weiner, I. Frieze, A. Kukla, S. Reed, and R. Rosenbaum, *Perceiving the Causes of Success and Failure* (Morristown, N.J.: General Learning Press, 1971).

7. K. Deaux and T. Emswiller, "Explanations of Successful Performance on Sex-Linked Tasks," *Journal of Personality and Social Psychology* 29(1974):80–85; and

T. Cash, B. Gillen, and D. Burns, "Sexism and 'Beautyism' in Personnel Consultant Decision Making," *Journal of Applied Psychology* 62(1977):301–310.

8. S. Feldman-Summers and S. Kiesler, "Those Who Are Number Two Try Harder: The Effect of Sex on Attributions of Causality," *Journal of Personality and Social Psychology* 30(1974):846–855; C. Etaugh and B. Brown, "Perceiving the Causes of Success and Failure of Male and Female Performers," *Developmental Psychology* 11(1975):103; and J. Taynor and K. Deaux, "Equity and Perceived Sex Differences: Role Behavior as Defined by the Task, the Mode and the Action," *Journal of Personality and Social Psychology* 32(1975):381–390.

9. C. Etaugh and B. Brown, "Perceiving the Causes of Success and Failure of Male and Female Performers," *Developmental Psychology* 11(1975):103; T. Cash, B. Gillen, and D. Burns, "Sexism and 'Beautyism' in Personnel Consultant Decision Making," *Journal of Applied Psychology* 62(1977):301–310; and N. Feather and J. Simon, "Reactions to Male and Female Success and Failure in Sex-linked Occupations: Impressions of Personality, Causal Attribution and Perceived Likelihood of Difference Consequences," *Journal of Personality and Social Psychology* 31(1975):20–31.

10. B. Rosen and T. Jerdee, "Influence of Sex-Role Stereotypes on Personnel Decisions," *Journal of Applied Psychology* 59(1974):9–14; T. Shaw, "Differential Impact of Negative Stereotypes on Employee Selection," *Personnel Psychology* 25(1974):333–338; J. Haefner, "Race, Age, Sex and Competence as Factors in Employee Selection of the Disadvantaged," *Journal of Applied Psychology* 62(1977):199–202; and B. Gutek and D. Stevens, "Differential Responses of Males and Females to Work Situations Which Evoke Sex-role Stereotypes," *Journal of Vocational Behavior* 14(1979):23–32.

11. B. Rosen, T. Jerdee, and T. Prestwich, "Dual Career Mutual Adjustment: Potential Effects of Discriminatory Managerial Attitudes," *Journal of Marriage and the Family* 37(1975):565–572; and B. Gutek and D. Stevens, "Differential Responses of Males and Females to Work Situations Which Evoke Sex-role Stereotypes," *Journal of Vocational Behavior* 14(1979):23–32.

12. L. Fidell, "Empirical Verification of Sex Discrimination in Hiring Practices in Psychology," *American Psychologist* 25(1970):1094–1098.

13. R. Dipboye, R. Arvy, and D. Terpstra, "Sex and Physical Attractiveness of Raters and Applicants as Determinants of Resume Evaluations," *Journal of Applied Psychology* 62(1977):228–234; and J. Terborg and D. Illgen, "A Theoretical Approach to Sex Discrimination in Traditionally Masculine Occupations," *Organizational Behavior and Human Performance* 13(1975):352–376.

14. Council of Chief State School Officers and the National Association of State Boards of Education, "Facing the Future: Education and Equity for Females and Males," (December 1980) cited in the Testimony of Mary Hatwood Futrell,

President of the National Education Association, before the United States House of Representatives Committee on the Judiciary, Subcommittee on Civil and Constitutional Rights, 13 September 1983; pp. 6–9. See also Sharon Epperson, "Studies Link Subtle Sex Bias in Schools with Women's Behavior in the Workplace," *Wall Street Journal*, 16 September 1988, p. 19.

15. "The Less Credible Sex," *The Judges' Journal* 24(1):16.

16. William Eich, "Gender Bias in the Courtroom: Some Participants are More Equal than Others," Judicature 69(6):339–343; p. 339.

17. Jeffrey Schmalz, "New York Courts Cited On Sex Bias," *New York Times*, 20 April 1986, p. 1, 19.

18. V. Nieva and Barbara Gutek, "Sex Effects on Evaluation," *Academy of Management Review* 5(1980):267–276.

19. Several selection studies have documented that, when asked to assess identical male and female candidates for scholarships and overseas study programs, the male candidates were judged to be more intelligent and likeable than their women candidates. R. Lao, W. Upchurch, W. Corwin, and W. Grossnickle, "Biased Attitudes toward Females as Indicated by Ratings of Intelligence and Likeability," *Psychological Reports* 37(1975):1315–1320; and K. Deaux and J. Taynor, "Evaluation of Male and Female Ability: Bias Works Two Ways," *Psychological Reports* 31(1973):20–31.

20. Sara Rix, ed., *The American Woman 1988–89: A Status Report* (New York: W.W. Norton, 1988).

21. "The United Nations Decade for Women, 1976–1985: Employment in the United States," U.S. Department of Labor, Women's Bureau, July 1985, p. 125.

22. D. Franklin and J. Sweeney, "Women and Corporate Power," in E. Boneparth and E. Stoper, eds., *Women, Power and Policy: Toward the Year 2000*, 2nd. ed. (New York: Pergamon Press, 1988), p. 50.

23. Ibid.

24. It should be noted that in a series of cases involving Title VII of the Civil Rights Act of 1964, which deals with racial discrimination in hiring and promotions, the United States Supreme Court has ruled that statistical evidence showing underrepresentation of protected minorities is sufficient to establish a prima facie case of racial discrimination. *United States v. Iron Workers Local 86; United States v. Hayes International Corporation; United States v. United Brotherhood of Carpenters and Joiners.*

25. F. K. Barasch has demonstrated that although women have earned approximately 20 percent of the Ph.D.s in the natural sciences since the early 1970s, they are seldom hired as university faculty in these fields. Indeed, women constitute less

than 5 percent of university faculty in the natural sciences. Women Ph.D.s are far more likely to be employed as laboratory technicians. "H.E.W., The University and Women," *Dissent* (Summer 1973):332–339. Reprinted in Barry Gross, ed., *Reverse Discrimination* (New York: Prometheus Books, 1977).

26. *Hazelwood School District v. United States*, 433 U.S. 299 (1977). To say that underutilization establishes a *prima facie* case of discrimination is to say that it becomes the burden of the institution or individual accused of discrimination to prove to the Court that women are underutilized for reasons other than discrimination. It should be noted that on June 5, 1989, the Supreme Court issued a ruling that may have a profound effect upon future discrimination cases. In *Wards Cove Packing v. Atonio*, the Rehnquist Court shifted the burden of proof in discrimination cases. Rather than requiring those employers/companies accused of discrimination to prove that their job requirements and practices are bona fide, necessary, and not discriminatory as had been the case since 1971 *(Griggs v. Duke Power Company)*, the Court shifted the burden to employees filing complaints to prove that the challenged practices are in fact not necessary. This case specifically involved job requirements that have the effect of discriminating; it did not address discriminatory hiring/promotion practices per se. Thus, should the Court choose to interpret the decision narrowly, it may have no effect on future cases involving underrepresentation or underutilization. On the other hand, that the Court is willing to reverse well-established standards of proof in discrimination cases does not bode well for women and minorities who continue to suffer from ongoing discrimination.

27. W. Kahn and J. Grune, "Pay Equity: Beyond Equal Pay for Equal Work," in E. Boneparth, ed., *Women, Power and Policy* (New York: Pergamon, 1982), p. 76; and Francine Blau, "The Economic Status of Women in the Labor Market," Testimony before the United States House of Representatives Committee on the Judiciary, Subcommittee on Civil and Constitutional Rights, 14 September 1983, p. 5.

28. W. Kahn and J. Grune, "Pay Equity: Beyond Equal Pay for Equal Work," in E. Boneparth, ed., *Women, Power and Policy* (New York: Pergamon, 1982), p. 77; and Robert Pear, "Women Reduce Lag in Earnings But Disparities With Men Remain," *New York Times* 3 September 1987, pp. 1,7.

29. Francine Blau, "The Economic Status of Women in the Labor Market," Testimony before the United States House of Representatives Committee on the Judiciary, Subcommittee on Civil and Constitutional Rights, 14 September 1983, p. 5.

30. Ibid., p. 6.

31. *Statistical Abstract of the United States: 1986* (Washington, D.C.: Bureau of the Census, U.S. Department of Commerce, 1986), p. 402.

32. These Census Bureau projections were cited in the Testimony of the National Federation of Business and Professional Women's Clubs (BPW/USA) before the United States House of Representatives Committee on the Judiciary, Subcommittee on Civil and Constitututional Rights, 14 September 1983, p. 10.

33. For a review of this literature, see Francine Blau, "Discrimination Against Women: Theory and Evidence," in W. Darity, ed., *Labor Economics: Modern Views* (Boston: Kluwer-Nijhoff, 1984).

34. National Academy of Sciences, *Women, Wages and Work: Equal Pay for Work of Equal Value* (Washington, D.C., 1981); and Blau, "Discrimination Against Women: Theory and Evidence," in W. Darity, ed., *Labor Economics: Modern Views* (Boston: Kluwer-Nijhoff, 1984).

35. See, for example, F. A. Hayek, *Individualism and Economic Order* (Chicago: University of Chicago Press, 1948).

36. Hilda Scott, *Women Work Their Way to the Bottom: The Feminization of Poverty* (Boston: Pandora Press, 1984), p. 19.

37. Steven Erie, Martin Rein and Barbara Wiget, "Women and the Reagan Revolution: Thermidor for the Social Welfare Economy," in Irene Diamond, ed., *Families, Politics and Public Policy* (New York: Longman, 1983), pp.94–119.

38. *Money Income and Poverty Status of Families and Persons in the United States, 1980* (U.S. Bureau of the Census, Current Population Reports Series P-60, No. 127, August 1981), Table 21.

39. Diana Pearce and Harriette McAdoo, *Women and Children: Alone and In Poverty* (Washington D. C.: National Advisory Council on Economic Opportunity, 1981).

40. Ellen Boneparth, *Women, Power and Policy* (New York: Pergamon Press, 1982), p. 207.

41. Lenore Weitzman, "The Economic Consequences of Divorce: Social and Economic Consequences of Property, Alimony and Child Support Awards," *UCLA Law Review* 28:1181–1251.

42. Testimony of Federally Employed Women before the United States House of Representatives Committee on the Judiciary, Subcommittee on Civil and Constitutional Rights, 14 September 1983, p. DR-5; and Scott, *Women Work Their Way to the Bottom*, p. 19.

43. Ibid. Studies of judicial attitudes indicate that judges rely upon a number of detrimental gender stereotypes in fixing divorce settlements. Among the myths that influence inequitable divorce settlements are these:

> support payments are payments to the wife, not the children, and like alimony or maintenance, when received will only go to indulge an indolent lifestyle;

any woman who wants to can go out and get a job and support herself; housework and childrearing isn't work; and a woman will always be able to find
another man to take care of her.

From William Eich, "Gender Bias in the Courtroom: Some Participants are More
Equal than Others," *Judicature* 69(6):339–343; p. 342. See also Norma Wikler, "On
the Judicial Agenda for the 80s: Equal Treatment for Men and Women in the
Courts," *Judicature* 64(1980):202–207; and R. Segal, *Proposed Project on Judicial Attitudes Toward Women* (New York: NOW Legal Defense and Education Fund Report,
1978).

44. *Money Income and Poverty Status of Families and Persons in the United States,
1980* (U.S. Bureau of the Census, Current Population Reports Series P-60, No.
127, August 1981), Table 18. Only 5 percent of families with employed male heads
of household live below the poverty level.

45. Kentucky ranks 49th in the United States in terms of level of benefit for
AFDC (Aid to Families with Dependent Children) recipients. At the current time
in Kentucky, a mother with two children receives $196 per month or $2,353 per
year in welfare assistance.

46. Kathleen K. Shortridge, "Poverty is a Woman's Problem" in Jo Freeman,
ed., *Women: A Feminist Perspective* 3rd ed. (Palo Alto, Calif.: Mayfield Publishing
Co., 1984).

· 47. Dorothy Ridings, President of the League of Women Voters, Testimony before the United States House of Representatives Committee on the Judiciary, Subcommittee on Civil and Constitutional Rights, 14 September 1983, p. 9.

48. Federally Employed Women, Testimony before the United States House of
Representatives Committee on the Judiciary, Subcommittee on Civil and Constitutional Rights, 14 September 1983, p. 16.

49. For an analysis of this phenomenon, see M. E. Hawkesworth, "Workfare
and the Imposition of Discipline," *Social Theory and Practice* 11(2):163–181.

50. Diana Pearce and Harriette McAdoo, *Women and Children: Alone and In
Poverty* (Washington D. C.: National Advisory Council on Economic Opportunity,
1981).

51. Joseph Pereira, "Women Allege Sexist Atmosphere in Offices Constitutes
Harassment," *Wall Street Journal,* 10 February 1988, p. 21.

52. Catherine MacKinnon's *The Sexual Harassment of Working Women: A Case
of Sex Discrimination* (New Haven: Yale University Press, 1979) was particularly instrumental to this effort. MacKinnon argued that Title VII of the 1964 Civil Rights
Act and Title IX of the 1972 Educational Amendments could provide the statutory
basis for the prohibition of sexual harassment as an illegal form of sex discrimina-

tion. In 1980, the Equal Employment Opportunity Commission issued guidelines (29 CFR Chapter XIV, § 1604.11 [a-f]) calling for the establishment of appropriate sanctions for sexual harassment.

53. Pereira, "Women Allege Sexist Atmosphere in Offices Constitutes Harassment," p. 21.

54. Lin Farley, *Sexual Shakedown* (New York: Warner Books, 1980) and Billy Dziech and Linda Weiner, *The Leacherous Professor: Sexual Harassment on Campus* (Boston: Beacon Press, 1984).

55. R. Hall and B. Sandler, *The Classroom Climate: A Chilly One for Women?* (Washington, D.C.: American Association of Colleges, 1982); R. Hall and B. Sandler, *Out of the Classroom: A Chilly Campus Climate for Women?* (Washington, D.C.: American Association of Colleges, 1984); and R. Hall and B. Sandler, *The Campus Climate Revisited: Chilly for Women Faculty, Administrators and Graduate Students* (Washington, D.C.: American Association of Colleges, 1986).

56. Billy Dziech, Sexual Harassment Workshop, The University of Louisville, 14 November 1987.

57. This study was conducted by Professors Terry Denny and Karen Arnold of the University of Illinois and was reported in an article, "In Career Goals, Female Valedictorians Fall Behind," *The New York Times*, 8 November 1987, Education Supplement, p. 7.

58. Barbara Gutek, *Sex and the Workplace: The Impact of Sexual Behavior and Harassment on Women, Men and Organizations* (San Francisco: Jossey Bass, 1985); Walter Kiechel, "The High Cost of Sexual Harassment," *Fortune*, 14 September 1987, p. 147; N. Epstein, "When Professors Swap Grades for Sex," *The Washington Post*, 6 September 1981, section 6, p. 1; and Hall and Sandler, *The Campus Climate Revisited*, p. 10.

59. Diana Russell and Nancy Howell, "The Prevalence of Rape in the United States Revisited," *Signs* 8(1983):688.

60. Barry Burkhardt obtained these results in a survey of students at Auburn University in Alabama. His findings are summarized in "A Distrubing Look at Rape," *National On Campus Report*, 23 September 1983, p. 1. Comparable studies have been conducted at other universities. At Cornell University, 19 percent of the women students surveyed reported that they had been forced to have intercourse against their will, but only 2 percent said they had been raped; at another small college near Ithaca, 18 percent of the women noted that they had had intercourse against their will, but only 9 percent said they had been raped. These studies were reported in *The Boston Herald*, 22 September 1985, p. 6. and *Parade Magazine*, 22 September 1985, p. 10. See also, Beth Sherman, "The New Realities of Date Rape," *The New York Times*, 23 October 1985, pp. 17, 19.

61. Susan Estrich, *Real Rape* (Cambridge: Harvard University Press, 1987) p. 10.

62. "A Disturbing Look at Rape," *National On Campus Report*, p.1.

63. Seymour Feshbach and Neal Malamuth, "Sex and Aggression: Proving the Link," *Psychology Today* 12(6):111–117, 122.

64. "The Date Who Rapes," *Newsweek*, April 9, 1984, p. 91.

65. Associated Press, "Some Junior High Pupils Say Rape May Be Justified," *The Toronto Star*, 6 July 1988.

66. Feshbeck and Malamuth, "Sex and Aggression," p. 116.

67. Eich, "Gender Bias in the Courtroom," p. 341. The judge was recalled as a result of this episode.

68. Ibid., p. 342.

69. Rape Awareness Fact Sheet (Louisville, Ky: YWCA Rape Relief Center, 1988). See also Susan Griffin, "Rape: The All-American Crime," *Ramparts* (September 1971):26–35; Susan Brownmiller, *Against Our Will: Men, Women and Rape* (New York: Simon and Schuster, 1975); Andrea Dworkin, "The Rape Atrocity and the Boy Next Door," in A. Dworkin, ed. *Our Blood: Prophesies and Discourses on Sexual Politics* (New York: Harper and Row, 1976) pp. 22–49; Diana Russell, *The Politics of Rape: The Victim's Perspective* (New York: Stein and Day, 1975); Noreen Connell and Cassandra Wilson, *Rape: The First Sourcebook for Women by New York Radical Feminists* (New York: New American Library, 1974); and Judith Ehrhart and Bernice Sandler, *Campus Gang Rape: Party Games?* (Washington, D.C.: Association of American Colleges, 1985).

70. In 1975, the highest court of appeal in Britain ruled that if a man believes a woman is consenting to sex, he cannot be convicted of rape, no matter how unreasonable his belief may be. Director of Public Prosecutions v. Morgan 2 W.L.R. 923 (H.L.). For feminist analyses of Morgan, see Carol Pateman, "Women and Consent," *Political Theory* 8(2):149–168; and Estrich, *Real Rape*, pp. 92–104.

71. Data produced by the Bureau of Justice Statistics indicates that 42–58 percent of rapes are reported to police. Susan Estrich notes that although most stranger rapes are reported, the majority of acquaintance rapes are not reported to police. *Real Rape*, pp. 10–15, 110 n.7.

72. Although domestic violence encompasses abuse of children in the home as well as abuse of women, I will be focusing upon women in this discussion. It is important to note, however, that certain forms of child abuse are also "gendered:" in cases of incest as well as sexual child abuse, 92 percent of the victims are female and 97 percent of the assailants are male. The language in which these issues are discussed has been criticized for masking the gender specificity of the assaults. See,

for example, Teresa De Lauretis, "The Violence of Rhetoric: Considerations on Representation and Gender," *Semiotica* 54(1985):11–31.

73. Louis Harris and Associates, *Survey of Spousal Violence Against Women in Kentucky,* July 1979. The study was commissioned by the Kentucky Commission on Women and funded by the Law Enforcement Assistance Administration. Comparable results have been found in the studies of a number of states.

74. Sandra Wexler, "Battered Women and Public Policy," in Ellen Boneparth, ed., *Women, Power and Policy* (New York: Pergamon Press, 1982), p. 187. For detailed discussions of the problem of domestic violence, see Richard Gelles, *The Violent Home,* rev. ed. (Beverly Hills: Sage, 1987); Suzanne Steinmetz and Murray Stauss, eds., *Violence in the Family* (New York: Dodd Mead, 1974); Maria Roy, ed., *Battered Women: A Psychological Study of Domestic Violence* (New York: Van Nostrand Reinhold, 1977); Terry Davidson, *Conjugal Crime: Understanding and Changing the Battered Wife Pattern* (New York: Hawthorne, 1978); Murray Strauss, Richard Gelles, and Suzanne Steinmetz, *Behind Closed Doors: Violence in the American Family* (Garden City, N.Y.: Doubleday, 1980); Lenore Walker, *The Battered Woman Syndrome* (New York: Springer, 1984); and Elizabeth Stanko, *Intimate Intrusions: Women's Experience of Male Violence* (London: Routledge and Kegan Paul, 1985).

75. A number of books have traced the historical practice of wife abuse in order to demonstrate that in most cultures the practice has been condoned or approved rather than condemned. See for example, R. E. Dobash and R. P. Dobash, *Violence Against Wives: A Case Against Patriarchy* (New York: Free Press, 1979); M. May, "Violence in the Family: An Historical Perspective," in J. Martin, ed., *Violence in the Family* (Chichester: Wiley, 1978); J. Sutton, "Modern and Victorian Battered Women," in *Battered Women and Abused Children* (Occasional Paper No. 4, University of Bradford, 1979); and N. Tomes, "A Torrent of Abuse: Causes of Violence Among Working Class Men and Women in London, 1840–1975," *Journal of Social History* 11(3):329–345.

76. Jan Pahl, *Private Violence and Public Policy* (London: Routledge and Kegan Paul, 1985), pp. 13–19.

77. Sandra Wexler quotes Senator Humphrey's (R-N.H.) response to proposed legislation for the prevention and treatment of domestic violence: "The federal government should not fund missionaries who would wage war on the traditional family and on local values." Cited in "Battered Women and Public Policy," p. 193.

78. Jan Pahl, "Police Response to Battered Women," *Journal of Social Welfare Law* (November 1982):337–343; A. Faragher, "The Response of the Police to the Problem of Marital Violence," in R. Frankenberg et al., *Battered Women Project* (University of Keele, Report to the Department of Health and Social Security, 1980); and M. D. Pagelow, *Woman Battering: Victims and Their Experience* (Beverly Hills: Sage, 1981).

79. For arguments of this sort, see Thomas Sowell, "Affirmative Action Reconsidered," and Sidney Hook, "The Bias of Anti-Bias Regulations," both in Barry Gross, ed., *Reverse Discrimination* (Buffalo, N.Y.: Prometheus Books, 1977), pp. 113–131 and 88–96; and Richard Lester, *Anti-Bias Regulations of Universities: Faculty Problems and their Solutions* (New York: McGraw Hill, 1974).

80. Justice Scalia advanced both these claims in his dissent in *Johnson v. Transportation Agency*, Santa Clara County, California. The text of the decision can be found in *United States Law Week* 55 LW 4379 (March 24, 1987). Johnson involved a charge of reverse discrimination by a white male who lost in a competition for the job of dispatcher to a white woman. The Court ruled that no reverse discrimination had occured in this case. It also held that it was permissible for employers to consider the sex of a job applicant as one qualification among others in promotion cases pertaining to traditionally sex-segregated job classifications. Although all the materials submitted in the case certified that the woman was well qualified for the position, Justice Scalia insisted upon referring to the woman as "unqualified" in his dissent, and emphatically lamented the consequences of hirings such as hers for the productivity of the American workforce and for the future protection of individual rights.

81. Sowell, "Affirmative Action Reconsidered," p. 129.

82. For the most recent articulation of this claim, see Nicholas Davidson, "The Revalidation of the Masculine and Feminine," in *The Failure of Feminism* (Buffalo, N.Y.: Prometheus Books), pp. 257–276.

83. A range of possible explanations advanced by feminists will be considered in the next chapter.

Chapter 3: Explaining Oppression: Matriarchy, Patriarchy, and the Defeat of the Female Sex

1. Alison Jaggar defines oppression as "the imposition of unjust constraints on the freedom of individuals or groups." *Feminist Politics and Human Nature* (Totowa, N. J.: Rowman and Allanheld, 1983), p.6.

2. The classic works of feminist theory are devoted to a clear exposition of the nature of women's oppression. The brief account that follows will not attempt to reproduce these systematic accounts, but merely to chart their contours. For insightful treatments of women's oppression, see Mary Wollstonecraft, *A Vindication of the Rights of Women* (New York: W. W. Norton, 1975); Simone de Beauvoir, *The Second Sex* (New York: Bantam Books, 1961); Eva Figes, *Patriarchal Attitudes* (London: New York: Stein and Day, 1970); Germaine Greer, *The Female Eunuch* (New York: McGraw-Hill, 1970); Sheila Rowbothan, *Woman's Consciousness, Man's World* (Hammondsworth: Penguin, 1973); Adrienne Rich, *Of Woman Born* (New York: Norton, 1976); Michele Barrett, *Women's Oppression Today* (London: Verso, 1980).

3. Iris Young, "Is Male Gender Identity the Cause of Male Domination?" in Joyce Trebilcot, ed., *Mothering: Essays in Feminist Theory* (Totowa, N. J.: Rowman and Allanheld, 1984), pp. 129–146, on p. 136.

4. Ibid.

5. Linda Nicholson, *Gender and History: The Limits of Social Theory in the Age of the Family* (New York: Columbia University Press, 1986), p. 206.

6. Janet Richards, *The Skeptical Feminist* (Harmondsworth: Penguin Books, 1982), p. 174.

7. The Berkeley-Oakland Women's Union Statement, "Principles of Unity," in Zillah Eisenstein, ed., *Capitalist Patriarchy and the Case for Socialist Feminism* (New York: Monthly Review Press, 1979), p. 355.

8. Janet Sayers, *Sexual Contradictions: Psychology, Psychoanalysis, and Feminism* (London: Tavistock Publications, 1986), p. 118.

9. Zillah Eisenstein, "Developing a Theory of Capitalist Patriarchy," in Zillah Eisenstein, ed., *Capitalist Patriarchy and the Case for Socialist Feminism* (New York: Monthly Review Press, 1979), pp. 5–40.

10. Michele Rosaldo, "The Use and Abuse of Anthropology," *Signs* 5(3):389–417, p. 394.

11. For a detailed analysis of psychological oppression, see Sandra Lee Bartky, "On Psychological Oppression," in Sharon Bishop and Marjorie Weinzweig, eds., *Philosophy and Women* (Belmont, Calif.: Wadsworth Publishing, 1979), pp. 33–41.

12. Rosaldo, "The Use and Abuse of Anthropology," p. 394.

13. Judith Andre, "Power, Oppression and Gender," *Social Theory and Practice* 11(1):107–122, p. 114.

14. Gayle Rubin. "The Traffic in Women: Notes on the 'Political Economy' of Sex," in Rayner Reiter, ed., *Toward an Anthropology of Women* (New York: Monthly Review Press), p. 157.

15. Some feminists have suggested that language causes women's oppression. See, for example, Dale Spender, *Man Made Language* (London: Routledge and Kegan Paul, 1980). The nature of this causal claim suggests a process of socialization in which language plays a pivotal role: it is through a language that trivializes, excludes, and insults women that women come to know their subordinate place in the world. Since this chapter focuses on historical claims concerning the origin of women's oppression, questions concerning the role of language in the reproduction of relations of dominance and subordination will not be examined here. Chapter 4 considers issues pertaining to language and belief systems and their relation to women's oppression in detail. For an insightful critique of the view that language itself

causes women's oppression, see Deborah Cameron, *Feminism and Linguistic Theory* (London: MacMillan Press, 1985).

16. See, for example, Nicholas Davidson, *The Failure of Feminism* (Buffalo, New York: Prometheus Books, 1988). Davidson insists that feminism is an "anti-male movement" that has "spewed up a whole demonology of new forces to fight against" by positing men and maleness as the enemy (p. 43). Suggesting that the "feminist perspective" can be reduced to "the idea that men are collectively responsible for all the evils of history," Davidson caricatures the feminist method of analysis in the following terms: "find something that bothers you and explore how it's caused directly or indirectly by men and by tradition" (p. 45). Davidson argues that because feminists use this "method" to generate anti-male propaganda, feminism must be understood as a new form of fascism. "Feminism, like Nazism, makes it fashionable to hate an entire category of people on the basis of a biological characteristic . . . this time, sex." (p. 48) Much of Davidson's analysis turns on a systematic misreading of a few feminist texts. But some of his claims gain credence among those unfamiliar with feminism because he can quote passages that seem to support his view. My hope in this chapter is to help feminists see that certain kinds of arguments are clearly self-defeating.

17. Arguments emphasizing biological differences in hormones and chromosomes do not fit this visibility model.

18. Arguments that invoke women's biological difference have been used not only as an explanation of women's oppression, but also as the foundation for claims concerning women's "natural superiority." See, for example, Ashley Montagu, *The Natural Superiority of Women* (New York: Macmillan, 1953); and Elizabeth Gould Davis, *The First Sex* (New York: Putnam, 1971). For more recent discussions of an inherent women's difference, see the analysis of the "rhetoric of difference" in the next chapter.

19. Shulamith Firestone, *The Dialectic of Sex* (New York: William Morrow and Company, 1970).

20. Ibid., p. 232.

21. Ibid., p. 226.

22. Ibid., pp. 8–9.

23. Ibid., p. 232.

24. Both Susan Brownmiller's *Against Our Will* (New York: Bantam Books, 1976) and Andrea Dworkin's *Intercourse* (New York: Free Press, 1987) come to mind here, for both tend to imply that a man's possession of a penis is the key to women's oppression. Rape becomes paradigmatic in male-female relations, both as cause and as symbol of male domination. Thus, the question "Why do men rape?" is of paramount importance. Yet, in both these works, the explanation offered reduces to

"because they can." Men dominate women through rape because they have the anatomical ability to do so.

25. Mary O'Brien, *The Politics of Reproduction* (London: Routledge and Kegan Paul, 1981). O'Brien develops an account of male supremacy not "wholly material, wholly ideal, or wholly psychological, but has aspects of all of these"—an account that is consonant with the multi-dimensional nature of male supremacy itself. Because of the complexity of her account, it is not altogether accurate to categorize her explanation in terms of biological determinism. I have chosen to do so, however, both because her dialectical method suggests that the material has explanatory primacy over the ideational and the psychological, and because she does claim that "for men, physiology is fate" (p. 62).

26. Ibid., p. 51.

27. Ibid.

28. Ibid., p. 52.

29. Ibid., p. 62.

30. Ibid., p. 49.

31. Ibid., p. 33.

32. Ibid., pp. 60–61.

33. Ibid., p.114.

34. Ibid.

35. Ibid., p. 23; see also pp. 189–190.

36. Ibid., p. 115.

37. For anthropological evidence concerning culturally mediated experiences of the body including menstruation, pregnancy, couvade, menopause, see the essays in Rayna Reiter, ed., *Toward An Anthropology of Women* (New York: Monthly Review Press, 1975); and Michele Zimbalist Rosaldo and Louise Lamphere, eds., *Women, Culture and Society* (Stanford: Stanford University Press, 1974).

38. Firestone, *The Dialectic of Sex*, p. 9.

39. For an exhaustive catalogue of such diversity, see Bettyann Kevles, *Females of the Species: Sex and Survival in the Animal Kingdom* (Cambridge: Harvard University Press, 1986).

40. Recognizing this problem, John Stuart Mill noted: "What women by nature cannot do, it is quite superfluous to forbid them from doing. . . . If women have a greater natural inclination for some things than for others, there is no need of laws

or social inculcation to make the majority of them do the former in preference to the latter." *Subjection of Women* (Cambridge: M.I.T. Press, 1970), pp. 27–28.

41. For an excellent discussion of this method and its problems, see Joan Smith, "Feminist Analysis of Gender: A Mystique," in Lowe and Hubbard, Woman's Nature, pp. 89–109.

42. Richards, *The Skeptical Feminist*, p. 82.

43. For arguments that neither childbearing nor childrearing rendered women dependent upon men in hunting and gathering societies, see Lila Leibowitz, "Origins of the Sexual Division of Labor," in Lowe and Hubbard, *Woman's Nature*, pp. 123–147.

44. In O'Brien's case, it is the female body that is depicted as naturally superior. Indeed, it is male inferiority that creates the need to compensate in turn producing male dominance. Such compensatory arguments will be discussed later in this chapter in the analysis of psychological explanations of women's oppression. What is important to note at this point is that O'Brien also posits a natural sexual hierarchy, not just sexual difference.

45. Michele Wittig has noted that the very determination to conceive of women as a "natural group" defined by their capacity to give birth "is a sophisticated, mythic construction, an imaginary formation" that reinterprets physical features through a network of social relationships. "One is Not Born a Woman," in Alison Jaggar and Paula Rothenberg, eds., *Feminist Frameworks* (New York: McGraw-Hill, 1984).

46. I have borrowed this phase from Joseph Margolis, "Robust Relativism," in Joseph Margolis, ed., *Philosophy Looks at the Arts*, 3rd ed. (Philadelphia: Temple University Press, 1987), p. 495.

47. Mary Wollstonecraft, *A Vindication of the Rights of Woman* (New York: W. W. Norton, 1975), p. 193.

48. Ibid., p. 26.

49. Ibid., p. 37.

50. Ibid., p. 38.

51. Harriet Taylor Mill, "The Enfranchisement of Women," *Westminster Review* (1851); reprinted in Alice Rossi, ed., *Essays on Sex Equality* (Chicago: University of Chicago Press, 1970), p. 99.

52. John Stuart Mill, *The Subjection of Women* (Cambridge: M.I.T. Press, 1970), pp. 6–7. This essay was originally published in 1869.

53. Harriet Taylor Mill, "The Enfranchisement of Women," p. 99. Compare John Stuart Mill, *The Subjection of Women*, p. 7.

54. Harriet Taylor Mill, "The Enfranchisement of Women," p. 99.

55. John Stuart Mill, The Subjection of Women, p. 21, cf. p. 8.

56. Harriet Taylor Mill, "The Enfranchisement of Women," p. 108.

57. Lerner, The Creation of Patriarchy, p.8; Charlotte Bunch, "Lesbians in Revolt," in Jaggar and Rothenberg, Feminist Frameworks, pp. 144–148; Janet Richards, The Skeptical Feminist, pp. 175–178; Susan Rae Peterson, "Coercion and Rape: The State as a Male Protection Racket" in Mary Vetterling Braggin, Frederick Elliston, and Jane English, eds., Feminism and Philosophy (Totowa, N.J.: Littlefield and Adams, 1977), pp. 330–371.

58. Richards, The Skeptical Feminist, p. 176.

59. This point is made by J. J. Rousseau in A Discourse on the Origin of Inequality (New York: E. P. Dutton, 1950), p. 232.

60. Charlotte Bunch, "Lesbians in Revolt," in Jaggar and Rothenberg, Feminist Frameworks, p. 145. See also Leibowitz, "Origins of the Sexual Divsion of Labor," and Kathleen Gough, "The Origin of the Family" Journal of Marriage and the Family 33:760–771 (1971). Lerner suggests that the critical technological innovations were related to militarism, which emerged much later than hunting. The Creation of Patriarchy, pp. 76–100.

61. Lerner, The Creation of Patriarchy, p. 87.

62. Susan Griffin, "Rape: The All-American Crime," Ramparts (September, 1971):26–35.

63. Susan Rae Peterson, "Rape and Coercion: The State as a Male Protection Racket," in Vetterling-Braggin, ed., Feminism and Philosophy (Totowa, N.J.: Littlefield and Adams, 1977), pp. 333–346. See also Dominique Poggi, "Une apologie des rapports de domination," in Elaine Marks and Isabelle de Courtivron, eds., New French Feminisms (New York: Schocken Books, 1981), pp. 76–78.

64. Lorenne Clark and Lynda Lange, The Sexism of Social and Political Theory: Women and Reproduction from Plato to Nietzsche (Toronto: University of Toronto Press, 1979), p. xii.

65. Although the degree of difference varies with muscle group, when strength is compared for people of equal weight, women are about three-quarters as strong as men of the same weight; when weight is not controlled for, women are about two-thirds as strong as men. Marian Lowe, "The Dialectic of Biology and Culture," in Lowe and Hubbard, Woman's Nature, p. 43; Robert Malina, "Quantification of Fat, Muscle and Bone in Man," Clinical Orthopaedics 65(1969):9–38; and Donald K. Mathews and Edward L. Fox, The Physiological Basis of Physical Education and Athletics, 2nd ed. (Philadelphia: W. B. Saunders, Co., 1976).

66. One need only read the details of the Athenian assault against the Melians recounted by Thucydides to comprehend exactly how old this tradition is. *The Peloponnesian War* (New York: Penguin Books, 1982), pp. 400–408.

67. This phrase is borrowed from Friedrich Engels, *The Origin of the Family, Private Property and the State*, ed., Eleanor Leacock (New York: International Publishers, 1972), pp. 120–121. Gerda Lerner has suggested that feminists should avoid the language of oppression, precisely because it fosters an image of power struggles resulting in male dominance. *The Creation of Patriarchy*, pp. 233–234.

68. Thucydides, *The Peloponnesian War*, p. 402.

69. Consider for example Rousseau's suggestion that the plight of the noble savage might require markedly different excellences than those recognized in eighteenth century France: "Where there is no love, of what advantage is beauty? Of what use wit to those who do not converse, or cunning to those who have no business with others?" *A Discourse on the Origin of Inequality* (New York: E. P. Dutton, 1950), p. 232.

70. The most systematic critiques are offered by Michele Barrett, *Women's Oppression Today* (London: Verso, 1980); Zillah Eisenstein, *Capitalist Patriarchy and the Case for Socialist Feminism* (New York: Monthly Review Press, 1979); Juliet Mitchell, *Women's Estate* (New York: Vintage Books. 1973); Alison Jaggar, *Feminist Politics and Human Nature* (Totowa, N.J.: Rowman and Allanheld, 1983); Christine Delphy, *Close To Home: A Materialist Analysis of Women's Oppression* (Amherst, Ma.: University of Massachusetts Press, 1984); Collette Guillamin, "The Practice of Power and Belief in Nature, Part I: the Appropriation of Women," *Feminist Issues* 1(1981):3–28 and "The Practice of Power and Belief in Nature, Part II: the Naturalist Discourse," *Feminist Issues* 1(1981):87–109.

71. As a methodology, historical materialism requires detailed investigation of the modes and relations of production in specific historical periods. Despite this clear mandate for historical investigation, some feminists have merely reproduced accounts of women's subordination advanced by Engels and Levi-Strauss, rather than engage in their own analyses of women's productive and reproductive roles in different societies. The following analysis emphasizes the works of Engels and Levi-Strauss precisely because of their continuing influence.

72. Engels, *The Origin of the Family, Private Property and the State*, p. 120.

73. Ibid., p. 121.

74. For insightful criticisms of Engels, see Paula Webster, "Matriarchy: A Vision of Power," and Gayle Rubin, "The Traffic In Women," in Rayna Reiter, ed., *Toward An Anthropology of Women* (New York: Monthly Review Press), pp. 141–156 and pp. 157–210; Marie Louise Janssen-Jurreit, *Sexism: The Male Monopoly on History and Thought* (London: Pluto Press, 1982); Eisenstein, *Capitalist Patriarchy and the Case for Socialist Feminism*; Lerner, *The Creation of Patriarchy*.

75. Webster, "Matriarchy: A Vision of Power," p. 143.

76. Lerner, *The Creation of Patriarchy,* p. 29.

77. Ibid., p. 30.

78. This account is developed by Marx and Engels jointly in *The Communist Manifesto,* by Marx in *The German Ideology,* and by Engels in *The Origin of Private Property, Family and State.*

79. The influence of Levi-Strauss can be seen in the works of Juliet Mitchell, *Women's Estate* and *Psychoanalysis and Feminism* (New York: Vintage Books, 1974); Gayle Rubin, "The Traffic in Women"; Batya Weinbaum, *The Curious Courtship of Women's Liberation and Socialism* (Boston: South End Press, 1979); Eisenstein, *Capitalist Patriarchy;* Lerner, *The Creation of Patriarchy;* as well as French Feminists, Delphy, *Close to Home;* Guillamin, "The Practice of Power;" and Luce Irigaray, *Speculum of the Other Woman,* trans. Gillian Gill (Ithaca: Cornell University Press, 1985) and *This Sex Which Is Not One,* trans. Catherine Porter (Ithaca: Cornell University Press, 1985).

80. Claude Levi-Strauss, "The Family," in H. Shapiro, ed., *Man, Culture and Society* (London: Oxford University Press, 1971).

81. Ibid., p. 48.

82. Rubin, "The Traffic in Women," p. 178.

83. Claude Levi-Strauss, *The Elementary Structures of Kinship* (Boston: Beacon Press, 1969).

84. Ibid., p. 481.

85. Ibid., p. 115.

86. Mitchell, *Psycholanalysis and Feminism,* p. 372.

87. Nicholson, *Gender and History,* pp. 100–101.

88. Gayle Rubin, "The Traffic in Women," p. 176.

89. Ibid.

90. Ibid., pp. 176–177.

91. For a lucid analysis of this phenomenon, see R. C. Tucker, "The Cunning of Reason in Hegel and Marx," *Review of Politics* 18(3):269–295; and Jose Sorzano, "David Easton and The Invisible Hand," *American Political Science Review* 69:91–106.

92. John Stuart Mill, *The Subjection of Women,* p. 80.

93. Virgina Woolf, *A Room of One's Own* (New York: Harcourt, Brace and World, 1957), p. 35.

94. Azizah Al-Hibri, "Reproduction, Mothering and The Origins of Patriarchy," in Joyce Trebilcot, ed., *Mothering: Essays in Feminist Theory* (Totowa, N.J.: Rowman and Allanheld, 1984), pp. 81–93. As a methodological point, it should be noted that it is thoroughly problematic to generalize about the experiences of all men on the basis of the contentious claims of three theorists.

95. Ibid., p. 84.

96. Ibid., pp. 84–85.

97. Ibid., p. 87.

98. Ibid.

99. Eva Feder Kittay, "Womb Envy: An Explanatory Concept," in Joyce Trebilcot, ed., *Mothering: Essays in Feminist Theory* (Totowa, N.J.: Rowman and Allanheld, 1984) pp. 94–128.

100. Ibid., p. 103.

101. Ibid., p. 97.

102. Ibid., p. 95.

103. The accounts by Nancy Chodorow, *The Reproduction of Mothering: Psychoanalysis and the Sociology of Gender* (Berkeley: University of California Press, 1978) and Dorothy Dinnerstein, *The Mermaid and the Minotaur* (New York: Harper and Row, 1983) have been enormously influential. It would take a small book to review the literature that relies upon the explanatory framework they introduce. Their psychological claims have been adopted by such notable feminist theorists as Nancy Hartsock, Sandra Harding, Jane Flax, Jean Elshtain, Evelyn Fox-Keller, and Gerda Lerner. Perhaps an even stronger indicator of their influence is how seldom these views have been criticized. For the few extant critiques of these views, see Judith Lorber, Rose Laub Coser, Alice S. Rossi, and Nancy Chodorow, "On the Reproduction of Mothering: A Methodological Debate," *Signs* 6(3):482–514 (1981); Iris Young, "Is Male Gender Identity the Cause of Male Domination," in Joyce Trebilcot, ed., *Mothering: Essays in Feminist Theory*, pp. 130–146; Roger Gottlieb, "Mothering and the Reproduction of Power: Chodorow, Dinnerstein and Social Theory," *Socialist Review* 77(1984):93–119; Nancy Chodorow, Dorothy Dinnerstein and Roger Gottleib, "Mothering and the Reproduction of Power: An Exchange," *Socialist Review* 78(1984): 121–130; and Janet Sayers, *Sexual Contradictions: Psychology, Psychoanalysis and Feminism* (London: Tavistock, 1986).

104. It is not altogether clear that Chodorow and Dinnerstein meant their views to be taken as an historical account of the origin of women's oppression. At several points, both theorists have suggested they intended only to offer an account of how

gender relations are reproduced in contemporary society. I am fully willing to grant that this limited objective was their primary intent. I believe that it is important to consider these psychoanalytic accounts within the general rubric of explanations of women's oppression, however, both because the quotes below support the larger claim and because other feminists tend to cite Chodorow and Dinnerstein in support of genetic explanations of women's oppression. Consider, for example, Gerda Lerner's appropriation of Chodorow's views. Although she prefaces her claim with caveats about projecting contemporary views onto the past, she nonetheless claims that within primitive societies "The ego formation of the individual male, which must have taken place within a context of fear, awe, and possibly dread of the female, must have led men to create social institutions to bolster their egos, strengthen their self-confidence, and validate their sense of self worth." *Creation of Patriarchy,* p. 45.

105. Chodorow, *The Reproduction of Mothering,* p. 169.

106. Ibid., p. 181–185.

107. Chodorow, "On the Reproduction of Mothering: A Methodological Debate," pp. 502–503.

108. Chodorow, *The Reproduction of Mothering,* p. 181.

109. Dinnerstein, *The Mermaid and the Minotaur,* p. 28.

110. Ibid., pp. 36–37.

111. Pauline Bart, "Review of Chodorow's *Reproduction of Mothering,*" in Trebilcot, ed., *Mothering,* p. 151.

112. Iris Young, "Is Male Gender Identity the Cause of Male Domination," in Joyce Trebilcot, ed., *Mothering,* p. 138.

113. Jaggar and Rothenberg, *Feminist Frameworks,* p. 82.

114. David Kirp, Mark Yudof and Marlene Franks, *Gender Justice* (Chicago: University of Chicago Press, 1986), p. 52.

115. For an insightful introduction to the philosophy of history, see Frank Manuel, *Shapes of Philosophical History* (Stanford: Stanford University Press, 1965).

116. Webster, "Matriarchy: A Vision of Power," p. 143.

117. Janssen-Jurreit, *Sexism,* pp. 51–59.

118. Ibid.

119. Cited by Tania Modleski, "Feminism and the Power of Interpretation: Some Critical Readings," in Teresa de Lauretis, ed., *Feminist Studies/Critical Studies*

(Bloomington: Indiana University Press, 1986), pp. 132–133. Modleski traces this Freudian vindication of the patriarchal principle in recent works of literary theory.

120. Lerner, *The Creation of Patriarchy,* p. 35.

121. Webster, "Matriarchy: A Vision of Power," p. 155.

Chapter 4: Feminist Rhetoric: Models of Politicization

1. An earlier version of this chapter appeared as "Feminist Rhetoric: Discourses on the Male Monopoly of Thought," *Political Theory* 16(3):444–467.

2. For a helpful introduction to the range of differences among contemporary feminists, see Alison Jaggar and Paula Rothenberg, *Feminist Frameworks* (New York: McGraw Hill, 1984). For more critical treatments of these diverse approaches, see Jean Elshtain, *Public Man, Private Woman* (Princeton: Princeton University Press, 1981) and Alison Jaggar, *Feminist Politics and Human Nature* (Totowa, N.J.: Rowman and Allanheld, 1983).

3. Rhetoric is traditionally defined as the art of persuasion, an art that consists in identifying the particular arguments necessary to convince a specific audience. In recent analyses, the development of suitably persuasive arguments has been linked to the production of a world in language—a production that requires the reinvention of the past in order to promote a determinate future. In this chapter, I shall be drawing upon both conceptions of rhetoric.

4. In order to identify various feminist rhetorics, I have focused upon stylistic and substantive similarities in the works of a large number of feminist writers. This necessarily results in a failure to do justice to the subtlety and sophistication of individual author's views. Because rhetorical strategies lack the drive toward systematicity and the commitment to consistency characteristic of theory, it is frequently the case that multiple rhetorical strategies coexist within the same text. And it is precisely for this reason that it is possible to identify common rhetorical strategies across texts regardless of the distinctions between liberal, radical, socialist, and psychoanalytic approaches to feminism. In developing descriptions of the rhetoric of oppression, the rhetoric of difference, the rhetoric of reason, and the rhetoric of vision, I have chosen bold examples in order to construct something of an "ideal type" to facilitate explication and analysis, but it is important to stress that in more subtle guises, these rhetorical strategies surface in a great deal of feminist analysis. Except in the case of direct quotations, the citations included in the following notes are intended to be representative rather than exhaustive.

5. Ti Grace Atkinson, "Radical Feminism and Love," unpublished manuscript, (1970); Mary Daly, *Gyn/Ecology: The Metaethics of Radical Feminism* (Boston, Beacon Press, 1978).

6. Shulamith Firestone, *The Dialectic of Sex* (New York: William Morrow, 1970); Kathleen Barry, *Female Sexual Slavery* (Englewood Cliffs, N.J.: Prentice Hall,

1979); Catherine MacKinnon, "Feminism, Marxism, Method and the State: An Agenda for Theory," *Signs* 7(3):515–544.

7. Mary Wollstonecraft, *Vindication of the Rights of Woman*, ed., Charles Hagelman (New York: W.W. Norton, 1967); John Stuart Mill, *The Subjection of Women* (Cambridge: M.I.T. Press, 1970).

8. Sheila Ruth, "Methodocracy, Misogyny and Bad Faith: The Response of Philosophy," *Men's Studies Modified: The Impact of Feminism on the Academic Disciplines*, ed., Dale Spender (Oxford: Pergamon, 1981), pp. 43–54.

9. Mary Daly, *Beyond God the Father* (Boston: Beacon Press, 1973), p. 9.

10. Gloria Joseph and Jill Lewis, *Common Differences: Conflicts in Black and White Feminist Perspectives* (New York: Kitchen Table/Women of Color Press, 1985).

11. Barry, *Female Sexual Slavery*; Daly, *Gyn/Ecology*; Susan Brownmiller, *Against Our Will: Men, Women and Rape* (New York: Bantam, 1976); Andrea Dworkin, *Women Hating* (New York: Dutton, 1974); Susan Griffin, *Woman and Nature: The Roaring Inside Her* (New York: Harper Colophon, 1980); Adrienne Rich, *Of Woman Born* (New York: Norton, 1976).

12. The phrase is borrowed from a passage in Nietzsche: "The spell which fights on our behalf, the eye of Venus that charms and blinds even our opponents, is the magic of the extreme, the seduction that everything extreme exercises." *The Will to Power*, trans., Walter Kaufman and R. J. Hollingdale (New York: Vintage Press, 1968), p. 749. For an insightful discussion of the role of hyperbole in Nietzsche's work, see Alexander Nehamas, *Nietzsche: Life As Literature* (Cambridge: Harvard University Press, 1985), pp. 13–41.

13. Andrea Dworkin has suggested that conservative women understand the world in terms strikingly similar to those deployed in the rhetoric of oppression but the starkness of the options provokes in them a collaborationist rather than a revolutionary response. Although I believe her argument assumes far too great a level of clairvoyance on the part of traditional women, her interpretation does at least recognize that the same image may produce a variety of responses. See her *Right-Wing Women* (New York: Perigree Books/Putnam, 1983).

14. Jean Elshtain, *Public Man, Private Woman* (Princeton: Princeton University Press, 1981).

15. Discussions of "difference" have surfaced in two disparate contexts within feminist analysis. The first usage long established in feminist circles emphasizes putative differences between men and women and provides a positive valuation for those characteristics deemed to be uniquely feminine/female/womanly. This is the usage I am calling the "rhetoric of difference." A second, far more sophisticated conception of "difference" (perhaps more accurately captured by the Derridean term *différance* that can be translated both as "difference" and "deferral") has been ad-

vanced recently by a number of feminist scholars working within the postmodern tradition. Informed by the theory of deconstruction, this approach emphasizes that binary oppositions, such as those manifested in the rigid separation of genders, represent ideological obfuscations that distort the multiplicity of differences characteristic of concrete individuals. The sensitivity to the ideological force of language, the insistence upon recognition of multiplicities and play of differences within each gendered subject as a subversive strategy, and the conscious refusal to countenance the reification of genders into one dichotomous opposition links this approach to the rhetorical strategy I have called the "rhetoric of vision." For examples of this view see Drucilla Cornell and Adam Thurschwell, "Feminism, Negativity, Inter-subjectivity," *Praxis International* 5(1986):484–504; Iris Young, "The Ideal of Community and the Politics of Difference," *Social Theory and Practice* 12 (1986):1–26; Jane Flax, "Gender as a Problem: In and For Feminist Theory," *American Studies/Amerika Studien* 31(1986):193–213; Joan Scott, "Gender: A Useful Category of Historical Analysis," *American Historical Review* 91(1986):1053–1075. The overlap in terminology is unfortunate not only for those of us who might wish to design systems of classification in which categories are mutually exclusive but also for those who deploy the language of "difference," for the disparate meanings are often conflated. Too often the postmodern conception is masked as it is uncritically appropriated by those who would revalue the "feminine," a problem discussed below.

16. For a discussion of these early feminist movements see Ellen DuBois, *Feminism and Suffrage: The Emergence of an Independent Women's Movement in America, 1848–1869* (Ithaca: Cornell University Press, 1978); Theresa McBride, *The Domestic Revolution, 1820–1920* (London: Croom Helm, 1976); David Morgan, *Suffragists and Liberals: The Politics of Women's Suffrage in England* (Totowa, N.J.: Rowman and Littlefield, 1975); Andrew Rosen, *Rise Up Women: The Militant Campaign of the Women's Social and Political Union* (London: Routledge and Kegan Paul, 1974).

17. The literature concerning the "gender gap" has grown extensively in the past few years. For a helpful guide to this literature, see Barbara Nelson, *American Women and Politics: A Bibliography and Guide to the Sources* (New York: Garland, 1983). Discussions that link women's difference to arguments concerning a unique women's perspective or standpoint can be found in Nancy Hartsock, *Money, Sex and Power: Toward a Feminist Historical Materialism* (Boston: Northeastern University Press), Alison Jaggar, *Feminist Politics and Human Nature* (Totowa, N.J.:Rowman and Allanheld, 1983), and in Mary O'Brien, *The Politics of Reproduction* (Boston: Routledge and Kegan Paul, 1983). The implications of a unique women's perspective for issues such as affirmative action are treated in Lorraine Code, "Is the Sex of the Knower Epistemologically Significant?" *Metaphilosophy* 12(1981):267–276; Marsha Schermer, "Comments on Attig's 'Why Are You, A Man, Teaching This Course on Philosophy and Feminism' " *Metaphilosophy* 11(1980):178–181; Alan Soble, "Feminist Epistemology and Women Scientists," *Metaphilosophy* 14(1983):291–307; Evelyn Fox Keller, *Reflections on Gender and Science* (New Ha-

ven: Yale University Press, 1984); Sandra Harding, *The Science Question in Feminism* (Ithaca: Cornell University Press, 1986). For a general overview of issues arising from discussions of women and knowledge, see M. E. Hawkesworth, "Feminist Epistemology: A Survey of the Field," *Women and Politics* 7(3):115–127. These issues are also taken up in the next chapter.

18. Nancy Chodorow, *The Reproduction of Mothering* (Berkeley: University of California Press, 1978); Jean Elshtain, "Against Androgyny," *Telos* 47(1981):13–20; Carol Gilligan, *In a Different Voice* (Cambridge: Harvard University Press 1982); Charlotte Perkins Gilman, *Herland* (New York: Pantheon, 1979); Marilyn French, *Beyond Power: On Women, Men and Morals* (New York: Summitt, 1985); Sara Ruddick, "Maternal Thinking," *Feminist Studies* 6(1980):342–367; Sara Ruddick, "Pacifying the Forces: Drafting Women in the Interests of Peace," *Signs* 8(1983): 171–189; Virginia Woolf, *Three Guineas* (New York: Harcourt, Brace and World, 1938).

19. Ruddick, "Maternal Thinking."

20. Gilligan, *In a Different Voice.*

21. Jean Elshtain, "Feminists Against the Family," *The Nation* (17 November 1979:481).

22. Indeed, suspicion of notions of equality has led many French theorists to explicitly repudiate the label "feminist" as inevitably bourgeois and assimilationist. For a discussion of this position, see Dorothy Kaufman-McCall, "Politics of Difference: The Women's Movement in France from May 1968 to Mitterand," *Signs* 9(1983):282–293.

23. It is important to note that the postmodern deconstructions typical of French theorists such as Cixous, Fouqué, Irigaray, and Kristeva do not always blend well with the presuppositions of the Anglo-American rhetoric of difference. It is quite likely that many of these authors would be quite dissatisfied with the appropriation of their ideas by Anglo-American feminists. For a discussion of these French theorists in relation to American feminism, see Patrice McDermott, *Differing/Deferring Politics: Contemporary French Feminist Theories* (New York: SUNY Press, forthcoming).

24. Luce Irigaray, *Speculum of the Other Woman*, trans., Gillian Gill (Ithaca: Cornell University Press, 1985) and *This Sex Which Is Not One*, trans. Catherine Porter (Ithaca: Cornell University Press, 1985).

25. Hélène Cixous, *La Jeune Née*, in collaboration with Catherine Clément (Paris: UGE, 10/18:1975); "Le Rire de la Méduse," *L'Arc* 61(1975):39–54; and *La Venue à l'écriture*, in collaboration with Annie Leclerc and Madeleine Gagnon (Paris: UGE 10/18:1977).

26. Irigaray, *This Sex Which Is Not One*, p. 76.

27. Cora Kaplan, "Pandora's Box: Subjectivity, Class and Sexuality in Socialist Feminist Criticism," *Making a Difference*, eds., Gayle Greene and Coppelia Kahn (New York: Methuen, 1985), p. 148.

28. It might be objected that although the charge of essentialism is warranted in the case of the Anglo-American rhetoric of difference, it is singularly inappropriate in the cases of Cixous and Irigaray, who are consciously deploying deconstructive techniques. There is certainly some merit in this objection. Yet, it is important to consider the possibility that prescriptions to "write the body" or to draw one's political and epistemological analogies from "women's sexuality" do themselves slip too easily into essentialist traps. For arguments that Cixous and Irigaray do indeed fall into essentialist metaphysics, see Toril Moi, "Hélène Cixous: An Imaginary Utopia" and "Patriarchal Reflections: Luce Irigaray's Looking Glass" in *Sexual/Textual Politics* (London: Methuen, 1985).

29. Michel Foucault, *The History of Sexuality*, vol. 1 (New York: Vintage Books, 1980).

30. The notion of treating women as a group for political purposes while simultaneously avoiding any metaphysical commitments has been discussed by Toril Moi, *Sexual/Textual Politics* and by Donna Haraway, "A Manifesto for Cyborgs: Science, Technology and Socialist Feminism in the 1980s," *Socialist Review* 80(1985):65–107.

31. Christine de Pizan's status as a feminist is not altogether unproblematic. For alternative views on this topic, see Diane Bornstein, "Ideals for Women in the Works of Christine de Pizan," Michigan Consortium for Medieval Studies, 1981; Sheila Delaney, "The Conservatism of Christine de Pizan," (Paper presented at the Modern Languages Association Annual Meeting, 1983); Joan Kelly, "Early Feminist Theory and the Querelles des Femmes, 1400–1879," *Signs* 8(1982):4–28; Ann McMillan, "The Angel in the Text: Christine de Pizan and Virginia Woolf," (Paper presented at the Modern Languages Association Annual Meeting, 1983); and Charity Willard, "A Fifteenth Century View of Women's Role in Medieval Society: Christine de Pizan's *Livre des Trois Virtus*," in *The Role of Women in the Middle Ages*, ed., Rosemarie Thee Morewedge (New York: SUNY Press, 1975).

32. Christine de Pizan, *The Book of the City of the Ladies*, trans. Earl Jeffrey Richards (New York: Persea, 1982), pp. 3–4.

33. Janet Richards, *The Skeptical Feminist* (London: Penguin, 1982), p. 40.

34. Mill, *The Subjection of Women*, p. 3.

35. Wollstonecraft, *A Vindication of the Rights of Woman*; Mill, *The Subjection of Women*; Gilman, *Herland*; Eva Figes, *Patriarchal Attitudes* (New York: Stein and Day, 1970); Michele Barrett, *Women's Oppression Today* (London: Verso, 1980); Richards, *The Skeptical Feminist*.

36. Dale Spender, *Men's Studies Modified: The Impact of Feminism on the Academic Disciplines* (Oxford: Pergamon, 1981).

37. For the sake of brevity, I shall only mention recent studies in political science. The literature of comparable undertakings in history, anthropology, psychology, sociology, philosophy, literature, literary theory, art history, and the natural sciences is now voluminous. For an introduction to some of these developments, see Spender, *Men's Studies Modified*; Sandra Harding and Merrill Hintikka, *Discovering Reality: Feminist Perspectives on Metaphysics, Methodology and Philosophy of Science* (Dordrecht: D. Reidel, 1983); Marion Lowe and Ruth Hubbard, *Women's Nature: Rationalizations of Inequality* (New York: Pergamon, 1963); Geraldine Finn and Angela Miles, *Feminism in Canada* (Montreal: Black Rose Books, 1982); Carol Pateman and Elizabeth Gross, *Feminist Challenges* (Boston: Northeastern University Press, 1986); as well as the detailed review essays of developments in particular disciplines in *Signs*.

38. S. C. Bourque and J. Grossholtz, "Politics as an Unnatural Practice: Political Science Looks at Female Participation," *Politics and Society* (Winter 1974):225–266; Diane Fowlkes, *How Feminist Theory Reconstructs American Government and Politics* (Washington, D.C.: American Political Science Association, 1983); Beverly Cook, Karen O'Connor, and Susette Talarico, *Women in the Judicial Process* (Washington, D.C.: American Political Science Association, 1983); Milda Hedblom, *Women and American Political Organizations and Institutions* (Washington, D.C.: American Political Science Association, 1983); Virginia Sapiro, *Women, Political Action and Political Participation* (Washington, D.C.: American Political Science Association, 1983); Mary L. Shanley and Shelby Lewis, *Feminism and the Growth of the American Polity* (Washington, D.C.: American Political Science Association, 1983); Judith Stiehm with Michele Saint-Germaine, *Men, Women and State Violence: Government and the Military* (Washington, D.C.: American Political Science Association, 1983); M. Goot and E. Reid, *Women and Voting Studies: Mindless Matrons or Sexist Scientism* (Beverly Hills, Calif.: Sage Professional Papers in Comparative Political Sociology, 1975); M. E. Currell, *Political Woman* (London: Croom Helm, 1974); J. Jaquette, *Women in Politics* (New York: Wiley, 1974); Joni Lovenduski, "Toward the Emasculation of Political Science: The Impact of Feminism," *Men's Studies Modified*, ed., Dale Spender (Oxford: Pergamon, 1981); Jeanne Kirkpatrick, *Political Woman* (New York: Basic Books, 1974); Elizabeth Valance, *Women in the House* (London: Humanities Press, 1982); Ethel Klein, *Gender Politics* (Cambridge: Harvard University Press, 1984).

39. "Scholarly Treatment of Women in Political Science Texts Subject of Study" *WCPS* (Women's Caucus for Political Science) *Quarterly*, 6 May 1979.

40. Moi, *Sexual/Textual Politics*, p. 82.

41. Fred Dallmayr, *Language and Politics* (Notre Dame: University of Notre Dame Press, 1984), p. 85.

42. For this reason, Sandra Harding has argued that "feminist empiricism" is internally inconsistent: it involves explicit adherence to the norms of value neutral-

ity, objectivity, and impartiality while simultaneously generating substantive research findings that call these values into question. *The Science Question in Feminism* (Ithaca: Cornell University Press, 1986).

43. Dallmayr, *Language and Politics*, p. 63.

44. Ibid., p. 101.

45. de Pizan, *City of the Ladies*, p. 65.

46. Due to the limitations of space, only the works of Wittig will be treated here. The works of a great number of contemporary feminist poets, novelists, and playwrights could be used equally well to illustrate the rhetoric of vision as could Donna Haraway's "Manifesto for Cyborgs," *Socialist Review* 80(1985):65–107 and the feminist theorists cited in note 14.

47. Monique Wittig, "One Is Not Born a Woman," *Proceedings of the Second Sex Conference* (New York: Institute for the Humanities 1979), p. 70.

48. Monique Wittig, *Les Guérillères* (New York: Avon, 1971).

49. Monique Wittig and Sande Zeig, *Lesbian Peoples: Material for a Dictionary* (New York: Avon, 1979).

50. Monique Wittig, *Lesbian Body* (New York: Avon, 1973).

51. Hayden White, *Tropics of Discourse* (Baltimore: Johns Hopkins University Press, 1978). White applies his theory of tropology to the works of a very wide range of thinkers in the fields of philosophy, history, literature, and psychology. The following analysis attempts to be faithful to his categories in applying them to feminist rhetoric.

52. Donna Haraway criticizes taxonomies constructed to validate one's preferred position as "telos" in the context of certain Socialist Feminist strategies in "Manifesto for Cyborgs."

Chapter 5: Feminist Theory and Claims of Truth

1. An earlier version of this chapter appeared as, "Knowers, Knowing, Known: Feminist Theory and Claims of Truth," *Signs* 14(3):533–557.

2. Sandra Harding and Merrill Hintikka, eds., *Discovering Reality: Feminist Perspectives on Epistemology, Metaphysics, Methodology and Philosophy of Science* (Dordrecht: D. Reidel, 1983); Dale Spender, ed., *Men's Studies Modified: The Impact of Feminism on the Academic Disciplines* (Oxford: Pergamon, 1981).

3. In addition to the works of Harding and Hintikka and Spender mentioned above, see also Sandra Harding, *The Science Question in Feminism* (Ithaca: Cornell University Press, 1986); Carol Pateman and Elizabeth Gross, eds., *Feminist Chal-*

lenges (Boston: Northeastern University Press, 1986); Marion Lowe and Ruth Hubbard, eds., *Women's Nature: Rationalizations of Inequality* (New York: Pergamon, 1983); Evelyn Fox Keller, *Reflections on Gender and Science* (New Haven: Yale University Press, 1984); and Jean Grimshaw, *Philosophy and Feminist Thinking* (Minneapolis: University of Minnesota Press, 1986).

4. Nancy Hartsock, "The Feminist Standpoint: Developing a Ground for a Specifically Feminist Historical Materialism," in Harding and Hintikka, eds., *Discovering Reality* (Dordrecht: D. Reidel, 1983), pp. 283–310; and Nancy Hartsock, *Money, Sex and Power: Towards a Feminist Historical Materialism* (Boston: Northeastern University Press, 1985); Alison Jaggar, *Feminist Politics and Human Nature* (Totowa, N.J.: Rowman and Allenheld, 1983); and Rita Mae Kelly, Bernard Ronan, and Margaret Cawley, "Liberal Positivistic Epistemology and Research on Women and Politics," *Women and Politics* 7(3):11–27.

5. Such challenges of men's claims to "know" women's nature have been a staple of feminist criticism since its inception. For examples of early critiques, see Christine de Pisan's fifteenth-century treatise, *The Book of the City of the Ladies*, trans. Earl Jeffrey Richards (New York: Persea, 1982); Mary Wollstonecraft, *A Vindication of the Rights of Woman*, ed., Charles Hagelman (New York: W. W. Norton, 1967); and John Stuart Mill, *The Subjection of Women* (Cambridge: M.I.T. Press, 1970). For more recent criticisms, see Mary Daly, *Gyn/Ecology: The Metaethics of Radical Feminism* (Boston: Beacon Press, 1978); Dale Spender, ed., *Women of Ideas and What Men Have Done to Them* (London: Ark Paperbacks, 1982).

6. Angela Davis, *Women, Race and Class* (New York: Random House, 1981); Gloria Joseph and Jill Lewis, *Common Differences: Conflicts in Black and White Feminist Perspectives* (New York: AnchorPress/Doubleday, 1981); Paula Giddens, *When and Where I Enter: The Impact of Black Women on Race and Sex in America* (New York: Bantam Books, 1984).

7. Genevieve Lloyd, *The Man of Reason: Male and Female in Western Philosophy* (London: Methuen, 1984); Carol McMillan, *Women, Reason and Nature* (Oxford: Basil Blackwell, 1982); Helen Weinrich-Haste, "Redefining Rationality: Feminism and Science," (Paper presented at the Ontario Institute for Studies in Education, Toronto, Ontario, 9 October 1986).

8. This characterization of the alternatives is developed most clearly by Sandra Harding in *The Science Question in Feminism*. For alternative characterizations of the options available to feminism, see Alison Jaggar, *Feminist Politics and Human Nature*, Eloise Buker, "Hermeneutics: Problems and Promises for Doing Feminist Theory," (Paper presented at the Annual Meeting of the American Political Science Association, New Orleans, 30 August 1985); and Susan Hekman, "The Feminization of Epistemology: Gender and the Social Sciences," *Women and Politics* 7(3):65–83.

9. For examples of feminist empiricist arguments, see Janet Richards, *The Skeptical Feminist* (London: Penguin, 1982); S.C. Bourque and J. Grossholtz, "Politics As An Unnatural Practice: Political Science Looks at Female Participation," *Politics and Society* (Winter 1974):225–266; M. Goot and E. Reid, *Women and Voting Studies: Mindless Matrons or Sexist Scientism* (Beverly Hills, Calif.: Sage Professional Papers in Comparative Political Sociology, 1975); Jill McCalla Vickers, "Memoirs of an Ontological Exile: The Methodological Rebellions of Feminist Research," in G. Finn and A. Miles, eds., *Feminism in Canada* (Montreal: Black Rose Books, 1982), pp. 27–46.

10. For examples of feminist standpoint arguments, see Hartsock, "The Feminist Standpoint," and *Money, Sex and Power*; Jaggar, *Feminist Politics and Human Nature*; Mary O'Brien, *The Politics of Reproduction* (London: Routledge and Kegan Paul, 1981); Hilary Rose, "Hand, Brain and Heart: A Feminist Epistemology for the Natural Sciences," *Signs* 9(1):73–90; Dorothy Smith, "Women's Perspective as a Radical Critique of Sociology," *Sociological Inquiry* 44(1):7–13.

11. Jane Flax, "Gender as A Social Problem: In and For Feminist Theory," *American Studies/Amerika Studien* 31(2):193–213.

12. For additional examples of feminist postmodernism, see Jane Flax, "Postmodernism and Gender Relations in Feminist Theory," *Signs* 12(4):621–643; Donna Haraway, "A Manifesto for Cyborgs: Science, Technology and Socialist Feminism in the 1980's," *Socialist Review* 80:65–107; Claudine Hermann, "The Virile System," in E. Marks and I. De Courtivron, eds., *New French Feminisms* (New York: Schocken Books, 1981), pp. 87–89; Susan Hekman, "The Feminization of Epistemology," *Women and Politics* 7(3):65–83; Luce Irigaray, *Speculum of the Other Woman*, trans. Gillian Gill (Ithaca: Cornell University Press, 1985); and Luce Irigaray, *This Sex Which Is Not One*, trans. Catherine Porter (Ithaca: Cornell University Press, 1985).

13. Harding, *The Science Question in Feminism*, p. 244; see also pp. 194–196. This ambivalence is also apparent in Jane Flax's article, "Postmodernism and Gender Relations in Feminist Theory," (*Signs* 12(4):621–643), which categorizes feminist theory as "a type of postmodern philosophy" (p. 624) while simultaneously illuminating some of the deficiencies of postmodernism for feminists committed to human emancipation. Thus, Flax concludes that "the relation of feminist theorizing to the postmodern project of deconstruction is necessarily ambivalent" (p. 625).

14. Mary Daly, *Beyond God the Father* (Boston: Beacon Press, 1973), p. 9.

15. Simone de Beauvoir, *The Second Sex*, trans. and ed., H. M. Parshley (New York: Bantam Books, 1960), p. 201.

16. Toril Moi traces this subtle shift in the work of a number of contemporary French feminists and offers an insightful critique of this slide; see *Sexual/Textual Politics: Feminist Literary Theory* (New York: Methuen, 1985), p. 28.

17. For a detailed and illuminating discussion of the arguments that sustain this claim, see Judith Grant, "I Feel Therefore I Am: A Critique of Female Experience as a Basis for Feminist Epistemology," *Women and Politics* 7(3):99–114.

18. Harding, *The Science Question in Feminism*, p. 63; for similar claims, see Susan Bordo, "The Cartesian Masculinization of Thought," *Signs* 11:439–456; and Kathy Ferguson, "Male Ordered Politics: Feminism and Political Science," (Paper presented at the Annual Meeting of the American Political Science Association, New Orleans, 30 August 1985).

19. Harding, *The Science Question in Feminism*, p. 229; see also Isaac Balbus, *Marxism and Domination* (Princeton: Princeton University Press, 1982); and Evelyn Fox Keller, *Reflections on Gender and Science* (New Haven: Yale University Press, 1984).

20. For a sustained consideration of the possibility that the "ideals of reason have incorporated an exclusion of the feminine," see Genevieve Lloyd, *The Man of Reason* (London: Methuen, 1982).

21. Elizabeth Fee, "Whither Feminist Epistemology?" (Paper presented at Beyond the Second Sex Conference, University of Pennsylvania, 1984); Hekman discusses a number of feminist works that link dichotomous thinking to gender hierarchy in "The Feminization of Epistemology," *Women and Politics* 7(3):65–83.

22. Irigaray, *Speculum of the Other Woman* and *The Sex Which is Not One*: Hélène Cixous, "Le Rire de la Meduse," *L'Arc* 61:39–54 (1975) and "Le Sex ou La Tete," *Les Cahier du GRIF* 13:5–15 (1976); and Ferguson, "Male-Ordered Politics."

23. Irigaray, *Speculum of the Other Woman*, p. 48.

24. Whether these contentious claims are drawn directly from the theories of Freud or indirectly from Freud by means of Klein, Winnicott, and Chodorow or by means of Lacan and Irigaray, the ultimate blame for the fragility of male identity is attributed to women *qua* mothers. Despite their theoretical complexities, the various interpretations of the "Oedipal conflict" manage to insinuate that it is women-only childcare practices that are the cause of psychic needs to oppress women. That a good deal of feminist theorizing should be premised upon such "blame-the-victim" assumptions is itself very puzzling.

25. For the purposes of developing a logical taxonomy, it might be preferable to identify psychological arguments as one form of functionalism, a form emphasizing the psychological needs and interests served by particular ideas. Because of the frequency with which psychological claims surface in feminist epistemology, in the foregoing analysis I have treated psychological claims independently, but they are also vulnerable to the kinds of problems identified below.

26. John Stuart Mill, *The Subjection of Women* (Cambridge: M.I.T. Press, 1970); Germaine Greer, *The Female Eunuch* (London: St. Albans, 1971).

27. Sara Ann Ketchum and Christine Pierce, "Separatism and Sexual Relationships," in S. Bishop and M. Weinsweig, eds., *Philosophy and Women* (Belmont, Calif.: Wadsworth Press, 1979), pp. 163–171.

28. Wally Seccombe, "The Housewife and Her Labour Under Capitalism," *New Left Review* 83:(January 1973):3–24; John Berger and Jean Mohr, *A Seventh Man* (London: Harmondsworth, 1975); Victoria Beechey, "Some Notes on Female Wage Labour in the Capitalist Mode of Production," *Capital and Class* 3(Fall 1977):45–64, and "Women and Production," in A. Kuhn and A. M. Wolpe, eds., *Feminism and Materialism* (London: Routledge and Kegan Paul, 1978), pp. 155–197.

29. Iris Young, "Impartiality and the Civic Public: Some Implications for Feminist Critiques of Moral and Political Theory," *Praxis International* 5(4):381–401, p. 384.

30. For critiques of functionalist arguments within feminism, see Richards, *The Skeptical Feminist*; and Michele Barrett, *Women's Oppression Today: Problems in Marxist Feminist Analysis* (London: Verso, 1980).

31. Feminist approaches to epistemology are not alone in reducing a variety of theoretical conceptions of reason to a monolithic notion of instrumental rationality. Richard Bernstein has argued that this is a problem in a number of postmodern theories. See "The Rage Against Reason," *Philosophy and Literature* 10(2):186–210. For an insightful critique of this tendency within feminism, see Jean Grimshaw, *Philosophy and Feminist Thinking* (Minneapolis: University of Minnesota Press, 1986).

32. For critiques of instrumental reason, see Max Weber, *The Protestant Ethic and the Spirit of Capitalism*, trans. Talcott Parsons (New York: Charles Scribner's Sons, 1958); Hans-Georg Gadamer, "Historical Transformations of Reason," in Theodore Geraets, ed., *Rationality Today* (Ottawa: University of Ottawa Press, 1979), pp. 3–14; Max Horkheimer and Theodor Adorno, *Dialectic of Enlightenment* (New York: Continuum, 1982); and Jürgen Habermas, "Dialectics of Rationalization," *Telos* 49(1981):5–31.

33. See, for example, Mary Daly, *Gyn/Ecology*; Marilyn French, *Beyond Power: On Women, Men and Morals* (New York: Summitt, 1984); Sara Ruddick, "Maternal Thinking," *Feminist Studies* 6(2):342–367 and "Pacifying the Forces: Drafting Women in the Interests of Peace," *Signs* 8(3):471–489. Several feminist scholars have recently noted the irony that this oppositional conception of male and female reason reproduces the caricatures of masculine and feminine that have marked patriarchal social relations; see, Grant, "I Feel Therefore I Am;" and Hekman, "The Feminization of Epistemology."

34. Consider Lorraine Code, "Is the Sex of the Knower Epistemologically Significant?" *Metaphilosophy* 12(1981):267–276; Cixous, "Le rire de la Meduse," and Le

sexe ou la tete;" Irigaray, *Speculum of the Other Woman*; H. K. Trask, *Eros and Power: The Promise of Feminist Theory* (Philadelphia: University of Pennsylvania Press, 1986); and Jane Flax, "Political Philosophy and the Patriarchal Unconscious: A Psychoanalytic Perspective on Epistemology and Metaphysics," in Harding and Hintikka, eds., *Discovering Reality* (Dordrecht: D. Reidel, 1983), pp. 245–282.

35. Compare, Mary Daly, *Gyn/Ecology*; Marilyn French, *Beyond Power*; and Susan Griffin, *Woman and Nature: The Roaring Inside Her* (New York: Harper Colophon, 1980).

36. It is important to note that in contrast to claims concerning the immediate apprehension of reality characteristic of discussions of women's embodiedness and intuition, standpoint theories emphasize that a "privileged" standpoint is "achieved rather than obvious, a mediated rather than an immediate understanding . . . an achievement both of science (analysis) and of political struggle" (Hartsock, "The Feminist Standpoint," p. 288). Thus, standpoint theories are far more sophisticated in their analysis of knowledge than feminist intuitionists and feminist empiricists. But standpoint theories still suffer from overly simplistic conceptions of the self and of science that sustain problematic claims concerning the "universal" experiences of women that afford a foundation for a "privileged" standpoint. The nature of these problems is discussed below.

37. Rose, "Hand, Brain and Heart."

38. Hartsock, "The Feminist Standpoint," and *Money, Sex and Power.*

39. Jaggar, *Feminist Politics and Human Nature.*

40. In an effort to illuminate the extent to which conceptions of the "body" are socially mediated, Monique Wittig has noted that

> in our [women's] case ideology goes far since our bodies as well as our minds are the product of this manipulation. We have been compelled in our bodies and our minds to correspond, feature by feature, with the idea of nature that has been established for us. Distorted to such an extent that our deformed body is what they call "natural," is what is supposed to exist as such before oppression. Distorted to such an extent that at the end oppression seems to be a consequence of this "nature" in ourselves (a nature which is only an idea).

"One is Not Born A Woman," Proceedings of the Second Sex Conference, (New York, Institute for the Humanities, 1979).

41. Hegel advances a detailed critique of intuitionism in his preface to the *Phenomenology*; see G. W. F. Hegel, *Phenomenology of Spirit*, trans. J. B. Baillie (New York: Harper Colophon, 1967), pp. 73–75.

42. This problem has been noted by Alan Soble, "Feminist Epistemology and Women Scientists," *Metaphilosophy* 14(1983):291–307 (1983); Judith Grant, "I Feel Therefore I Am;" and Sandra Harding, *The Science Question in Feminism.*

43. In *The Science Question in Feminism*, Sandra Harding defines gender symbolism as the attribution of dualistic gender metaphors to distinctions that rarely have anything to do with sex differences, for example, "male" reason versus "female" intuition (p. 17).

44. Foundationalism is an epistemological stance, which asserts that an ultimate grounding of knowledge, science, philosophy, and language is possible. Since Descartes introduced the metaphor of the indubitable "foundation," modern philosophy has devoted a great deal of effort to the search for an Archimedean point upon which to ground knowledge. Many rationalists, empiricists, phenomenologists, and analytic philosophers have shared the conviction that they had finally discovered the "method" that could clearly differentiate knowledge (episteme) from shifting opinions (doxai); they differ however, in their depictions of the nature of the correct "method."

45. See for example, Hans Albert, *Treatise on Critical Reason*, trans. Mary Varney Rorty (Princeton: Princeton University Press, 1985); Richard Bernstein, *Beyond Objectivism and Relativism* (Philadelphia: University of Pennsylvania Press, 1983); Stanley Cavell, *The Claim of Reason* (New York: Oxford University Press, 1979); Richard Rorty, *Philosophy and the Mirror of Nature* (Princeton: Princeton University Press, 1979).

46. These arguments were developed forcefully by David Hume in his *Enquiry Concerning Human Understanding* (Oxford: Clarendon Press, 1975). For more recent treatment of the issues, see Albert, *Treatise on Critical Reason*.

47. Albert, *Treatise on Critical Reason*; and Karl Popper, *Conjectures and Refutations* (New York: Basic Books, 1962).

48. Albert, *Treatise on Critical Reason*.

49. The "myth of the given" is discussed by Wilfred Sellars in *Science, Perception and Reality* (New York: Humanities Press, 1963), p. 64. For helpful introductions to Sellars' work, see Gibson Winter, *Elements for a Social Ethic: Scientific and Ethical Perspectives on Social Process* (New York: Macmillan, 1966), pp. 61–166; Richard Bernstein, *The Restructuring of Social and Political Theory* (Philadelphia: University of Pennsylvania Press, 1976), pp. 121–135; and John Gunnell, *Between Philosophy and Politics* (Amherst: University of Massachusetts Press, 1986), pp. 68–90.

50. For a detailed discussion of the conception of practice invoked here, see Alaisdair MacIntyre, *After Virtue* (Notre Dame: University of Notre Dame Press, 1981), pp. 174–189.

51. In *Beyond Objectivism and Relativism*, Bernstein characterizes this erroneous conclusion as the "myth of the framework" (p. 84).

52. For an intriguing discussion of some of the most fundamental presuppositions that have shaped Western cognitive practices since the seventeenth century,

see Michel Foucault, *The Order of Things: An Archaeology of the Human Sciences* (New York: Vintage Books, 1973).

53. See Popper, *Conjectures and Refutations*; Harold Brown, *Perception, Theory and Commitment: The New Philosophy of Science* (Chicago: Precedent Publishing Company, 1977); and Norman Stockman, *Anti-Positivist Theories of Science: Critical Rationalism, Critical Theory and Scientific Realism* (Dordrecht: D. Reidel, 1983).

54. Albert, *Treatise on Critical Reason*; Popper, *Conjectures and Refutations*; Brown, *Perception, Theory and Commitment*; and Stockman, *Anti-Positivist Theories of Science*.

55. Seyla Benhabib, *Critique, Norm and Utopia* (New York: Columbia University Press, 1986); Charles Taylor, "Foucault on Freedom and Truth," *Political Theory* 12(2):152–183; William E. Connolly, "Taylor, Foucault and Otherness," *Political Theory* 13(3):365–376.

56. See for example, Alan Megill, *Prophets of Extremity: Nietzsche, Heidegger, Foucault, Derrida* (Berkeley: University of California Press, 1985); Iris Young, "Impartiality and the Civic Public: Some Implications of Feminist Critiques of Moral and Political Theory," *Praxis International* 5(4):381–401.

57. Michel Foucault, *Discipline and Punish* (New York: Vintage Books, 1977) and *The History of Sexuality*, vol. I (New York: Vintage Books, 1980).

58. Cavell, *The Claim of Reason*.

59. For a detailed discussion of this problem, see Seyla Benhabib, *Critique, Norm, and Utopia*.

60. In suggesting that an understanding of cognition as a human practice can help feminist analysis avoid the problems of feminist empiricism and feminist standpoint theories while simultaneously illuminating fruitful strategies of inquiry for feminist analysis, I do not mean to suggest that the notion of cognition as a human practice itself could or should supplant feminist investigations of knowledge claims. Feminist inquiry remains as important in the field of epistemology as in any other traditional academic area of investigation, precisely because most contemporary practitioners in these fields, like their predecessors in the Western tradition, suffer from a peculiar form of gender blindness. Even those most sensitive to the politics of knowledge in contexts involving race and class remain remarkably unaware of the unique issues raised by the problem of gender. Feminist analysis serves as a crucial corrective for this acute and pervasive form of masculinist myopia.

61. See, for example, Buker, "Hermeneutics: Problems and Promises for Doing Feminist Theory"; and Moi, *Sexual/Textual Politics*.

62. Hayden White, *Tropics of Discourse* (Baltimore: Johns Hopkins University Press, 1978), p. 3.

63. For a helpful introduction to and critique of the postmodern shift from world to text, see Allan Megill, *Prophets of Extremity: Nietzsche, Heidegger, Foucault, Derrida* (Berkeley, University of California Press, 1985).

64. The conception of cognition as a human practice requires a coherence theory of truth. Due to the limitations of space, it is not possible to explore the dimensions of this conception in detail here; nor is it possible to provide a systematic defense of this conception of truth against the charge of relativism. For works that do undertake both those tasks, see Richard Bernstein, *Beyond Objectivism and Relativism* (Philadelphia: University of Pennsylvania Press, 1983); Stanley Cavell, *The Claim of Reason* (New York: Oxford University Press, 1979); Don Herzog, *Without Foundations: Justification in Political Theory* (Ithaca: Cornell University Press); and William E. Connolly, *Appearance and Reality in Politics* (Cambridge: Cambridge University Press, 1981).

Chapter 6: Re/Vision: Feminist Theory Confronts the Polis

1. Josephine Donovan, ed., *Feminist Literary Criticism: Explorations in Theory* (Lexington: University of Kentucky Press, 1975).

2. Michele Barrett, *Women's Oppression Today: Problems in Marxist Feminist Analysis* (London: Verso Press, 1980); Eloise Buker, "Hermeneutics: Problems and Promises for Doing Feminist Theory," (Paper presented at the Annual Meeting of the American Political Science Association, New Orleans, 1985); Lorenne Clark and Lynda Lange, eds., *The Sexism of Social and Political Theory: Women and Reproduction from Plato to Nietzsche* (Toronto: University of Toronto Press, 1979); Jean Bethke Elshtain, *Public Man, Private Woman* (Princeton: Princeton University Press, 1981); Sandra Harding and Merrill Hintikka, eds., *Discovering Reality: Feminist Perspectives on Epistemology, Metaphysics and the Philosophy of Science* (Dordrecht: D. Reidel, 1983); Luce Irigaray, *Speculum of the Other Woman*, trans. by Gillian Gill (Ithaca: Cornell University Press, 1985); Alison Jaggar, *Feminist Politics and Human Nature* (Totowa, N. J.: Rowman and Allanheld, 1983); Mary Mahowald, *Philosophy of Women: Classical to Current Concepts* (Indianapolis: Hackett Publishing, 1978); Linda Nicholson, *Gender and History: The Limits of Social Theory in the Age of the Family* (New York: Columbia University Press, 1986); Mary O'Brien, *The Politics of Reproduction* (London: Routledge and Kegan Paul, 1983); Susan Moller Okin, *Women in Western Political Thought* (Princeton: Princeton University Press, 1979); Martha Osborne, *Women in Western Thought* (New York: Random House, 1979); Carol Pateman and Elizabeth Gross, eds., *Feminist Challenges: Social and Political Theory* (Boston: Northeastern University Press, 1986); Dale Spender, *Women of Ideas and What Men Have Done to Them* (London: Ark Paperbacks, 1983); Jill Mc-Calla Vickers, "Memoirs of an Ontological Exile: The Methodological Rebellions of Feminist Research," in Geraldine Finn and Angela Miles, eds., *Feminism in Canada* (Montreal: Black Rose Books, 1982), pp. 27–46.

3. In addition to the works cited above, see Nancy Chodorow, *The Reproduction of Mothering: Psychoanalysis and the Sociology of Gender* (Berkeley: University of California Press, 1978); Mary Daly, *Gyn/Ecology: The Metaethics of Radical Feminism* (Boston: Beacon Press, 1978); Simone de Beauvoir, *The Second Sex*, trans. and ed., H. M. Parshley (New York: Bantam Books, 1961); Zillah Eisenstein, *Capitalist Patriarchy and the Case for Socialist Feminism* (New York: Monthly Review Press, 1979); Carol Gilligan, *In A Different Voice: Psychological Theory and Women's Development* (Cambridge: Harvard University Press, 1982); Carol Gould, *Beyond Domination: New Perspectives on Women and Philosophy* (Totowa, N. J.: Rowman and Allanheld, 1984); Juliet Mitchell, *Women's Estate* (New York: Vintage Books, 1973); Juliet Mitchell, *Psychoanalysis and Feminism* (New York: Vintage Books, 1974); Kate Millett, *Sexual Politics* (New York: Avon Books, 1971); Janet Richards, *The Skeptical Feminist* (London: Penguin, 1982).

4. An earlier version of this chapter appeared as "Re/Vision: Feminist Theory Confronts the Polis," *Social Theory and Practice* 13(2):155–186.

5. The little discussion available on this topic tends to operate at a very general level concerning the comparative merits of capitalist, socialist, or social democratic polities for advancing women's rights. These discussions tend to focus upon ideological differences rather than institutional arrangements within these systems that "ought" to contribute to the advancement of women. See, for example, the essays in Eisenstein's *Capitalist Patriarchy*, the final two chapters in Barrett's *Women's Oppression Today*, and Chapter 9 in Richards' *The Skeptical Feminist*. When one moves from ideological debate to studies of existing systems, one finds remarkable similarities concerning the subordination of women in all these systems. For a helpful guide to the extensive empirical literature, see Sharon Wolchik, "Women and Politics in Comparative Perspective: Europe and the Soviet Union," *Women and Politics* 1(2):65–83.

6. Jaggar, *Feminist Politics and Human Nature*, p. 344.

7. Gloria Joseph and Jill Lewis, *Common Differences: Conflicts in Black and White Feminist Perspectives* (New York: Anchor Press/Doubleday 1981), p. 172.

8. Elaine Marks and Isabelle De Courtivron, eds., *New French Feminisms* (New York: Schocken, 1981); Luce Irigaray, *Speculum of the Other Woman*, trans. Gillian Gill (Ithaca: Cornell University Press, 1985) and Luce Irigaray, *This Sex Which Is Not One*, trans. Catherine Porter (Ithaca: Cornell University Press, 1985).

9. Mary Daly, *Gyn/Ecology*; Marilyn French, *Beyond Power: On Men, Women and Morals* (New York: Summit, 1985); Susan Griffin, *Women and Nature: The Roaring Inside Her* (New York: Harper Colophon, 1980); Haunani-Kay Trask, *Eros and Power: The Promise of Feminist Theory* (Philadelphia: University of Pennsylvania Press, 1986). For a critique of this association of reason and masculinity, see Judith

Grant, "I Feel Therefore I Am: A Critique of Female Experience as the Basis for a Feminist Epistemology," *Women and Politics* 7(3):99–114.

10. Lynne Farrow, "Feminism as Anarchism," *Aurora* (1974):7, 11; currently available as Black Bear Pamphlet 2 (London: 76 Peckham Road, SE5). Both Mary O'Brien and Judith Grant have cautioned against too facile a rejection of all theory on this ground, suggesting instead a distinction between good theory that arises from feminist praxis and "abstract" theory that loses contact with the immediate problems confronting feminism. See O'Brien's *The Politics of Reproduction* (London: Routledge and Kegan Paul, 1983), pp. 1–15, 188; and Grant's "Fundamental Feminism: Core Concepts in American Theory of the Second Wave," Ph.D. diss., Rutgers University, 1986, pp. 288–293.

11. Jaggar, *Feminist Politics and Human Nature*, p. 202; Nicholson, *Gender and History*, pp. 24, 35; Barrett, *Women's Oppression Today*, pp. 227–247; and Sheila Rowbotham, "The British Women's Movement and the State" (Paper presented at the Women's Studies Resource Center, Ontario Institute for Studies in Education, Toronto, Ontario, 9 November 1986).

12. O'Brien, "Feminist Praxis," in Angela Miles and Geraldine Finn, eds., *Feminism in Canada: From Pressure to Politics* (Montreal: Black Rose Books, 1982), p. 261.

13. Richards, *The Skeptical Feminist*, pp. 50, 52.

14. Jaggar, *Feminist Politics and Human Nature*, pp. 377–389; O'Brien, *The Politics of Reproduction*, pp. 22–23; Sandra Harding, *The Science Question in Feminism* (Ithaca: Cornell University Press, 1986), pp. 243–247.

15. Jaggar, *Feminist Politics and Human Nature*, p. 387.

16. For an insightful discussion of this point, see Seyla Benhabib, *Critique, Norm, and Utopia* (New York: Columbia University Press, 1986).

17. Plato, *The Republic*, VII, 518a–520d.

18. It is interesting to note that for purposes of conversion or "purification," Plato recommends a process of de-urbanization and rural rehabilitation with chilling similarities to the policies adopted by the Khmer Rouge in Kampuchea from 1975–1979 as one possible strategy. See *The Republic*, VII, 541a–b.

19. Ibid., II, 369a–383c; III, 402d–417b; IV, 441d–444d.

20. Aristotle, *The Politics*, I. i, 1252a §2. Ernest Barker, trans. and ed. (London: Oxford University Press, 1958).

21. Ibid., I. xii, 1259b §2.

22. Ibid., III. v, 1278a §2. In this passage, Aristotle discusses "mechanics and laborers" as examples of those who are "necessary conditions" of the state's exis-

tence but who could not qualify for citizenship because they are incapable of achieving excellence.

23. Within the classical liberal tradition, "negative liberty" refers to freedom from governmental intrusion. The term is associated with the creation of a "private sphere" in which the individual is free to act without any interference from the state. Negative liberty is typically contrasted with notions of "positive liberty," which suggest that true freedom requires individual participation in decision making about collective concerns. Positive liberty requires citizens to participate actively in governance. It is an inherently democratic conception. Negative liberty, on the other hand, is compatible with any form of regime, since it requires only that some sphere—no matter how small—be insulated from governmental intrusions.

24. Zillah Eisenstein, *The Radical Future of Liberal Feminism* (New York: Longman, 1981); Jean Bethke Elshtain, *Public Man, Private Woman*; Jaggar, *Feminist Politics and Human Nature*.

25. There has been a tendency to interpret the liberal feminist assumption of human equality in Lockean terms, that is, to root equality in a conception of rationality. See, for example, Jaggar, "Liberal Feminism and Human Nature" in *Feminist Politics and Human Nature*, pp. 27–50 and Nicholson, *Gender and History*, pp. 20–26. The liberal tradition is however far more varied than this reduction suggests. Indeed, a good deal of liberal theory explicitly rejects rationality as the basis of human equality. Hobbes offers the subjectivity of the passions and the capacity to kill as alternatives; Rousseau identifies a capacity for autonomous existence as the basis for equality; and Hume identifies self-interest and limited generosity as the traits which humans have in common.

26. This point was central to Rousseau's critique of earlier formulations of liberal theory. See his *Discourse on the Origin of Inequality* and *The Social Contract*.

27. Both Locke in *The Second Treatise on Government* and Madison in *The Federalist Papers* suggest a number of pragmatic considerations to justify representative government.

28. My interpretation of the function of the private sphere in liberal discourse differs markedly from that of Zillah Eisenstein who argues that the public/private split provided the means for the perpetuation of patriarchy within emergent bourgeois culture (*The Radical Future of Liberal Feminism*); from that of Jean Elshtain who suggests that public life in general, and politics in particular, "is in part an elaborate defense against the tug of the private, against the lure of the familial, against the evocations of female power" (*Public Man, Private Woman*, pp. 15–16); and from that of Linda Nicholson who suggests that the institutionalization of the private sphere constituted a mechanism to depoliticize kinship and thereby consolidate the power of the bourgeois state (*Gender and History*, pp. 106–135).

29. Rawls argues that

The basis for self-esteem in a just society is not one's income share but the publicly affirmed distribution of fundamental rights and liberties. And this distribution being equal, everyone has a similar and secure status when they meet to conduct the common affairs of the wider society. No one is inclined to look beyond the constitutional affirmation of equality for further political ways of securing his status . . . In a well-ordered society, then, self-respect is secured by the public affirmation of the status of equal citizenship for all.

A Theory of Justice (Cambridge: Belknap Press, 1971), pp. 544–545.

30. Thus, I disagree with both Zillah Eisenstein *(The Radical Future of Liberal Feminism)* and Alison Jaggar *(Feminist Politics and Human Nature)* in their arguments that liberal feminism, in carrying the principle of equality to its logical conclusion, necessarily pushes beyond liberalism towards radical democracy.

31. For a full discussion of this point, see Richard Sennett and Jonathan Cobb, *The Hidden Injuries of Class* (New York: Alfred A. Knopf, 1972) and Michael Lewis, *The Culture of Inequality* (New York: American Library, 1978).

32. For the remainder of this chapter, I shall use the term "radical feminist" to designate all three of these groups for they all share the belief that men have power as men in a society organized into sexual spheres and that the elimination of this male privilege presupposes the *radical* transformation of human relations as well as social and political structures. Although the differences among these approaches to feminism are of great importance in their analyses of the causes of women's oppression, they are much less clear cut when one focuses upon political prescriptions for the good society. For detailed discussion of these differences, see Elshtain, *Public Man, Private Woman*; Jaggar and Struhl, *Feminist Frameworks: Alternative Theoretical Accounts of the Relations Between Men and Women* (New York: McGraw Hill, 1978); and Jaggar, *Feminist Politics and Human Nature*. For an argument that the tendency to emphasize differences among feminists rather than their similarities contributes to a notion that feminist views are merely adjuncts to traditional political theories incapable of autonomous existence, see Judith Grant, "Fundamental Feminism: Core Concepts in American Theory of the Second Wave" Ph.D. diss., Rutgers University, 1986).

33. Sandra Bartky defines this phenomenon as the essence of psychological oppression. "On Psychological Oppression," in Sharon Bishop and Marjorie Weinzweig, eds., *Philosophy and Women* (Belmont, Calif.: Wadsworth Publishing, 1979), pp. 33–41.

34. Carol Smart and Barry Smart, *Women, Sexuality and Social Control* (London: Routledge and Kegan Paul, 1978), p. 1.

35. Joan Roberts, *Beyond Intellectual Sexism* (New York: David McKay Company, 1976), p. 6.

36. Juliet Mitchell, *Psychoanalysis and Feminism*; and Nancy Chodorow, *The Reproduction of Mothering*.

37. Anne Koedt, "Lesbianism and Feminism," in Anne Koedt, Ellen Levine and Anita Rapone, eds., *Radical Feminism* (New York: Quadrangle Press, 1973), pp. 246–258.

38. Joan Roberts, *Beyond Intellectual Sexism*; Mary Daly, *Gyn/Ecology*; Susan Griffin, *Woman and Nature*; Adrienne Rich, *Of Woman Born* (New York: W.W. Norton, 1976).

39. Robin Lakoff, *Language and Woman's Place* (New York: Harper and Row, 1975); Mary Daly, *Gyn/Ecology*; Rosemary Reuther, *New Woman, New Earth* (New York: Seabury Press, 1975); Juliet Mitchell, *Psychoanalysis and Feminism*.

40. Nancy Chodorow, *Reproduction of Mothering*; Susan Griffin, *Woman and Nature*.

41. Zillah Eisenstein, *Capitalist Patriarchy*; Margaret Benston, "The Political Economy of Women's Liberation," *Monthly Review* 21(4):13–25; Batya Weinbaum, *The Curious Courtship of Women's Liberation and Socialism* (Boston: South End Press, 1979).

42. Adrienne Rich, *Of Woman Born*; Chodorow, *The Reproduction of Mothering*; Smart and Smart, *Women, Sexuality and Social Control*.

43. Charlotte Bunch, "Lesbians in Revolt," in Jaggar and Struhl, eds., *Feminist Frameworks*; Sarah Ann Ketchum and Christine Pierce, "Separatism and Sexual Relationships," in Bishop and Weinzweig, eds., *Philosophy and Women*; Ti Grace Atkinson, *Amazon Odyssey*; Jill Johnston, *Lesbian Nation*; Adrienne Rich, "Compulsory Heterosexuality and Lesbian Existence," *Signs* (1980):631–660.

44. Daly, *Gyn/Ecology*: Mary MacIntosh, "The State and the Oppression of Women," in Annette Kuhn and Ann Marie Wolpe, eds., *Feminism and Materialism* (London: Routledge and Kegan Paul, 1978), pp. 254–289; Carol Pateman, "Women and Consent" *Signs* 8(2):149–168.

45. Sara Ruddick, "Maternal Thinking" *Feminist Studies* 6(2):342–367; Sarah Ruddick, "Pacifying the Forces: Drafting Women in the Interests of Peace," *Signs* 8(3):471–489; Marilyn French, *Beyond Power: On Men, Women and Morals* (New York: Summit, 1985); Haunani-Kay Trask, *Eros and Power* (Philadelphia: University of Pennsylvania Press, 1986); Joyce Trebilcot, ed., *Mothering: Essays in Feminist Theory* (Totowa, N. J.: Rowman and Allanheld, 1984); Stephanie Leland, "Feminism and Ecology: Theoretical Connections," in Leonie Caldecott and Stephanie Le-

land, eds., *Reclaim the Earth* (Boston: Salem House Publishers/The Women's Press, 1984). It could be argued that "feminist standpoint" theories represent a weaker form of this model, which would explain claims that it is possible for sympathetic men to adopt the "standpoint of women." See Jaggar, *Feminist Politics and Human Nature*; Nancy Hartsock, "The Feminist Standpoint: Developing a Ground for a Specifically Feminist Historical Materialism," in Harding and Hintikka, eds., *Discovering Reality*; Nancy Hartsock, *Money, Sex and Power: Towards A Feminist Historical Materialism*; and Mary O'Brien, *The Politics of Reproduction*.

46. For insightful critiques of this model, see Iris Young "The Ideal of Community and the Politics of Difference," *Social Theory and Practice* 12(1):1–26 and Mary Dietz, "Citizenship With A Feminist Face: The Problem with Maternal Thinking," *Political Theory* 13(1): 19–37. It is interesting to note that Dietz explicitly calls for a return to an Aristotelian conception of politics as an alternative to the maternal model; she does not discuss the possibility that the Aristotelian model of equality may be too restrictive for easy adaptation to feminist ends.

47. Shulamith Firestone's *Dialectic of Sex* (New York: William Morrow, 1970) is perhaps the most famous articulation of this position. Marge Piercy's *Woman on the Edge of Time* provides a fictional account of the same possibility. In addition, in *The Politics of Reproduction*, Mary O'Brien has suggested that women's use of contraception could afford women the same distance from reproduction that men have always had; and Nancy Chodorow argues in *The Reproduction of Mothering* that elimination of the division of labor with respect to childrearing could have the same benign effect.

48. Indeed one could argue that Christine de Pisan's fifteenth-century treatise *The Book of the City of the Ladies* was the first to envision this possibility. Subsequent visions have surfaced in Charlotte Perkins Gilman's *Herland* and Monique Wittig's *Les Guérillères*.

49. The rhetoric of "difference" that has surfaced recently within feminism has generated a wide range of epithets for "assimilationist" feminists who are said to merely emulate male modes of behavior. Jean Elshtain, for example, has argued that such approaches constitute "expressions of contempt for the female body, for pregnancy, for childbirth, and childrearing" ("Feminists Against the Family," *The Nation*, 17 November 1979: 481). Luce Irigaray rejects the term "feminism" altogether, arguing that women must "denounce women's movements which aim simply for a change in the distribution of power, leaving intact the power structure itself, for these are resubjecting themselves, deliberately or not, to a phallocratic order" (*This Sex Which Is Not One*, p. 81).

50. In addition to the works cited in note 41, see Catherine McKinnon, "Feminism, Marxism, Method and the State: An Agenda For Theory," *Signs* 7(3):515–544. One could also interpret the recent debates concerning appropriate forms of lesbian sexuality as the development of additional restrictions upon the kinds of persons who would be welcome in an ideal political community. For alternative

views on this topic see, *What Color Is Your Handkerchief: A Lesbian SM Reader* (San Francisco: Samois, 1979) and Robin Linden, Darlene Pagano, Diane Russell, and Susan Leigh Star eds., *Against Sadomasochism* (Palo Alto, Calif.: Frog in the Wall, 1982).

51. Zillah Eisenstein, *Feminism and Sexual Equality* (New York: Monthly Review Press, 1984), p. 241.

52. Jaggar, *Feminist Politics and Human Nature*, p. 344.

53. The term "reproductive democracy" was introduced by Clark and Lange, *The Sexism of Social and Political Theory* and subsequently criticized by Rosalind Petchesky in "Reproductive Freedom: Beyond a Woman's Right to Choose," *Signs* 5(4):662. Alison Jaggar summarizes these views in *Feminist Politics and Human Nature*, pp. 148, 341.

54. Rousseau has presented the most direct discussion of this problem of attempting to secure substantive results for political decisions by establishing procedural rules for participation in his treatment of the General Will in *The Social Contract*.

55. Elshtain, *Public Man, Private Woman*, p. 222.

56. Concern for the oppressive implications of the model of community advanced within certain strains of feminist analysis has led Iris Young to call for the abandonment of the notion of community and the development of a conception of the political ideal based upon a model of the "unoppressive city." See "The Ideal of Community and the Politics of Difference," *Social Theory and Practice* 12(1):1–26.

57. Edith Altbach, ed., *German Feminism: Readings in Politics and Literature* (New York: SUNY Press, 1984), p. 273; De Beauvoir, "Interview with Alice Schwarzer," in Marks and de Courtivron, eds., *New French Feminism*, p. 146; Mary O'Brien, *The Politics of Reproduction*, pp. 201–210.

58. Ketchum and Pierce, "Separatism and Sexual Relationships."

59. Millett, *Sexual Politics*, pp. 362–363.

60. Both Mary O'Brien and Judith Grant have criticized this optimism concerning consciousness raising, indicating the extent to which it involves a retreat from materialist analysis to idealism. See *Politics of Reproduction*, pp. 188–190 and "Fundamental Feminism," pp. 271–293.

61. Sheila Rowbotham, "The Woman's Movement and Organizing for Socialism," in Rowbotham, Segal and Wainwright, eds., *Beyond the Fragments: Feminism and the Making of Socialism* (London: Merlin, 1979), p. 41.

62. Sara Evans, *Personal Politics* (New York: Knopf, 1979), p.223.

63. Iris Young, "The Ideal of Community and the Politics of Difference," p.13.

64. Michel Foucault, *The History of Sexuality* (New York: Vintage Books, 1980), p. 89.

65. Michel Foucault, *Discipline and Punish* (New York: Vintage Books, 1977), p. 201.

66. Steven Salkever, "Virtue, Obligation and Politics," *American Political Science Review* 68(1):78–92.

67. M. E. Hawkesworth, "Freedom and Virtue: The Covert Connection," *Cogito* 2(1):73–106.

Chapter 7: A Constitutional Proposal

1. Such tactics are typically associated with "liberal feminism" and have been central to the political efforts of organizations such as NOW (The National Organization for Women), WEAL (Women's Equality Action League), the Women's Political Caucus, and the League of Women Voters. For an academic discussion of women and politics that falls clearly within these parameters, see Ethel Klein, *Gender Politics* (Cambridge: Harvard University Press, 1984). For more critical discussions of the assumptions underlying, and the limitations of, liberal feminism, see Jean Elshtain, *Public Man, Private Woman* (Princeton: Princeton University Press, 1981); Zillah Eisenstein, *The Radical Future of Liberal Feminism* (New York: Longman, 1981); and Alison Jaggar, *Feminist Theory and Human Nature* (Totowa, N.J.: Rowman and Allanheld, 1983).

2. David L. Kirp, Mark G. Yudof, and Marlene Strong Franks, *Gender Justice* (Chicago: University of Chicago Press, 1986), p. 131.

3. Ibid., p.3.

4. For excellent examples of this approach, see Irene Diamond, ed., *Families, Politics and Public Policy* (New York: Longman, 1983); Joyce Gelb and Marian Lief Palley, *Women and Public Policies* (Princeton: Princeton University Press, 1987); Ellen Boneparth and Emily Stoper, eds., *Women, Power and Policy: Toward the Year 2000* (New York: Pergamon, 1988).

5. See, for example, Zillah Eisenstein, *Capitalist Patriarchy and the Case for Socialist Feminism* (New York: Monthly Review Press, 1979); Michele Barrett, *Women's Oppression Today* (London: Verso, 1980); and Christine Delphy, *Close to Home: A Materialist Analysis of Women's Oppression* (Amherst: University of Massachusetts Press, 1984).

6. Adrienne Rich, "Compulsory Heterosexuality and Lesbian Existence," *Signs* 5(4):631–651; Ti Grace Atkinson, *Amazon Odyssey* (New York: Links Books, 1984); Charlotte Bunch, "Lesbians in Revolt," *Lesbianism and the Women's Movement* (Oakland, Calif.: Diana Press, 1975); Andrea Dworkin, *Intercourse* (Free Press, 1987).

7. Edith Altbach, ed., *German Feminism: Readings in Politics and Literature* (Albany: SUNY Press, 1984), p. 273; Simone De Beauvoir, "Interview with Alice Schwarzer," in Marks and De Courtivron, *New French Feminisms* (New York: Schocken, 1981), p. 146; and Mary O'Brien, *The Politics of Reproduction* (London: Routledge and Kegan Paul, 1981), pp. 201–210.

8. Drawing parallels between slaves and women has been a recurrent tactic within feminist argument from J. S. Mill's *Subjection of Women* (Cambridge: M.I.T. Press, 1970) through Kathleen Barry's *Female Sexual Slavery* (Englewood Cliffs, N.J.: Prentice-Hall, 1979); although the extent to which the analogy has been pushed has varied markedly.

9. For a detailed critique of biological determinism, see Chapter 2.

10. Judith Evans, "An Overview of the Problem for Feminist Political Theorists," in Judith Evans, Jill Hills, Karen Hunt, Elizabeth Meehan, Tessa ten Tusscher, Ursula Vogel and Georgina Waylen, *Feminism and Political Theory* (London: Sage, 1986), p. 12. For additional criticisms of radical feminism, see Barrett, *Women's Oppression Today*; Elshtain, *Public Man/Private Woman*; and Janet Richards, *The Skeptical Feminist* (London: Penguin, 1982).

11. Shulamith Firestone is perhaps best known for prescribing reproductive technology as a remedy for sex oppression in *The Dialectic of Sex* (New York: William Morrow, 1970). Firestone's treatment of the parallels between race and sex itself demonstrates critical dysanalogies between the two. Her attempt to analyze racism in terms of a family metaphor drawn from the Oedipal complex fails to grasp unique dimensions of racism and trades on certain reprehensible racist stereotypes. For separatist proposals, see the works cited in note 6.

12. For arguments to support the view that this quest is futile, see Chapter 3.

13. Perhaps the most notorious example of this possibility is the Supreme Court case that ruled that excluding medical expenses related to normal pregnancy from disability and health insurance plans did not discriminate against women, because the distinction was not based on sex but merely divided "potential recipients into two groups—pregnant women and non-pregnant persons." *Geduldig v. Aiello*, 417 U.S. 484, 496–97, n.20 (1974). The rejection of maternity leaves as a form of "special pleading for women" that is nothing more than the "latest version of paternalism" also suffers from this defective logic. Kirp et al., *Gender Justice*, p. 41.

14. See O'Brien, *The Politics of Reproduction* (London: Routledge and Kegan Paul, 1981); Jaggar, *Feminist Politics and Human Nature* (Totowa, N. J.: Rowman and Allanheld, 1983); Delphy, *Close to Home: A Materialist Analysis of Women's Oppression* (Amherst: University of Massachusetts Press, 1984); as well as Nancy Hartsock, "The Feminist Standpoint: Developing a Ground for a Specifically Feminist Historical Materialism," in Harding and Hintikka, eds., *Discovering Reality* (Dordrecht: D. Reidel, 1983), pp. 283–310, and *Money, Sex and Power* (Boston: Northeastern University Press, 1985).

15. Karen Hunt has traced this development in the context of the British Labor party in "Crossing the River of Fire: The Social Construction of Women's Politicization," in Evans et al., *Feminism and Political Theory*, pp. 47–65.

16. This difficulty is manifested in the struggles that socialist feminists have had with affirmative action policies. See, for example, the discussions of Barrett, *Women's Oppression Today* (London: Verso, 1980) and Harding *The Science Question in Feminism* (Ithaca: Cornell University Press, 1986).

17. Kirp et al., *Gender Justice*, pp. 120–121.

18. The implications of the privatization of religion are discussed at length by Marx in his essay "On the Jewish Question," in Robert Tucker, ed., *The Marx-Engels Reader* (New York: W.W. Norton, 1978).

19. For detailed discussions of this problem, see Jan Pahl, ed., *Private Violence and Public Policy* (London: Routledge and Kegan Paul, 1985) and Elizabeth Stanko, *Intimate Intrusions: Women's Experience of Male Violence* (London: Routledge and Kegan Paul, 1985).

20. This formulation of distributive justice is drawn from Aristotle.

21. This phrase is borrowed from Deborah Cameron who provides an excellent discussion of this problem in *Feminism and Linguistic Theory* (London: Macmillan Press, 1985), p. 84–88.

22. Ibid., p. 86.

23. It might be objected that to view religion in terms of the promotion of interests is itself a secular mistake that fails to grasp the essence of faith and the role of religion in an individual's life. Yet, to the extent that religion promotes salvation, fellowship, community, or a host of other values, it would make sense to say "that it is in an individual's interest to join a church" or that "in the interest of salvation (fellowship, etc.) an individual decided to join a congregation." What is important to my point here is only that it is possible to make sense of such statements in relation to religion, but not in relation to gender.

24. The case of transsexuals is pertinent here for one might argue that such individuals do indeed choose their gender. But published statements of transsexuals suggest that these individuals feel that their gender is "fixed" and that they need to alter their bodies to conform to that sense of gendered self. Thus, a "woman locked in a man's body" undergoes surgery to attain a body consonant with her self-understanding.

25. Judith Evans makes this point in "Feminist Theory and Political Analysis," in Evans et al., *Feminism and Political Theory*, p. 107.

26. For historical examples of this phenomenon, see Joan W. Scott, "Gender: A Useful Category for Historical Analysis," *American Historical Review* 91(5):1053–1075.

27. What counts as a defining characteristic of race is a subject that should be considered with great caution, for many of the differences that have been ascribed to people of color involve the same process of invention and reification discussed in Chapter 1 with reference to gender.

28. This idea was first advanced by David Hume in his essay "On the Idea of a Perfect Commonwealth." It was subsequently elaborated by James Madison in "Federalist #51." For Madison's full argument, see Alexander Hamilton, James Madison and John Jay, *The Federalist* (Oxford: Basil Blackwell, 1948), p. 265. For an analysis of the similarities between the views of Hume and Madison, see Douglass Adair, *Fame and the Founding Fathers* (New York: W. W. Norton, 1974).

29. In *Gender Justice*, Kirp et al. insist that men were acting benevolently in imposing restrictions upon women: "However misguided their actions might seem to the contemporary observer, men sought to dignify women by elevating and protecting them;" and for this reason women are not entitled to the same kinds of compensation as blacks, pp. 42–45.

30. Madison, "Federalist #51," in Alexander Hamilton, James Madison and John Jay, *The Federalist* (Oxford: Basil Blackwell, 1948), p. 265.

31. For a detailed discussion of the dimensions of representation, see Hanna Pitkin, *The Concept of Representation* (Berkeley: University of California Press, 1967).

32. John Adams, "Letter to John Penn," *Works IV* (Boston, 1852–1865), p. 205. Cited in Pitkin, *The Concept of Representation*, p.60.

33. Pitkin, *The Concept of Representation*, p. 81.

34. Charles Hyneman advanced this objection against discussions of the demographic characteristics of legislators that merely noted the extent to which legislators were unlike their constituents without showing the relevance of such differences to political action. It should be noted that he was concerned more with characteristics pertaining to income, occupation, race, and religion than sex. Indeed, the passage excerpted begins: "Facts about the men who enact statutes are, presumably, significant . . ." But precisely because of the presumed irrelevance of gender, it is important to consider this objection directly. "Who Makes Our Laws," *Political Science Quarterly* 55: 556–581.

35. It is important to recognize the gap between procedural mechanism and substantive result to undermine stereotypical notions that women are necessarily committed to sisterhood, social justice, and peace, to offset unrealistic expectations of women in public office, and to set aside men's fears that sex equality in office would result in a cohesive voting bloc of women tantamount to women's dominance. Women are neither more moral than men nor less prone to the pressures of office than their male colleagues.

36. The peculiarity of the locution "men's interests" is itself indicative of entrenched sex bias. If a typical political scientist were pushed to explicate such a concept, I suspect that it would be defined in relation to issues such as defense, the economy, and national security—issues that are surely of equal importance to women.

37. Cameron, *Feminism and Linguistic Theory*, p. 113.

38. This connection between the private sphere and women's privation of public roles is discussed by Elizabeth Wolgast, *The Grammar of Justice* (Ithaca: Cornell University Press, 1987), p. 69.

39. Recent research attributes the underrepresentation of women in elective office and as candidates for elective office to "male hostility to the intrusion of women into such positions and the refusal of male party bosses to field women candidates for 'safe' or winnable seats in electoral contests." For a review of this literature, see Bernice Caroll, "Review Essay: Political Science, Part I," *Signs* 5(2):289–306. See also M. M. Lee, "Why So Few Women Hold Public Office: Democracy and Sex Roles," *Political Science Quarterly* 91(1976):297–314; Susan Welch, "Women as Political Animals: A Test of Some Explanations for Male-Female Political Participation Differences," *American Journal of Political Science* 21(1977):711–730; Elizabeth Valance, *Women in the House* (London: Humanities Press, 1982); Joni Lovenduski, "Toward the Emasculation of Political Science: The Impact of Feminism," in Dale Spender, ed., *Men's Studies Modified* (Oxford: Pergamon Press, 1981), pp. 83–97; and Rita Kelly, Bernard Ronan, and Margaret Cawley, "Liberal Positivistic Epistemology and Research on Women and Politics," *Women and Politics* 7(3):11–28.

40. William E. Connolly, *Appearance and Reality in Politics* (Cambridge: Cambridge University Press, 1981), p. 120.

41. I do not mean to suggest that feminists must abandon other forms of consciousness raising or cease providing critical assistance to women in rape crisis centers, domestic violence shelters, welfare rights organizations, and sex discrimination cases. My point is simply that if it is to succeed, a political campaign for constitutional reform must address different issues and different constituencies, and adopt different strategies than many feminists have in the past.

42. For an insightful argument that passage of an Equal Rights Amendment would produce symbolic rather than substantive gains for women, see Jane Mansbridge, *Why We Lost the ERA* (Chicago: University of Chicago Press, 1988).

43. Connolly, *Appearance and Reality in Politics*, p. 77.

44. To this point, I have focused upon strategies for constitutional reform within elective political systems in order to emphasize that sex parity in office is a feasible feminist objective in existing liberal democratic systems. But a constitu-

tional mandate for sex parity in office is compatible with virtually any form of regime. The strategies necessary to initiate constitutional reforms in socialist systems, military dictatorships, theocracies, etc., would necessarily vary from those needed in liberal democracies, but it is perfectly conceivable that women could play an equal role in the political leadership of any system.

45. For extensive analyses of historical and theoretical relations between the public and the private, see Jean Elshtain, *Public Man, Private Woman* (Princeton: Princeton University Press, 1981); Linda Nicholson, *Gender and History: The Limits of Social Theory in the Age of the Family* (New York: Columbia University Press, 1986); Linda Kerber, "Separate Spheres, Female Worlds, Woman's Place: The Rhetoric of Women's History," *Journal of American History* 75(1):9–39.

46. Virginia Woolf, *Three Guineas* (New York: Harcourt, Brace and World, 1938).

47. This conception of privacy is advanced and defended as central to feminist objectives by Anita Allen, *Uneasy Access: Privacy for Women in A Free Society* (Totowa, N.J.: Rowman and Littlefield, 1988), p. 3.

48. Ibid., p. 37.

49. Because women tend to live longer than men and because infant mortality rates for males are slightly higher than those of females, women constitute 52 percent of the world population. Thus, it might be said that to work to achieve a situation in which women hold 50 percent of all public offices is to demand too little, to fight for less than what women deserve. I grant the validity of the mathematical point. Nevertheless, since winning rough sex parity in office would be such a vast improvement over women's current situation and since it strikes a symbolic blow for the sexual equality of men and women, I believe that it constitutes a worthy conception of gender justice.

50. I am indebted to Philip Alperson, Christine de Stefano, and Judith Grant for calling this issue to my attention.

51. This image of the United States as a nation of minorities was advanced by Justice Powell, speaking for a majority of the Supreme Court in *Regents of the University of California v. Bakke* (438 U.S. 265, 1978). The Supreme Court used this image to challenge the legitimacy of a voluntarily created, preferential admissions program for disadvantaged students at the University of California, Davis, Medical School. The U.C. Davis program established special admission standards for racial minorities and for economically disadvantaged students. The Supreme Court ruled that in the absence of a judicial or administrative finding of intentional discrimination on the part of the school, a race-conscious remedy was unconstitutional. For a detailed discussion of the assumptions that sustained the Court's decision, see M. E. Hawkesworth, "The Affirmative Action Debate and Conflicting Conceptions of Individuality," *Hypatia/Women's Studies International Forum* 7(5):335–347.

52. For arguments that compensatory justice is an inadequate conception for feminist objectives, see Chapter 3.

53. It is important to recognize that it is possible to identify varying degrees of oppression. All women suffer from sexism in contemporary societies: they are devalued simply because they are women. That does not imply that all women are oppressed to the same degree. Those women who constitute the 4 percent of their sex earning incomes greater than $35,000 per year do not suffer the same degree of oppression as poor women, much less as poor women of color.

54. In the United States, a number of agencies have developed strategies for investigating discrimination complaints. The Office of Civil Rights, the Equal Employment Opportunity Commission, and the Office of Federal Contract Compliance as well as Human Rights Commissions at the state level have developed criteria for assessing the merits of such complaints. Agencies such as these could easily be charged with the responsibility to investigate group claims concerning ongoing discrimination.

55. Justice Powell, *Regents of the University of California v. Bakke* (438 U.S. 265, 1978).

56. In the United States for example, blacks and hispanics would have little difficulty documenting continuing discrimination.

57. A "safe" seat is one that the party of the incumbent is virtually certain to win in any election. In the United States, the vast majority of seats (approximately 80 percent) are "safe."

58. To identify all the possible strategies by which sex parity in elective office could be achieved would require a book in itself. What is important to note is simply that the mechanics of implementation are neither particularly difficult nor unique to the issue of sex parity in office. For offices that are typically filled by one individual, for example, the institutionalization of a pattern of sex rotation in office could meet the objectives of the sex parity provision. In one election, all contending parties would nominate women for the office; in the following election, all the nominees would be men. This principle of rotation in office has been used in nations such as Colombia in order to guarantee that opposing parties have "equal time" in public office. Ample mechanisms for the achievement of sex parity in elective office could be generated by the creative extrapolation from existing electoral rules.

59. Virginia Held, "Reasonable Progress and Self-Respect," in Tom Beauchamp, ed., *Ethics and Public Policy* (Englewood Cliffs, N.J.: Prentice-Hall, 1975), p. 34.

60. Although a constitutional provision such as this does not directly address the underrepresentation of women in the corporate, business, or academic sectors,

it could have an important indirect effect. The literature on political appointees suggests the existence of a "revolving door" between government office and corporate board room and between government post and university appointment. If 50 percent of all offices were held by women, then those women too would have to go somewhere after completing their terms in office. It is likely that the desire to benefit from the political knowledge, experience and connections of such individuals would offset lingering sexist prejudices within corporate and university administrations. Thus, sex parity in public office might have impovtant spillover effects on the private sector.

Bibliography

Albert, Hans. 1985. *Treatise on Critical Reason.* Mary Varney Rorty, trans. Princeton: Princeton University Press.

Altbach, Edith, ed. 1984. *German Feminism: Readings in Politics and Literature.* New York: SUNY Press.

Aquinas, Thomas. 1947. *Summa Theologica.* New York: English Dominican Province.

Aristotle. 1941. *The Basic Works.* Richard McKeon, ed. New York: Random House.

Atkinson, Ti Grace. 1970. Radical Feminism and Love. Unpublished manuscript.

Augustine. 1948. *The Basic Writings.* Whitney Oates, ed. New York: Random House.

Ayim, Maryann, and Barbara Houston. 1985. The Epistemology of Gender Identity: Implications for Social Policy. *Social Theory and Practice* 11(1):260.

Balbus, Isaac. 1982. *Marxism and Domination.* Princeton: Princeton University Press.

Barasch, F. K. 1977. H. E. W., The University and Women. In *Reverse Discrimination,* Barry Gross, ed. New York: Prometheus Books.

Barrett, Michele. 1980. *Women's Oppression Today: Problems in Marxist Feminist Analysis.* London: Verso.

Barry, Kathleen. 1979. *Female Sexual Slavery.* Englewood Cliffs, N.J.: Prentice-Hall.

255

Bartky, Sandra. 1979. On Psychological Oppression. In *Philosophy and Women*, S. Bishop and M. Weinzweig, eds. Belmont, Ca.: Wadsworth Publishing.

Beauvoir, Simone de. 1961. *The Second Sex*. H. M. Parshley, trans. and ed. New York: Bantam Books.

————. 1981. Interview with Alice Schwarzer. In *New French Feminisms*, E. Marks and I. de Courtivron, eds. New York: Schocken.

Beechey, Victoria. 1977. Some Notes on Female Wage Labour in the Capitalist Mode of Production. *Capital and Class* 3:45–64.

————. 1978. Women and Production. In *Feminism and Materialism*, A. Kuhn and A. Wolpe, eds. London: Routledge and Kegan Paul.

Benhabib, Seyla. 1986. *Critique, Norm and Utopia*. New York: Columbia University Press.

Benston, Margaret. 1969. The Political Economy of Women's Liberation. *Monthly Review* 21(4):13–25.

Berger, John, and Jean Mohr. 1975. *A Seventh Man*. Harmondsworth: Penguin.

Bernstein, Richard. 1976. *The Restructuring of Social and Political Theory*. New York: Harcourt, Brace, Jovanovich.

————. 1983. *Beyond Objectivism and Relativism: Science Hermeneutics and Praxis*. Philadelphia: University of Pennsylvania Press.

————. 1986. The Rage Against Reason. *Philosophy and Literature* 10(2):186–210.

Bishop, Sharon, and Majorie Weinzweig, eds. 1979. *Philosophy and Women*. Belmont, Calif.: Wadsworth Publishing.

Blau, Francine. 1983. The Economic Status of Women in the Labor Market. Testimony Before the United States House of Representatives Committee on the Judiciary, Subcommittee on Civil and Constitutional Rights, September 14.

————. 1984. Discrimination Against Women: Theory and Evidence. In *Labor Economics: Modern Views*, W. Darity, ed. Boston: Kluwer-Nijhoff.

Boneparth, Ellen. 1982. *Women, Power and Policy*. New York: Pergamon.

————, and Emily Stoper. 1988. *Women, Power and Policy: Toward the Year 2000*. New York: Pergamon.

Bornstein, Diane. 1981. Ideals for women in the Work of Christine de Pizan. Michigan Consortium for Medieval Studies.

Borreson, Elizabeth. 1968. *Subordination and Equivalence: Nature et role de la femme d'apres Augustin et Thomas d'Aquin*. Oslo: Universitets-forlaget.

Bourque, S.C., and J. Grossholtz. 1974. Politics As An Unnatural Practice: Political Science Looks at Female Participation. *Politics and Society* 4(2):225–266.

Brownmiller, Susan. 1976. *Against Our Will: Men, Women and Rape.* New York: Bantam.

Buker, Eloise. 1985. Hermeneutics: Problems and Promises for Doing Feminist Theory. Paper presented at the Annual Meeting of the American Political Science Association. New Orleans.

Bunch, Charlotte. 1978. Lesbians in Revolt. In *Feminist Frameworks*. A. Jaggar and P. Struhl, eds. New York: McGraw Hill.

Burkhardt, Barry. 1983. A Disturbing Look at Rape. *National On Campus Report.* 23 September:1.

Cameron, Deborah. 1985. *Feminism and Linguistic Theory.* London: MacMillan Press.

Cash, T., B. Gillen, and D. Burns. 1977. Sexism and 'Beautyism' in Personnel Consultant Decision Making. *Journal of Applied Psychology* 62:301–310.

Cavell, Stanley. 1979. *The Claim of Reason: Wittgenstein, Skepticism, Morality and Tragedy.* New York: Oxford University Press.

Chodorow, Nancy. 1978. *The Reproduction of Mothering: Psychoanalysis and the Sociology of Gender.* Berkeley: The University of California Press.

Cixous, Hélène. 1975. Le Rire de La Meduse. *L'Arc* 61:39–54.

———. 1976. Le Sexe ou La Tete. *Les Cahiers du GRIF* 13:5–15.

Clark, Lorenne, and Lynda Lange, 1979. *The Sexism of Social and Political Theory: Women and Reproduction from Plato to Nietzsche.* Toronto: University of Toronto Press.

Code, Lorraine. 1981. Is the Sex of the Knower Epistemologically Significant? *Metaphilosophy* 12:267–276.

Connell, Noreen, and Cassandra Wilson. 1974. *Rape: The First Sourcebook for Women by New York Radical Feminists.* New York: New American Library.

Connolly, William E. 1981. *Appearance and Reality in Politics.* Cambridge: Cambridge University Press.

———. 1985. Taylor, Foucault and Otherness. *Political Theory* 13(3):365–376.

Cornell, Drucilla, and Adam Thurschwell. 1986. Femininsm, Negativity, Intersubjectivity. *Praxis International* 5(4):484–504.

Council of Chief State School Officers and the National Association of State Boards of Education. 1980. *Facing the Future: Education and Equity for Females and Males.* Washington, D.C.: NASBE.

Currell, M. E. 1974. *Political Woman,* London: Croom Helm.

Dallmayr, Fred. 1984. *Language and Politics.* Notre Dame: University of Notre Dame Press.

Daly, Mary. 1973. *Beyond God the Father.* Boston: Beacon Press.

——. 1978. *Gyn/Ecology: The Metaethics of Radical Feminism.* Boston: Beacon Press.

Davidson, Nicholas. 1988. *The Failure of Feminism.* Buffalo, New York: Prometheus Books.

Davidson, Terry. 1978. *Conjugal Crime: Understanding and Changing the Battered Wife Pattern.* New York: Hawthorne.

Davis, Angela. 1981. *Women, Race and Class.* New York: Random House.

Delaney, Sheila. 1983. The Conservatism of Christine de Pizan. Paper presented to the Modern Languages Association Annual Convention.

de Lauretis, Teresa. 1985. The Violence of Rhetoric: Considerations on Representation and Gender. *Semiotica* 54:11–31.

——. 1986. *Feminist Studies/Critical Studies.* Bloomington: University of Indiana Press.

Delphy, Christine. 1984. *Close to Home: A Materialist Analysis of Women's Oppression.* Amherst: University of Massachusetts Press.

Deaux, K., and J. Taynor. 1973. Evaluation of Male and Female Ability: Bias Works Two Ways. *Psychological Reports* 31:20–31.

——, and T. Emswiller. 1974. Explanations of Successful Performance on Sex-Linked Tasks. *Journal of Personality and Social Psychology* 29:80–85.

Derrida, Jacques. 1979. *Spurs/Eperons.* Chicago: University of Chicago Press.

——. 1980. *The Archaeology of the Frivolous.* Pittsburgh: Duquesne University Press.

——. 1981a. *Dissemination.* Chicago: University of Chicago Press.

——. 1981b. *Positions.* Chicago: University of Chicago Press.

Dietz, Mary. 1985. Citizenship with a Feminist Face: The Problem of Maternal Thinking. *Political Theory* 13(1):19–37.

Dinnerstein, Dorothy. 1983. *The Mermaid and the Minotaur.* New York: Harper and Row.

Dipboye, R., R. Arvy, and D. Terpstra. 1977. Sex and Physical Attractiveness of Raters and Applicants as Determinants of Resume Evaluations. *Journal of Applied Psychology* 62:228–234.

Director of Public Prosecutions v. Morgan 2 W.L.R. 923 (H.L.).

Dobash, R. E., and R. P. Dobash. 1979. *Violence Against Wives: A Case Against Patriarchy.* New York: Free Press.

Donovan, Josephine, ed. 1975. *Feminist Literary Criticism: Explorations in Theory.* Lexington: University of Kentucky Press.

DuBois, Ellen. 1978. *Feminism and Suffrage: The Emergence of an Independent Women's Movement in America, 1848–1869.* Ithaca: Cornell University Press.

Dworkin, Andrea. 1974. *Woman Hating.* New York: Dutton.

———. 1976. The Rape Atrocity and the Boy Next Store. In *Our Blood: Prophesies and Discourses on Sexual Politics,* A. Dworkin, ed. New York: Harper and Row.

———. 1983. *Right Wing Women.* New York: Perigree/Putnam.

———. 1987. *Intercourse.* New York: Free Press.

Dziech, Billy, and Linda Weiner. 1984. *The Leacherous Professor: Sexual Harassment on Campus.* Boston: Beacon Press.

Ehrhart, Judith, and Bernice Sandler. 1985. *Campus Gang Rape: Party Games?* Washington, D.C.: Association of American Colleges.

Eich, William. 1985. Gender Bias in the Courtroom: Some Participants are More Equal than Others. *Judicature* 69(6):339–343.

Eisenstein, Zillah. 1979. *Capitalist Patriarchy and the Case for Socialist Feminism.* New York: Monthly Review Press.

———. 1981. *The Radical Future of Liberal Feminism.* New York: Longman.

———. 1984. *Feminism and Sexual Equality.* New York: Monthly Review Press.

Elshtain, Jean Bethke. 1979. Feminists Against the Family. *The Nation.* November 17.

———. 1981a. Against Androgeny. *Telos* (47):5–21.

———. 1981b. *Public Man, Private Woman.* Princeton University Press.

Engels, Freidrich. 1972. *The Origin of the Family, Private Property and the State.* New York: International Publishers.

Epperson, Sharon. 1988. Studies Link Subtle Sex Bias in Schools with Women's Behavior in the Workplace. *The Wall Street Journal.* 16 September:19.

Epstein, N. 1981. When Professor Swap Grades for Sex. *The Washington Post.* 6 September, section 6:1.

Erie, Steven, Martin Rein, and Barbara Wiget. 1983. Women and the Reagan Revolution: Thermidor for the Social Welfare Economy. In *Families, Politics and Public Policy,* Irene Diamond, ed. New York: Longman.

Estrich, Susan. 1987. *Real Rape.* Cambridge: Harvard University Press.

Etaugh, C., and B. Brown. 1975. Perceiving the Causes of Success and Failure of Male and Female Performers. *Developmental Psychology* 11:103–110.

Evans, Judith, Jill Hills, Karen Hunt, Elizabeth Meehan, Tessa ten Tusscher, Ursula Vogel, and Georgina Weylen. 1986. *Feminism and Political Theory.* London: Sage.

Faragher, A. 1980. The Response of the Police to the Problem of Marital Violence. In *Battered Women Project,* R. Frankenberg, et al., eds. University of Keele. Report to the Department of Health and Social Security.

Farley, Lin. 1980. *Sexual Shakedown.* New York: Warner Books.

Farrow, Lynne. 1974. *Feminism as Anarchism.* London: Black Bear Pamphlet 2.

Feather, T., and J. Simon. 1975. Reactions to Male and Female Success and Failure in Sex-linked Occupations: Impressions of Personality, Causal Attribution and Perceived Likelihood of Difference Consequences. *Journal of Personality and Social Psychology* 31:20–23.

Fee, Elizabeth. 1983. Women's Nature and Scientific Objectivity. In *Women's Nature Rationalizations of Inequality,* M. Lowe and R. Hubbard, eds. New York: Pergamon.

———. 1984. Whither Feminist Epistemology of Science. Paper presented at Beyond the Second Sex Conference, University of Pennsylvania.

Feldman-Summers, S., and S. Kiesler. 1974. Those Who Are Number Two Try Harder: The Effect of Sex on Attributions of Causality. *Journal of Personality and Social Psychology* 30:846–855.

Ferguson, Kathy. 1985. Male Ordered Politics: Feminism and Political Science. Paper presented at the Annual Meeting of the American Political Science Association, New Orleans.

Feshbach, Seymour, and Neal Malamuth. 1978. Sex and Aggression: Proving the Link. *Psychology Today* 12(6):111–117, 122.

Feyerabend, Paul. 1970. *Against Method: Outline for an Anarchistic Theory of Knowledge.* In *Minnesota Studies in the Philosophy of Science.* vol. 4., Radner and Winokur, eds. Minneapolis: University of Minnesota Press.

Fidell, L. 1970. Empirical Verification of Sex Discrimination in Hiring Practices in Psychology. *American Psychologist* 25:1094–1098.

Figes, Eva. 1970. *Patriarchal Attitudes.* New York: Stein and Day.

Finn, Geraldine, and Angela Miles, eds. 1982. *Feminism in Canada.* Montreal: Black Rose Books.

Firestone, Shulamith. 1970. *The Dialectic of Sex: The Case for Feminist Revolution.* New York: William Morrow.

Flax, Jane. 1983. Political Philosophy and the Patriarchal Unconscious: A Psychoanalytic Perspective on Epistemology and Metaphysics. In *Discovering Reality,* S. Harding and M. Hintikka, eds. Dordrecht: D. Reidei.

————. 1986. Gender as a Social Problem: In and For Feminist Theory. *American Studies/Amerika Studien* 31(2):193–213.

Foucault, Michel. 1977. *Discipline and Punish.* New York: Vintage Books.

————. 1980. *The History of Sexuality.* New York: Vintage Books.

Fowlkes, Diane. 1983. *How Feminist Theory Reconstructs American Government and Politics.* Washington, D.C.: American Political Science Association.

Fox-Keller, Evelyn. 1984. *Reflections on Gender and Science.* New Haven: Yale University Press.

Franklin, D. and J. Sweeney. 1988. Women and Corporate Power. In *Women, Power and Policy: Toward the Year 2000.* 2d ed., E. Boneparth and E. Stoper, eds. New York: Pergamon Press.

Freeman, Jo. 1984. *Women: A Feminist Perspective.* Palo Alto: Mayfield Publishing Company.

French, Marilyn. 1985. *Beyond Power: On Women, Men and Morals.* New York: Summitt.

Gadamer, Hans-Georg. 1979. Historical Transformations of Reason. In *Rationality Today,* Theodore Geraets, ed. Ottawa: University of Ottawa Press.

Gelles, Richard. 1987. *The Violent Home.* Rev. ed. Beverly Hills: Sage.

Giddens, Paula. 1984. *When and Where I Enter: The Impact of Black Women on Race and Sex in America.* New York: Bantam Books.

Gilligan, Carol. 1982. *In A Different Voice: Psychological Theory and Women's Development.* Cambridge: Harvard University Press.

Gilman, Charlotte. 1979. *Herland.* New York: Pantheon.

Goldberg, P. 1968. Are Women Prejudiced Against Women. *Transaction* 5:28–30.

Goldman, Emma. 1971. *The Traffic in Women.* Ojai, Calif.: Times Change Press.

Goot, M., and E. Reid. 1975. *Women and Voting Studies: Mindless Matrons or Sexist Scientism.* Sage Professional Papers in Comparative Political Sociology.

Gould, Carol. 1984. *Beyond Domination: New Perspectives on Women and Philosophy.* Totowa, N.J.: Rowman and Allenheld.

————, and Marx Wartofsky. 1976. *Women and Philosophy: Toward a Theory of Liberation.* New York: G.P. Putnam and Sons.

Grant, Judith. 1987. I Feel Therefore I Am: A Critique of Female Experience as the Basis for a Feminist Epistemology. *Women and Politics* 7(3):99–114.

Greene, Gayle, and Coppelia Kahn, eds. 1985. *Making a Difference: Feminist Literary Criticism.* New York: Methuen.

Greer, Germaine. 1970. *The Female Eunuch.* New York: McGraw-Hill.

Griffin, Susan. 1980. *Woman and Nature: The Roaring Inside Her.* New York: Harper Colophon.

————. 1971. Rape: The All-American Crime. *Ramparts.* September:26–35.

Grimshaw, Jean. 1986. *Philosophy and Feminist Thinking.* Minneapolis: University of Minnesota Press.

Gross, Barry. 1977. *Reverse Discrimination.* Buffalo, N.Y.: Prometheus.

Gutek, Barbara. 1985. *Sex and the Workplace: The Impact of Sexual Behavior and Harassment on Women, Men and Organizations.* San Francisco: Jossey Bass.

————, and D. Stevens. 1979. Differential Responses of Males and Females to Work Situations Which Evoke Sex-role Stereotypes. *Journal of Vocational Behavior* 14:23–32.

Habermas, Jürgen. 1981. Dialectics of Rationalization. *Telos* 49:5–31.

Haefner, J. 1977. Race, Age, Sex and Competence as Factors in Employee Selection of the Disadvantaged. *Journal of Applied Psychology* 62:199–202.

Hall, R., and B. Sandler. 1982. *The Classroom Climate: A Chilly One for Women?* Washington, D.C.: American Association of Colleges.

————. 1984. *Out of the Classroom: A Chilly Campus Climate for Women?* Washington, D.C.: American Association of Colleges.

————. 1986. *The Campus Climate Revisited: Chilly for Women Faculty, Administrators and Graduate Students.* Washington, D.C.: American Association of Colleges.

Haraway, Donna. 1985. A Manifesto for Cyborgs: Science, Technology and Socialist Feminism in the 1980's. *Socialist Review* 80:65–107.

Harding, Sandra. 1986. *The Science Question in Feminism.* Ithaca: Cornell University Press.

————, and Merrill Hintikka, eds. 1983. *Discovering Reality: Feminist Perspectives on Epistemology, Metaphysics, Methodology and Philosophy of Science.* Dordrecht: D. Reidel.

Hartsock, Nancy. 1983. The Feminist Standpoint: Developing A Ground for a Specifically Feminist Historical Materialism. In *Discovering Reality*, S. Harding and M. Hintikka, eds. Dordrecht: D. Reidel.

————. 1985. *Money, Sex and Power: Towards A Feminist Historical Materialism.* Boston: Northeastern University Press.

Hawkesworth, M. E. 1984a. Freedom and Virtue: The Covert Connection. *Cogito* II(1):73–106.

————. 1984b. The Affirmative Action Debate and Conflicting Conceptions of Individuality. *Hypatia/Women Studies International Forum* 7(5):335–347.

————. 1985. Workfare and the Imposition of Discipline. *Social Theory and Practice* 11(2):163–181.

Hayek, F. A. 1948. *Individualism and Economic Order.* Chicago: University of Chicago Press.

Hazelwood School District v. United States, 433 U.S. 299 (1977)

Hegel, G. W. F. 1977. *Phenomenology of Spirit,* trans. A. V. Miller. Oxford: Oxford University Press.

Hekman, Susan. 1987. The Feminization of Epistemology: Gender and The Social Sciences. *Women and Politics* 7(3):65–84.

Hermann, Claudine. 1981. The Virile System. In *New French Feminisms.* E. Marks and I. De Courtivron, eds. New York: Schocken Books.

Herzog, Don. 1985. *Without Foundations: Justification in Political Theory.* Ithaca: Cornell University Press.

Hesse, Mary. 1980. *Revolutions and Reconstructions in the Philosophy of Social Science.* Brighton, England: Harvester Press.

Horkheimer, Max and Theodor Adorno. 1982. *Dialectic of Enlightenment.* New York: Continuum.

Irigaray, Luce. 1985a. *Speculum of the Other Woman,* trans. Gillian Gill. Ithaca: Cornell University Press.

———, 1985b. *This Sex Which Is Not One,* trans. Catherine Porter. Ithaca: Cornell University Press.

Jaggar, Alison. 1983. *Feminist Politics and Human Nature.* Totowa, N.J.: Rowman and Allenheld.

———, and Paula Rothenberg Struhl. 1978. *Feminist Frameworks: Alternative Theoretical Accounts of the Relations Between Men and Women.* New York: McGraw-Hill.

Janssen-Jurreit, Marielouise. 1982. *Sexism: The Male Monopoly on History and Thought.* London: Pluto Press.

Jaquette, J., ed. 1974. *Women in Politics.* New York: Wiley.

Jones, Ann. 1981. Writing the Body: Toward an Understanding of "l'ecriture feminine." *Feminist Studies* 7:247–263.

Joseph, Gloria, and Jill Lewis. 1981. *Common Differences: Conflicts in Black and White Feminist Perspectives.* New York: Anchor Press/Doubleday.

Kahn, W., and J. Grune. 1982. Pay Equity: Beyond Equal Pay for Equal Work. In *Women, Power and Policy,* E. Boneparth, ed. New York: Pergamon.

Kant, Immanuel. 1965. *Observations on the Feeling of the Beautiful and Sublime.* Berkeley: University of California Press.

Kaplan, Cora. 1985. Pandora's Box: Subjectivity, Class and Sexuality in Socialist Feminist Criticism. In *Making a Difference,* G.Greene and C. Kahn, eds. New York: Methuen.

Kaufman-McCall, Dorothy. 1983. Politics of Difference: The Women's Movement in France from May 1968 to Mitterand. *Signs* 9:282–293.

Kelly, Joan. 1982. Early Feminist Theory and the Querelles des Femmes, 1400–1789. *Signs* 8(1):4–28.

Ketchum, Sara Ann, and Christine Pierce. 1979. Separatism and Sexual Relationships. In *Philosophy and Women,* S. Bishop and M. Weinzweig, eds. Belmont, Calif.: Wadsworth.

Kevles, Bettyann. 1986. *Females of the Species: Sex and Survival in the Animal Kingdom*. Cambridge: Harvard University Press.

Kiechel, Walter. 1987. The High Cost of Sexual Harassment. *Fortune*, 14 September:147.

Kirkpatrick, Jeanne. 1974. *Political Woman*. New York: Basic Books.

Kirp, David, Mark Yudof, and Marlene Franks. 1986. *Gender Justice*. Chicago: University of Chicago Press.

Koedt, Anne. 1973. Lesbianism and Feminism. In *Radical Feminism*, A. Koedt, E. Levine and A. Rapone, eds. New York: Quadrangle.

Kress, Paul. 1979. Against Epistemology. *Journal of Politics* 41:526–542.

Krupnick, Mark. ed. 1983. *Displacement*. Bloomington: Indiana University Press.

Lakoff, Robin. 1975. *Language and Women's Place*. New York: Harper and Row.

Lao, R., W. Upchurch, W. Corwin, and W. Grossnickle. 1975. Biased Attitudes toward Females as Indicated by Ratings of Intelligence and Likeability. *Psychological Reports* 37:1315–1320.

Lerner, Gerta. 1986. *The Creation of Patriarchy*. New York: Oxford University Press.

Levi-Strauss, Claude. 1969. *The Elementary Structures of Kinship*. Boston: Beacon Press.

————. 1971. The Family. In *Man, Culture and Society*, H. Shapire, ed. London: Oxford University Press.

Lloyd, Genevieve. 1984. *The Man of Reason: Male and Female in Western Philosophy*. London: Methuen.

Locke, John. 1974. *Two Treatises on Government*. New York: Hafner.

Lovenduski, Joni. 1981. Toward the Emasculation of Political Science: The Impact of Feminism. In *Men's Studies Modified*, Dale Spender, ed. Oxford: Pergamon.

Lowe, Marian, and Ruth Hubbard. 1983. *Woman's Nature: Rationalizations of Inequality*. New York: Pergamon.

Lupri, Eugene. 1983. *The Changing Position of Women in Family and Society: A Cross National Comparison*. Leiden: E. J. Brill.

MacKinnon, Catherine. 1979. *The Sexual Harassment of Working Women: A Case of Sex Discrimination*. New Haven: Yale University Press.

————. 1987. *Feminism Unmodified*. Cambridge: Harvard University Press.

Madison, James. 1961. *Federalist Papers*. Ed. Clinton Rossiter. New York: New American Library.

Mahowald, Mary. 1978. *Philosophy of Women: Classical to Current Concepts*. Indianapolis: Hackett Publishing.

Margolis, Joseph. 1987. Robust Relativism. In *Philosophy Looks at the Arts*. 3rd ed., Joseph Margolis, ed. Philadelphia: Temple University Press.

Marks, Elaine, and Isabelle de Courtivron, eds. 1981. *New French Feminisms*. New York: Schocken.

May, M. 1978. Violence in the Family: An Historical Perspective. In *Violence in the Family*, J. Martin, ed. Chichester: Wiley.

McBride, Theresa. 1976. *The Domestic Revolution, 1820–1920*. London: Croom Helm.

McDermott, Patrice. 1985a. The Epistemological Challenge of Post-Lacanian French Feminist Theory: Luce Irigaray. Paper presented at the Annual Meeting of the American Political Science Association.

———. 1985b. Not Born A Woman: French Materialist Feminist Thought. Paper presented at the Annual Meeting of the Southern Political Science Association.

McMillan, Ann. 1983. The Angel in the Text: Christine de Pizan and Virginia Woolf. Paper presented at the Modern Languages Association Annual Convention.

Megill, Allan. 1985. *Prophets of Extremity: Nietzsche, Heidegger, Foucault, Derrida*. Berkeley: University of California Press.

Mill, Harriet Taylor. 1851. The Enfranchisement of Women. *The Westminster Review*.

Mill, John Stuart. 1970. *The Subjection of Women*. Cambridge: M.I.T. Press.

Millet, Kate. 1971. *Sexual Politics*. New York: Avon Books.

Mitchell, Juliet. 1973. *Women's Estate*. New York: Vintage Books.

———. 1974. *Psychoanalysis and Feminism*. New York: Vintage Books.

Moi, Toril. 1985. *Sexual/Textual Politics: Feminist Literary Theory*. New York: Methuen.

Moon, J. Donald. 1975. The Logic of Political Inquiry. In *Handbook of Political Science*. Vol. I, F. Greenstein and N. Polsby, eds. Reading, Mass.: Addison-Wesley.

Morgan, David. 1975. *Suffragists and Liberals: The Politics of Woman Suffrage in England*. Totowa, N.J.: Rowman and Littlefield.

National Academy of Sciences. 1981. *Women, Wages and Work: Equal Pay for Work of Equal Value*. Washington, D.C.

National Women's Conference Committee. 1985. *Report of the World Conference to Review and Appraise the Achievements of the United Nations Decade for Women: Equality, Development and Peace*. New York: United Nations.

Nehamas, Alexander. 1985. *Nietzsche: Life as Literature*. Cambridge: Harvard University Press.

Nicholson, Linda. 1986. *Gender and History: The Limits of Social Theory in the Age of the Family*. New York: Columbia University Press.

Nietzsche, Friedrich. 1968. *Basic Writings*. New York: Modern Library.

Nieva, V., and Barbara Gutek. 1980. Sex Effects on Evaluation. *Academy of Management Review* 5:267–276.

O'Brien, Mary. 1981. *The Politics of Reproduction*. London: Routledge and Kegan Paul.

————. 1982. Feminist Praxis: Feminism and Revolution; Feminist Theory and Feminist Practice. In *Feminism in Canada*, G. Finn and A. Miles, eds. Montreal: Black Rose Books.

Okin, Susan Moller. 1979. *Women in Western Political Thought*. Princeton: Princeton University Press.

Osborne, Martha. 1979. *Women in Western Thought*. New York: Random House.

Pagelow, M.D. 1981. *Woman Battering: Victims and Their Experience*. Beverly Hills: Sage.

Pahl, Jan. 1982. Police Response to Battered Women. *Journal of Social Welfare Law*. November:337–343.

————. 1985. *Private Violence and Public Policy*. London: Routledge and Kegan Paul.

Pateman, Carole. 1982. Women and Consent. *Signs* 8(2):149–168.

————, and Elizabeth Gross. 1986. *Feminist Challenges: Social and Political Theory*. Boston: Northeastern University Press.

Pear, Robert. 1987. Women Reduce Lag in Earnings But Disparities With Men Remain. *New York Times* 3 September:1,7.

Pearce, Diana, and Harriette McAdoo. 1981. *Women and Children: Alone and In Poverty.* Washington D. C.: National Advisory Council on Economic Opportunity.

Pereira, Joseph. 1988. Women Allege Sexist Atmosphere in Offices Constitutes Harassment. *Wall Street Journal* 10 February:21.

Pheterson, G., S. Kiesler, and P. Goldberg. 1971. Evaluation of the Performance of Women as a Function of their Sex. *Journal of Personality and Social Psychology* 19:110–114.

Pitkin, Hanna. 1967. *The Concept of Representation.* Berkeley: University of California Press.

Pizan, Christine de. 1982. *The Book of the City of the Ladies,* trans. Earl Jeffrey Richards. New York: Persea.

Plato. 1961. *The Collected Dialogues,* eds. Edith Hamilton and Huntington Cairns. Princeton: Princeton University Press.

Polanyi, Michael. 1958. *Personal Knowledge.* Chicago: University of Chicago Press.

Popper, Karl. 1962. *Conjectures and Refutations.* New York: Basic Books.

Rawls, John. 1971. *A Theory of Justice.* Cambridge, Mass.: Belknap Press.

Reiter, Rayner. 1975. *Toward An Anthropology of Women.* New York: Monthly Review Press.

Reuther, Rosemary. 1974. *Religion and Sexism.* New York: Simon and Schuster.

———. 1975. *New Woman, New Earth.* New York: Seabury Press.

Rich, Adrienne. 1976. *Of Woman Born.* New York: Norton.

———. 1980. Compulsory Heterosexuality and Lesbian Existence. *Signs* 5(4):631–651.

Richards, Janet. 1982. *The Skeptical Feminist.* London: Penguin.

Rix, Sara. 1988. *The American Woman 1988–89: A Status Report.* New York: W. W. Norton.

Roberts, Joan. 1976. *Beyond Intellectual Sexism.* New York: David McKay Co.

Rogers, Katherine. 1966. *The Troublesome Helpmate: A History of Misogyny in Literature.* Seattle: University of Washington Press.

Rorty, Richard. 1979. *Philosophy and the Mirror of Nature.* Princeton: Princeton University Press.

Rosaldo, Michele Zimbalist, and Louise Lamphere. 1974. *Women, Culture and Society.* Stanford: Stanford University Press.

Rose, Hilary. 1983. Hand, Brain and Heart: A Feminist Epistemology for the Natural Sciences. *Signs* 9(1):73–90.

Rosen, Andrew. 1974. *Rise Up Women! The Militant Campaign of the Women's Social and Political Union.* London: Routledge and Kegan Paul.

Rosen, B., and T. Jerdee. 1974. Influence of Sex-Role Stereotypes on Personnel Decisions. *Journal of Applied Psychology* 59:9–14.

———, and T. Prestwich. 1975. Dual Career Mutual Adjustment: Potential Effects of Discriminatory Managerial Attitudes. *Journal of Marriage and the Family* 37:565–572.

Rossi, Alice. 1970. *Essays on Sex Equality.* Chicago: University of Chicago Press.

Rousseau, Jean Jacques. 1950. *The Social Contract and the Discourses.* New York: E. P. Dutton.

———. 1955. *Emile.* New York: E.P. Dutton.

Rowbotham, Sheila. 1973. *Woman's Consciousness, Man's World.* Harmondsworth: Penguin Books.

———. 1979. The Women's Movement and Organizing for Socialism. In *Beyond the Fragments: Feminism and the Making of Socialism,* S. Rowbotham, L. Segal and H. Wainwright, eds. London: Merlin.

Roy, Maria, ed. 1977. *Battered Women: A Psychological Study of Domestic Violence.* New York: Van Nostrand Reinhold.

Rubin, Gayle. 1975. The Traffic in Women: Notes on the Political Economy of Sex. In *Toward An Anthropology of Women,* Rayner Reiter, ed. New York: Monthly Review Press.

Ruddick, Sara. 1980. Maternal Thinking. *Feminist Studies* 6(2):342–367.

———. 1983. Pacifying the Forces: Drafting Women in the Interests of Peace. *Signs* 8(3):471–489.

Russell, Diana. 1975. *The Politics of Rape: The Victim's Perspective.* New York: Stein and Day.

———, and Nancy Howell. 1983. The Prevalence of Rape in the United States Revisited. *Signs* 8(4):688–695.

Ruth, Sheila. 1981. Methodocracy, Mysogyny and Bad Faith: The Response of Philosophy. In *Men's Studies Modified,* Dale Spender, ed. Oxford: Pergamon.

Salkever, Steven. 1978. Virtue, Obligation and Politics. *American Political Science Review* 68:78–92.

Sartre, Jean Paul. 1966. *Being and Nothingness*. New York: Washington Square Press.

Saxonhouse, Arlene. 1985. *Women in the History of Political Thought*. New York: Praeger.

Sayers, Janet. 1986. *Sexual Contradictions: Psychology, Psychoanalysis and Feminism*. London: Tavistock Publications.

Schmalz, Jeffrey. 1986. New York Courts Cited On Sex Bias. *New York Times*. 20 April:1, 19.

Schopenhauer, Arthur. 1964. *The Pessimist's Handbook*. Lincoln: University of Nebraska Press.

Scott, Hilda. 1984. *Women Work Their Way to the Bottom: The Feminization of Poverty*. Boston: Pandora Press.

Scott, Joan. 1986. Gender: A Useful Category for Historical Analysis. *American Historical Review* 91(5):1053–1075.

Seccombe, Wally. 1974. The Housewife and her Labour Under Capitalism. *New Left Review* 83:3–24.

Shaktini, Namascar. 1982. Displacing the Phallic Subject: Wittig's Lesbian Writing. *Signs* 8(1):29–44.

Shaw, T. 1974. Differential Impact of Negative Stereotypes on Employee Selection. *Personnel Psychology* 25:333–338.

Sherman, Beth. 1985. The New Realities of Date Rape. *New York Times*, 23 October:17, 19.

Shortridge, Kathleen K. 1984. Poverty is a Woman's Problem. In *Women: A Feminist Perspective*. 3rd ed., Jo Freeman, ed. Palo Alto, Calif.: Mayfield Publishing Co.

Smart, Carol, and Barry Smart. 1978. *Women, Sexuality and Social Control*. London: Routledge and Kegan Paul.

Smith, Dorothy. 1974. Women's Perspective as a Radical Critique of Sociology. *Sociological Inquiry* 44(1):7–13.

Soble, Alan. 1983. Feminist Epistemology and Women Scientists. *Metaphilosophy* 14:291–307.

Spender, Dale. 1980. *Man Made Language*. London: Routledge and Kegan Paul.

———. 1981. *Men's Studies Modified: The Impact of Feminism on the Academic Disciplines*. Oxford: Pergamon.

———. 1983. *Women of Ideas and What Men Have Done to Them.* London: Ark Paperbacks.

Stanko, Elizabeth. 1985. *Intimate Intrusions: Women's Experience of Male Violence.* London: Routledge and Kegan Paul.

Steinmetz, Suzanne, and Murray Stauss, eds. 1974. *Violence in the Family.* New York: Dodd Mead.

Strauss, Murray, Richard Gelles, and Suzanne Steinmetz. 1980. *Behind Closed Doors: Vioence in the American Family.* Garden City, N.Y.: Doubleday.

Sullerot, Evelyn. 1981. Preface to the Feminine. In *New French Feminisms,* E. Marks and I. de Courtivron, eds. New York: Schocken Books.

Sutton, J. 1979. Modern and Victorian Battered Women. In *Battered Women and Abused Children.* Occasional Paper No. 4, University of Bradford.

Taylor, Charles. 1984. Foucault on Freedom and Truth. *Political Theory* 12(2):152–183.

Taynor, J., and K. Deaux. 1975. Equity and Perceived Sex Differences: Role Behavior as Defined by the Task, the Mode and the Action. *Journal of Personality and Social Psychology* 32:381–390.

Terborg, J., and D. Illgen. 1975. A Theoretical Approach to Sex Discrimination in Traditionally Masculine Occupations. *Organizational Behavior and Human Performance* 13:352–376.

Thucycdides. 1982. *The Peloponnesian War.* New York. Penguin.

Tomes, A. 1982. A Torrent of Abuse: Causes of Violence Among Working Class Men and Women in London, 1840–1975. *Journal of Social History* 11(3):329–45.

Trask, H. K. 1986. *Eros and Power: The Promise of Feminist Theory.* Philadelphia: University of Pennsylvania Press.

Valance, Elizabeth. 1982. *Women in the House.* London: Humanities Press.

Vetterling-Braggin, Mary, Frederick Elliston, and Jane English, eds. 1977. *Feminism and Philosophy.* Totowa, N.J.: Littlefield and Adams.

Vickers, Jill McCalla. 1982. Memoirs of an Ontological Exile: The Methodological Rebellions of Feminist Research. In *Feminism In Canada.* G. Finn and A. Miles, eds., Montreal: Black Rose Books.

Walker, Lenore. 1984. *The Battered Woman Syndrome.* New York: Springer.

WCPS (Women's Caucus for Political Science) *Quarterly.* 1979. Scholarly Treatment of Women in Political Science Texts Subjects of Study. May 6.

Weber, Max. 1958. *The Protestant Ethic and the Spirit of Capitalism,* trans. Talcott Parsons. New York: Charles Scribner's Sons.

Weinbaum, Batya. 1979. *The Curious Courtship of Women's Liberation and Socialism.* Boston: South End Press.

Weiner, B., I. Frieze, A. Kukla, S. Reed, and R. Rosenbaum. 1971. *Perceiving the Causes of Success and Failure.* Morristown, N.J.: General Learning Press.

Weinrich-Haste, Helen. 1986. Redefining Rationality: Feminism and Science. Paper presented at the Ontario Institute for Studies in Education. Toronto. October 9.

Weitzman, Lenore. 1983. The Economic Consequences of Divorce: Social and Economic Consequences of Property, Alimony and Child Support Awards. *UCLA Law Review* 28:1181–1251.

Wexler, Sandra. 1982. Battered Women and Public Policy. In *Women, Power and Policy,* Ellen Boneparth, ed. New York: Pergamon Press.

White, Hayden. 1978. *Tropics of Discourse.* Baltimore: Johns Hopkins University Press.

Wikler, Norma. 1980. On the Judicial Agenda for the 80s: Equal Treatment for Men and Women in the Courts. *Judicature* 64:202–207.

Willard, Charity. 1975. A Fifteenth Century View of Women's Role in Medieval Society: Christine de Pizan's Livre des Trois Virtus. In *The Role of Women in the Middle Ages.* Rosemarie Thee Morewedge, ed., New York: SUNY Press.

Wittig, Monique. 1971. *Les Guérillères.* New York: Avon.

———. 1973. *Lesbian Body.* New York: Avon.

———. 1979a. One is Not Born A Woman. *Proceedings of the Second Sex Conference.* New York: Institute for the Humanities.

———, and Sande Zeig. 1979b. *Lesbian Peoples: Material for A Dictionary.* New York: Avon.

Wollstonecraft, Mary. 1975. A *Vindication of the Rights of Woman.* Ed. Carol H. Poston. New York: W. W. Norton.

Women's Bureau. U.S. Department of Labor. 1985. The United Nations Decade for Women, 1976–1985: Employment in the United States. Washington, D.C.: General Printing Office.

Woolf, Virginia. 1929. A Room of One's Own. New York: Harcourt, Brace and World.

———. 1938. Three Guineas. New York: Harcourt, Brace and World.

Young, Iris. 1984. Is Male Gender Identity the Cause of Male Domination? In Mothering: Essays in Feminist Theory, Joyce Trebilcot, ed. Totowa, N.J.: Rowman and Allenheld.

———. 1986. Impartiality and the Civic Public: Some Implications of Feminist Critiques of Moral and Political Theory. Praxis International 5(4):381–401.

———. 1987. The Ideal of Community and the Politics of Difference. Social Theory and Practice 12(1):1–26.

Index

275